ESSENTIALS FOR THE LONG-TERM CARE NURSE

Charlotte Eliopoulos, PhD, MPH, RN, is executive director of the American Association for Long-Term Care Nursing (AALTCN) and works in private practice. She serves as a consultant on education and speaks on the topics of long-term care, geriatric nursing, integrative and holistic care of chronic conditions, culture change, staff development in long-term care, writing for publication, and self-care for nursing staff.

Dr. Eliopolous has authored 20 books on the topics of gerontology, long-term care, administration, culture change, holistic nursing, and complementary and alternative therapies, among others. She has been awarded six AJN Book of the Year awards for her publications.

Previous positions Dr. Eliopoulos has held include executive director, The Wellspring Program for Culture Change; interim executive director, National Association Directors of Nursing Administration in Long-Term Care (NADONA/LTC); president, American Holistic Nurses Association; director of education, Health Education Network; director of nursing and vice president for clinical services, Levindale Geriatric Center and Hospital, Baltimore, MD; associate faculty, Department of Health Policy and Management, Johns Hopkins University and Johns Hopkins School of Hygiene and Public Health, Baltimore, MD; clinical specialist in gerontological nursing, Johns Hopkins Hospital, Baltimore, MD; and consultant, Geriatric Care Services, Maryland Department of Health and Mental Hygiene.

ESSENTIALS FOR THE LONG-TERM CARE NURSE

A Guide for Nurses in Nursing Homes and Assisted Living Settings

Charlotte Eliopoulos, PhD, MPH, RN

SPRINGER PUBLISHING COMPANY
NEW YORK

Springer Publishing Company, LLC
11 West 42nd Street
New York, NY 10036
www.springerpub.com

Acquisitions Editor: Elizabeth Nieginski
Production Editor: Kris Parrish
Composition: S4Carlisle

ISBN: 978-0-8261-6093-5

39.16

The author and the publisher of this Work have made every effort to use sources believed to be reliable to provide information that is accurate and compatible with the standards generally accepted at the time of publication. Because medical science is continually advancing, our knowledge base continues to expand. Therefore, as new information becomes available, changes in procedures become necessary. We recommend that the reader always consult current research and specific institutional policies before performing any clinical procedure. The author and publisher shall not be liable for any special, consequential, or exemplary damages resulting, in whole or in part, from the readers' use of, or reliance on, the information contained in this book. The publisher has no responsibility for the persistence or accuracy of URLs for external or third-party Internet websites referred to in this publication and does not guarantee that any content on such websites is, or will remain, accurate or appropriate and does not guarantee that any content on such websites is, or will remain, accurate or appropriate.

Special discounts on bulk quantities of our books are available to corporations, professional associations, pharmaceutical companies, health care organizations, and other qualifying groups. If you are interested in a custom book, including chapters from more than one of our titles, we can provide that service as well.

For details, please contact:
Special Sales Department, Springer Publishing Company, LLC
11 West 42nd Street, 15th Floor, New York, NY 10036-8002
Phone: 877-687-7476 or 212-431-4370; Fax: 212-941-7842
E-mail: sales@springerpub.com

The ESSENTIALS series was published in the United States by Springer Publishing Company, LLC, as the FAST FACTS series.

Contents

Part III: Clinical Challenges

Part IV: Residents With Dementia

Part V: Management and Leadership

Preface

Long-term care consists of a continuum of services and supports that assist people with health and living needs over an extended period of time. Today more than 10 million people require some form of long-term care and the aging of the baby boomer population, coupled with increased longevity, will heighten the demand for this form of care for decades to come. Growing numbers of nurses will be working in long-term care and playing a major role in the provision of long-term care services.

Individuals who are living with chronic conditions and disabilities require ongoing monitoring, assessment, and care that fall within the scope of nursing practice. Further, nurses are ideally suited to address holistic needs that promote the highest possible quality of life for these individuals. Due to the wide range of conditions that people in need of long-term care possess, the diversity of this population, and the reality that long-term care nurses often work without close proximity to medical providers, nurses working in this specialty must be highly clinically competent. In addition, nurses working in long-term care often must delegate to and supervise other staff, requiring that they also demonstrate managerial competencies. When the realities of long-term care nursing are considered, it is one of the most challenging specialties for nurses. It also can be one of the most rewarding specialties in that nurses establish long-term relationships with the people they serve, which enables them to have a greater impact on their lives and well-being.

This book provides an overview of the unique aspects of long-term care with a specific focus on nurses working in nursing home and assisted living settings. It offers a review of the unique aspects and settings for long-term care, special needs of the population served, and clinical challenges. As a significant number of individuals who need long-term care services have cognitive impairment, a section is devoted to the care of residents with dementias. Management skills, legal risks, and issues pertaining to surveys are presented. In recognition of the stresses that can arise in long-term care nursing, a chapter is dedicated to the important topic of self-care.

The book is intended to serve as a quick reference for the wide range of clinical and managerial issues that a long-term care nurse may face. Boxes and tables are provided for quick reference, and the feature "Essential Facts" highlights special points. Resources for exploring additional information are listed at the end of the book. The range of topics covered in this text will contribute to enhancing the competencies of nurses working in this specialty and promoting a greater appreciation of the complexities of long-term care nursing.

Charlotte Eliopoulos

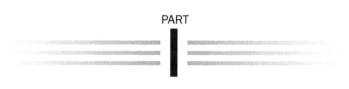

The Basics of Long-Term Care

Unique Aspects of Long-Term Care

Long-term care consists of services to assist persons with chronic conditions or disabilities who are unable to meet routine self-care activities and the demands of health conditions. As the name implies, care is needed over an extended period of time. Long-term care can be provided in individuals' private homes by home health agencies and informal caregivers or in residential facilities such as nursing homes and assisted living communities. With increasing life expectancies and more people living to ages at which the need for caregiving assistance heightens, reduced birth rates that decrease the potential caregivers available to older individuals, and improved medical care that enables people to live longer with complex conditions, the need for long-term care will continue to grow. Accompanying this will be the need for more nurses prepared in the unique aspects of this type of care.

This chapter should enable you to:

1. Compare and contrast acute and long-term care
2. Describe characteristics of a holistic approach to care
3. List characteristics of a therapeutic environment
4. Describe components of basic, holistic, and healing needs
5. List characteristics of assisted living and nursing home residents
6. Describe characteristics of long-term care nursing

A UNIQUE MODEL OF CARE

Nursing students and other health professionals receive most of their clinical experience in acute care settings. It is understandable, therefore, that they may lack an understanding of the unique aspects of long-term care.

In many acute care situations the focus is on diagnosing and treating health conditions. Patients can be treated without the nursing staff knowing their family relationships, living arrangements, scheduling preferences, spiritual practices, interests, personal desires, and occupational history. Consistent with the short duration of the encounter, the focus is on diagnosing and treating the condition.

The situation is quite different in long-term care settings. Owing to the extended time that most individuals reside in a nursing home or assisted living community, be it on a temporary or permanent basis, this setting will become a *home* for them. For this reason, quality of life joins quality of care as an important focus of services; a holistic approach supports this focus. Table 1.1 contrasts some of the characteristics of acute and long-term care.

TABLE 1.1 Similarities and Differences Between Acute and Long-Term Care

	Acute Care	Long-Term Care
Care provided	Treatment of urgent/emergency conditions, injuries, and acute illness; diagnostic workup for new conditions, surgeries, and related care	Treatment of stable conditions; rehabilitative therapies; assistance with activities of daily living; maintenance and, when possible, improvement of physical, emotional, mental, and social function and well-being; provision of highest possible quality of life
Nurses' role	Assess and plan care for immediate needs; monitor; administer medications and treatments; assess and plan for discharge needs	Assess and plan care for physical, mental, emotional, social, and spiritual needs; administer medications and treatments; monitor status; promote maximum patient/resident decision making; plan and provide interventions to support high quality of life; support family
Location	Office, urgent care center, emergency department, outpatient care/surgical center, hospital	Home, day care/treatment center, assisted living community, nursing home, subacute care center

(continued)

TABLE 1.1 Similarities and Differences Between Acute and Long-Term Care (*continued*)

	Acute Care	Long-Term Care
Time frame	Short term	Weeks to permanent stay
Staffing	Primarily professional staff	Primarily unlicensed caregivers under supervision of licensed nurses
Environment	Supports interventions, technical	Supports caregiving needs and provision of homelike environment

Holism is a theoretical approach that views the whole as being greater than its parts. In the context of health care, this means that in order to care for the whole person, the various parts of the person—physical, emotional, mental, social, spiritual—must be addressed. When they are, the resulting synergy creates an outcome more powerful than would be achieved by attention only to a part. A holistic approach:

- Recognizes that a person is a complex combination of physical, emotional, mental, spiritual, and social components that interact to influence total health and well-being
- Strives to achieve a balance of body, mind, and spirit rather than merely focusing on removing or managing the signs and symptoms of disease
- Fosters empowerment of the individual to actively participate in and, to the degree realistically possible, direct care

🌀 Clinical Snapshot

Two men have similar cardiovascular conditions. One receives expert medical attention, including medications, instruction in an exercise program and dietary modifications, and regular monitoring. The other receives similar medical attention, but also is afforded opportunities to discuss the impact of the diagnosis on family roles and responsibilities, his desire to strengthen his relationship with God, and his concern about his ability to engage in sexual activity.

The first man complies with the medical regimen and has normal diagnostic tests, yet carries emotional burdens that have a negative impact on his quality of life, produce stress, and threaten his motivation for ongoing compliance. The second man is able to discuss and work through issues that strengthen his motivation to adhere to the treatment plan and carve out a meaningful life.

The holistic approach used in the care of the second man enables him to live in harmony with his cardiovascular condition, potentially resulting in improved health outcomes and a higher quality of life.

There are additional considerations when care is provided in nursing homes and assisted living communities in that for many residents, these facilities will become their home. For this reason, attention must be given to the human and material factors that create a therapeutic environment promoting a sense of "home."

A therapeutic environment promotes holistic health, function, and healing. Characteristics of a long-term care facility that support a therapeutic environment are that it:

- Meets regulatory standards
- Is clean, safe, and free from odors and clutter
- Supports ease of use for persons with various mental and physical disabilities
- Provides space and opportunities for privacy, socialization, and solitude
- Offers sensory stimulation
- Incorporates nature (e.g., pets, plants)
- Is visually appealing
- Uses scents, sounds, and lighting therapeutically
- Affords residents the opportunity to personalize their rooms
- Is comfortable and inviting to visitors
- Facilitates easy interaction with the local community

The culture change movement has brought about considerable transformation in nursing homes that have contributed to creating a higher quality of life and more homelike environment. This is discussed more fully in Chapter 6.

Part of what constitutes home for many individuals is the relationship with family and significant others. Typically, a home is welcoming to these individuals and provides a nucleus for socialization. By contrast, a long-term care facility is a new and unusual environment for most people. Privacy is often limited, and exposure to certain sights, sounds, and odors can make both residents and visitors uncomfortable. To address holistic needs and promote continuity of relationships, nursing staff must act to foster visitation and continued meaningful relationships among residents and their loved ones.

In addition to making the nursing home or assisted living community welcoming and comfortable to family members, nurses also must consider the needs of the family. Family members may face challenges when their relative is admitted to a nursing home or assisted living facility, such as financial burdens, decisions about selling a home and relocating, and depression and anxiety at losing the companion or adjusting to the changed status of their relative. Nurses need to explore these issues with family members and provide guidance and assistance to them as necessary. (Chapter 13 offers a full discussion of caring for families.)

When examining the many facets of long-term care and its unique features compared with acute care, nurses can envision that their activities will involve:

- Ensuring that basic and therapeutic needs are met
- Promoting holistic care for health and harmony of the body, mind, and spirit
- Supporting healing by helping the person achieve optimal physical, mental, emotional, social, and spiritual well-being and function

ESSENTIAL FACTS

Healing is not limited to curing. Individuals with chronic conditions and disabilities can achieve healing by establishing a meaningful, satisfying life with their conditions and reaching their optimal level of physical, mental, emotional, social, and spiritual function.

Although having basic needs met, medications administered, and treatments performed are important and necessary to people with long-term care needs, these activities do not necessarily assure a satisfying, fulfilling life. Long-term care nursing interventions exceed these basic activities to support holistic care and quality of life (Figure 1.1).

THE LONG-TERM CARE POPULATION

Most of the long-term care population is of advanced age. Although at any given time less than 5% of older adults are in a nursing home or assisted living community, approximately one fourth of this population will spend some time in these facilities during their lifetimes. Assisted living and nursing home residents tend to be non-Hispanic white females in their early 80s or older who have at least one chronic condition, demonstrate limitations in meeting at least two activities of daily living, and need assistance with managing their medications. More than half suffer from dementia. Other common diagnoses are hypertension, heart disease, depression, arthritis, osteoporosis, diabetes, chronic obstructive pulmonary disease (COPD), cancer, and stroke.

ESSENTIAL FACTS

Currently there are more than 15,000 nursing homes with 1.7 million beds and twice that number of assisted living communities serving nearly one million individuals.

HEALING NEEDS

Achievement of peak potential of physical, mental, emotional, social, and spiritual functioning or peaceful dying process, or both

Spiritual awareness and growth

Self-discovery through use of illness as an opportunity to seek growth and purpose

Establishment of meaningful, purposeful life

HOLISTIC NEEDS

Attainment of harmony of mind, body, and spirit

Prevention of avoidable decline and dysfunction

Maximum possible responsibility for self-care

Exercise of individual rights and decision-making capacity

Interconnection with community within and outside facility

BASIC NEEDS

Satisfaction of physiological needs

Restoration or stabilization of physical and mental health, or both

Assurance of safety of human and physical environment

Treatment of conditions

Information for informed decision making

FIGURE 1.1   Levels of needs of long-term care residents.

LONG-TERM CARE NURSING

Long-term care is provided in various settings (see Chapter 2), and although some nursing roles and responsibilities are unique to specific settings, these general nursing activities are common to all:

- *Assessment:* The assessment process examines the individual in a holistic manner to determine the extent to which basic, holistic, and healing needs are being met (see Figure 1.1). As a person would not be admitted to a nursing home or assisted living community without the need for assistance, the deficits in the person's ability to independently fulfill total needs must be identified, followed by a more in-depth assessment of factors contributing to the deficits.

- *Care planning:* This leads to the development of the care plans with goals to address the needs and deficits, along with related actions. Nursing actions could include one or more of the following: strengthening the person's ability to meet needs independently, removing or minimizing factors that contribute to the person's limitations in meeting needs, or partially or totally providing the care necessary to meet the needs. Figure 1.2 demonstrates how this process flows.

Assessment of ability to meet basic physiological needs, protect self, self-administer medications and treatments, socialize, fulfill spiritual needs, make informed decisions, express needs and preferences

↓   ↓

Person able to fulfill needs   Person unable to fulfill needs; deficit or need identified

↓   ↓

Nursing actions to support resident's current level of function and regularly reassesses ongoing ability to meet needs

Reason for inability to meet need determined

↓

Measurable goals developed

↓

Nursing actions to address needs or deficits determined (strengthening person's ability to meet needs independently, removing or minimizing factors that contribute to person's limitations in meeting needs, and/or partially or totally providing care necessary to meet needs)

↓

Ongoing monitoring and reassessment of effectiveness of goals and plans; revisions as needed

FIGURE 1.2 The flow of nursing actions based on the assessed needs of the individual.

- *Management:* In addition to direct clinical services, most nurses in long-term care settings must perform a variety of management functions. Typically, most direct care staff in long-term care settings are nursing assistants who have limited preparation. The supervision, coaching, and guidance of nursing assistants are performed by licensed nurses. In addition, nursing home settings are highly regulated, and nurses must ensure that these regulations are consistently adhered to.

Box 1.1 describes some of the basic nursing responsibilities in long-term care settings.

Box 1.1 Basic Nursing Responsibilities in Long-Term Care Settings

Clinical

- Assess residents
- Develop or participate in development of care plans
- Communicate resident's care plan to caregivers
- Monitor and evaluate effectiveness of plans and actions
- Identify changes in status of resident
- Communicate changes in resident's status to health care provider
- Administer, observe reactions to, and evaluate effectiveness of medications
- Perform treatments and direct care activities
- Coordinate diagnostic tests; communicate test results to health care provider
- Review, accept, communicate, and implement orders from health care providers
- Document as needed and according to protocols
- Assist in emergency situations
- Facilitate admission and discharge of resident
- Assist in emergency care
- Comply with infection prevention and control policies and procedures
- Ensure residents' rights are respected
- Instruct residents and significant others as needed
- Provide emotional support
- Assist resident in fulfilling spiritual needs

Managerial

- Accept and give shift reports; communicate new orders and changes to staff and residents

(continued)

Box 1.1 *(continued)*

- Develop assignments; delegate activities; supervise staff to whom activities are delegated
- Monitor needs of staff
- Intervene when violations of standards of care, policies, or procedures are detected
- Administer disciplinary actions as needed and according to organizational policies
- Identify and take actions to resolve staff, operational, or environmental problems
- Inspect environment and equipment for safety and cleanliness
- Ensure appropriate amount and condition of equipment and supplies
- Provide instruction to direct care staff as needed
- Document meetings and counseling sessions
- Participate in committees
- Communicate problems and need to administrative staff
- Promote positive customer service

ESSENTIAL FACTS

Staffing in nursing homes and assisted living communities differs from that of hospitals in that most direct care providers are nursing assistants. Registered nurses constitute a small percentage of staff and often fill managerial and administrative positions. In addition, the total number of hours of nursing care provided per resident is considerably less than that in hospital settings.

Occasionally, people unfamiliar with the realities of nursing homes and assisted living communities comment that working in these settings must be dull or easier than acute care. In reality, to provide competent nursing services in long-term care settings, nurses must utilize a wide range of knowledge and skills. Consider that, on an average day, long-term care nurses may be providing care for residents with cardiovascular, pulmonary, neurological, endocrine, gastrointestinal, genitourinary, musculoskeletal, psychiatric, and cognitive disorders. They may have to administer a wide range of medications, ensure adherence to proper isolation technique, assist with dialysis, reinforce exercises prescribed by therapists, respond to a cardiac arrest, support a dying resident, and manage the behaviors of an agitated resident. Long-term care nursing is indeed challenging and complex.

To adequately fulfill their responsibilities in nursing homes and assisted living communities, nurses in these settings must be highly competent; this includes possessing:

- Evidence-based knowledge of common chronic conditions and age-appropriate care
- Critical thinking and problem-solving skills
- Expert assessment skills that address holistic needs and well-being
- Strategies to promote resident-centered and resident-directed care
- Ability to access, use, and evaluate information from a wide range of sources
- Effective written and verbal communication skills
- Ability to prioritize and plan nursing interventions
- Current management and coaching skills
- Knowledge of practices and technology that support safe practice
- Ability to manage their own time and that of others effectively
- Team leadership, collaboration, and facilitation skills
- Knowledge and use of codes of ethics affecting practice
- Ability to use information technology
- Analytical skills to utilize data
- Interest and actions that support quality improvement
- Knowledge of current regulations, laws, policies, and procedures that affect their practice
- Awareness and sensitivity to the needs and issues of people with diverse cultural, racial, spiritual, and sexual-orientation backgrounds
- Self-initiative to keep abreast of changed and new practices
- Positive self-care behaviors, and modeling of these behaviors to others
- Accountability for their own behaviors and practice

The diversity of conditions that residents possess helps make long-term care settings a clinically challenging practice setting for nurses. Long-term care nursing also provides the opportunity to offer whole-person care and develop meaningful relationships with residents and their significant others. It can be a very satisfying and rewarding branch of nursing.

2

Settings for Long-Term Care

The continuum of long-term care options for people who need nursing and medical care assistance on an extended basis includes home health care, continuing care retirement communities, assisted living communities, and nursing homes. Various factors influence the selection of the setting for service, such as the anticipated period of time for which care is to be provided, type of treatments and related care needed, degree of independence of the individual, family support, insurance plans, and financial resources.

This chapter should enable you to:

1. List services provided in home health care
2. Describe the options offered by continuing care retirement communities
3. Describe nurses' roles in assisted living communities
4. Identify tasks that registered nurses can and cannot delegate to comply with their scope of practice
5. List factors that increase a person's risk for nursing home admission
6. Describe nurses' roles in nursing homes
7. Identify payment sources for various long-term care services

HOME HEALTH CARE

Home health care provides medically ordered services at the skilled level on an intermittent basis under the direction of licensed health professionals. Services can include:

- Nursing care
- Intravenous (IV) and enterostomal therapy
- Rehabilitative therapies (physical therapy, occupational therapy, speech therapy, nutritional therapy)
- Counseling and other psychological therapies

Home health care is reimbursed by Medicare, Medicaid, the Department of Veterans Affairs, and private insurance; each payment source has specific conditions for reimbursement.

ESSENTIAL FACTS

Services that provide assistance with housekeeping, meal preparation or delivery, telephone reassurance, shopping, laundry, transportation, and personal care are considered home care rather than home health care. Home care does not need to be ordered by a physician and usually is paid directly by the recipient of services or through long-term care insurance. These services can be offered by health departments, social service agencies, private agencies, and faith communities.

In the United States, women use home health care services at a higher rate than men and those who do typically are 85 years of age and older. Men tend to have a spouse available as a primary caregiver whereas most women receiving home health services are widowed and rely on an adult child or other family member for assistance. The most common diagnoses of these patients are essential hypertension, heart disease, diabetes mellitus, chronic obstructive pulmonary disease (COPD), osteoarthritis, dementia, malignant neoplasms, and cerebrovascular disease.

Although the purpose for their visits may involve the provision of a treatment or monitoring of a condition, home health nurses need to be aware of other factors that can have an impact on patients' health and healing, such the lack of food, unsanitary or unsafe conditions in the home, unpaid bills, and decline in the availability or health of family caregivers. Home health nurses can serve an important function by guiding or referring patients to services and agencies that can provide assistance (Table 2.1).

CONTINUING CARE RETIREMENT COMMUNITIES

Continuing care retirement communities (CCRCs) provide a variety of living and care services for older adults, including independent living, assisted living, and nursing home care. Also known as life care communities,

TABLE 2.1 Services to Assist Community-Based Individuals

Adult Day Services

Public agencies, religious organizations, and private companies	Provide health and social services to people with moderate physical or mental disabilities and give respite to their caregivers during a portion of the day.

Care and Case Management

Private agencies, health departments	Offer registered nurses or social workers who assess an individual's needs, identify appropriate services, and help the person obtain and coordinate these services. Services coordinated can include medical care, home health services, socialization programs, financial planning and management, and housing.

Financial Aid

Social Security Administration	Can assist in obtaining retirement income, disability benefits, supplemental security income, and Medicare or other health insurances. Contact local office of the Social Security Administration.
Veterans Administration (VA)	Can provide financial aid to older veterans and their families. Contact the local VA office.
Other	Department stores, pharmacies, restaurants, banks, and other merchants offer discounts to older adults. Local departments of aging often have listings.

Food

Departments of social services	Can provide assistance with applications for food stamps.
Senior centers	Offer lunch programs.
Meals on Wheels	Provides home delivery of meals.

Home Monitoring

Private companies	Provide home monitoring and medical alarm systems, whereby the older adult wears a small remote alarm that can be pressed in the event of a fall or other emergency. The alarm triggers a central monitoring station to call designated contacts or the police.
Home health agencies, hospitals	Can provide telemanagement to enable people to have vital signs, blood glucose levels, and other physiological measurements communicated from the home to providers.

(continued)

TABLE 2.1 Services to Assist Community-Based Individuals (*continued*)

Housing

Local departments of housing and community development	Can aid older people in locating affordable housing and, for older homeowners, can provide information on tax discounts and direct them to resources to assist in home repairs and provide information regarding property tax discounts.

Social Support and Activities

Faith communities	Can offer health and social services such as congregate eating programs, home visitation, and chore assistance.
Senior centers	Provide clubs and activities.
Local chapters of the American Association of Retired Persons (AARP)	Can provide information on leisure pursuits, as well as many other resources.

Telephone Reassurance

Private companies, volunteers, health departments, social service agencies	Provide a daily telephone call, usually at a mutually agreed on time, to provide older people with social contact and ensure that they are safe and well.

Transportation

Public transportation	Many communities offer older adults discounts for bus, taxicab, subway, and train services; individual agencies should be contacted for more information.
Departments of aging, health and social services departments	Offer or can direct older adults to transportation services accommodating wheelchairs and other special needs.

CCRCs attract older adults who are able to live independently upon admission, but who want to plan for and determine where and how they live and receive care should their needs intensify. Older adults can live in a setting with people their own age and have opportunities for socialization, recreation, and oversight of health care needs. CCRCs offer the advantage that relocation will not be necessary as changes in function and care requirements occur. Housing structures can consist of apartments, condominiums, cottages, duplexes, or individual homes in a campus setting.

Contracts vary for CCRCs and can be structured as all-inclusive coverage, basic housing cost and added fee for service, or total fee for service. Most CCRCs require an entrance fee in addition to a monthly fee.

CCRCs vary in terms of policies related to refund of entrance fees and financial obligations should the older adult want to leave or when he or she dies. It is important that the older adult review the terms carefully prior to signing the contract.

Assisted Living Communities

Referred to as assisted living communities, residences, or facilities, these settings offer housing that is designed to accommodate the needs of older and disabled individuals, along with assistance with personal care and health management. There is variation in the models of assisted living communities (ALCs) in the degree of health care services offered; some focus more on the housing aspect while others emphasize health care services.

ESSENTIAL FACTS

ALCs are regulated on the state level; thus, there can be differences among the states in terminology used to refer to ALCs, level of care that can be provided, and the survey process used to monitor their performance.

Nursing practice in ALCs typically includes:

- Comprehensive assessment at admission, annually, and whenever there is a change in condition
- Monitoring and oversight of the resident's function and status in order to identify changes in care and service needs
- Planning for care needs and other services
- Administration of treatments
- Coordination and oversight of care
- Supervision of nursing caregivers
- Management of medications, including medication administration and oversight of the resident's self-administration of medications or of other staff who may administer medications
- Development, coordination, and implementation of health promotion programs
- Monitoring of safety and general status of the physical environment
- Communication of plans and changes to resident, health care team, caregivers, and family members or proxies

ESSENTIAL FACTS

A proxy is a person legally authorized to act on behalf of another person should that person become incapable of making decisions. The proxy is responsible for implementing the resident's wishes; therefore, residents should be encouraged to select a proxy who can be trusted to do so and to make the proxy fully aware of all health care preferences.

The focus of ALCs is to maximize the resident's independence. This requires that the nurse:

- Identify factors that may restrict independence and self-care ability and intervene to eliminate or minimize them
- Reinforce the resident's efforts to function independently
- Respect the resident's care and scheduling preferences
- Prevent complications that could jeopardize independence
- Ensure that caregivers promote maximum independent function in the resident
- Foster a homelike environment that promotes as normal a lifestyle and high a quality of life as possible

ESSENTIAL FACTS

In ALCs and many long-term care settings, registered nurses (RNs) are few in number and often are in the position of assigning functions to licensed practical or vocational nurses (LPNs or LVNs) and unlicensed nursing personnel. RNs can delegate to LPNs or LVNs the authority to assign certain tasks to unlicensed nursing staff, but the RNs still have the responsibility and accountability for those tasks.

Assessment and care plan development are within the scope of RN practice and cannot be delegated to LPNs or LVNs, or to unlicensed staff, although these other levels of nursing staff can contribute to data collection and care plan development.

Nurse practice acts specify legal restrictions relating to delegation, and nurses need to be familiar with scope of practice limitations. The nurse practice act for a specific state can be found on that state's board of nursing website.

The American Assisted Living Nurses Association has developed standards for assisted living nurses that can be found on the organization's website, at www.alnursing.org.

Nursing Homes

The highest level of long-term care services is offered in nursing homes. In the past few decades the acuity level of nursing home residents has increased, and many nursing homes are now caring for residents who would previously have been treated in an acute hospital. Factors that increase the risk for nursing home admission include:

- Loss of independent function
- Decreased cognitive function
- Medical condition that requires close supervision or regular treatments
- Immobility
- Living alone; lack of informal or family caregivers
- Hospitalization
- Advanced age
- Being a woman
- Diagnoses of dementia, hypertension, cerebrovascular accident, or heart disease

Nursing home care can be reimbursed by Medicare, Medicaid, private insurance, or private payments. Medicare pays only for *skilled nursing* care, meaning the resident must require medical care by licensed health care providers or rehabilitative therapy, or both. Skilled care is not required by Medicaid, which pays for most nursing home care; less than 5% of nursing home residents pay privately for their care.

The federal government certifies nursing homes to qualify for Medicare or Medicaid reimbursement, or both. Nursing homes that do not receive Medicare or Medicaid reimbursement are licensed by the state. To remain licensed and certified, nursing homes must meet standards expressed through regulations, and to ensure the homes meet these standards surveys are conducted by the state health department (which acts as an agent for the federal government). Current regulations were developed through legislation known as the Omnibus Budget Reconciliation Act of 1987 (OBRA '87), also known as the Nursing Home Reform Law, and require the following:

- Use of a standardized Resident Assessment Instrument (RAI) called the Minimum Data Set (MDS)
- Timely development of a written comprehensive care plan
- Specific minimum levels of staffing
- Protection of residents' rights
- Reduction in the use of restraints and psychotropic drugs
- Training and certification for nursing assistants
- A resident-centered survey process

ESSENTIAL FACTS

> In addition to being a site in which complex conditions can be treated, nursing homes are challenged to provide a homelike setting that offers residents a high quality of life along with a high quality of care.

The rising acuity levels of nursing home residents and multitude of diagnoses that can be present,coupled with the reality that medical staff are typically not present most of the time, demand that nursing home nurses be clinically competent to assess and manage residents' care. In addition, the fact that residents will reside in the nursing home for an extended time or, in some cases, the remainder of their lives requires that nurses ensure residents experience the highest possible quality of life. This includes optimum individualization of care, honoring the resident's personal preferences, creating a homelike environment, and offering the resident a meaningful life. Culture change programming has promoted these types of efforts. (Culture change is discussed in Chapter 6.)

Nurses fill a variety of roles in nursing homes, such as director of nursing, staff development director, quality assurance coordinator, infection control coordinator, clinical consultant, geropsychiatric nurse specialist, wound care specialist, rehabilitative nurse, and unit manager. Each of these roles requires special expertise to be integrated with basic nursing competencies. The American Association for Long Term Care Nursing (www.ltcnursing.org) offers education and certification programs that assist long-term care nurses in preparing for specialized roles.

3

Reimbursement for Long-Term Care

Often, the types of long-term care services that people use are influenced by the source of payment. There are differences among major third-party payers as to the services that qualify for payment, length of time services are covered, and conditions that must be met for the provider to be reimbursed.

This chapter should enable you to:

1. Describe Parts A, B, C, and D of the Medicare program
2. Describe the Medicaid program
3. Identify differences between Medicare and Medicaid in eligibility and services covered
4. List qualifications for and services covered by the Program for All-Inclusive Care of the Elderly (PACE)

MEDICARE

Medicare, Title 18 of the Social Security Act, was launched in 1965 as a health insurance program for individuals aged 65 years and older and younger individuals who receive Social Security Disability or Railroad Retirement Board benefits, or who have end-stage renal disease. In addition, a recipient must have been a U.S. citizen or permanent legal resident for 5 continuous years and be eligible for Social Security benefits with at least 10 years of payments contributed into the system. The Social Security Administration determines whether a person is eligible for Medicare.

ESSENTIAL FACTS

Medicare is primarily funded through payroll taxes collected through the Federal Insurance Contributions Act (FICA) and the Self-Employment Contributions Act.

Medicare consists of several parts:

- *Part A*: This is available to qualified individuals at no cost and covers:
  - Hospitalizations
  - Home health care (nursing or physical, occupational, or speech therapy) that is deemed medically necessary and provided on a part-time basis
  - Skilled nursing care for limited periods of time
  - Hospice
  - Certain medical equipment
- *Part B*: Also known as Supplemental Medical Insurance (SMI) is optional insurance that requires a monthly premium (that can be deducted from the recipient's monthly Social Security check) and has a deductible that must be met. It pays for:
  - Medically necessary physician visits
  - Medically necessary outpatient hospital services
  - Diagnostic tests
  - Certain immunizations
  - Chemotherapy
  - Blood transfusions
  - Immunosuppressive drugs following organ transplantation
  - Prosthetic devices
  - Some home health services
- *Part C*: Also known as Medicare Advantage, this is an optional plan that provides coverage beyond Parts A and B. It includes health maintenance organization (HMO) plans, preferred provider organization (PPO) plans, special needs plans (SNPs), and private fee-for-service plans.
- *Part D*: Offers a prescription drug plan administered by a private company. Plans vary depending on the company providing them.
- *Medigap supplemental insurance*: Provided by companies authorized by the Centers for Medicare and Medicaid Services (CMS), these plans cover medical expenses and services not covered through Medicare, such as deductibles and copayments.

Medicare covers long-term care services on a limited basis, and it does not cover basic, custodial level care. Although Medicare will not pay for residency in an assisted living community (ALC), it will cover the cost of medically necessary care that is provided in an ALC, as it would home health services in a person's private home in the community.

The CMS administers the Medicare and Medicaid programs. The federal government funds Medicare and benefits are similar throughout the United States. Because Medicaid is supported by matching state and federal funds, benefits can vary from state to state.

MEDICAID

Medicaid, a health insurance program for people of all ages who have limited income and assets, is Title 19 of the Social Security Act of 1965. It is jointly funded by the federal and state governments. States may vary in eligibility requirements and in the benefit packages they offer recipients.

Most Medicaid programs pay Medicare Part B premiums and coinsurance costs. Whereas Medicare offers only limited coverage for skilled nursing home care, Medicaid pays for all levels of nursing home care. Growing numbers of Medicaid programs are reimbursing for care in ALCs. It is not uncommon for people to pay privately for the costs of nursing home care that Medicare does not cover but then become eligible for Medicaid after their personal funds are depleted.

ESSENTIAL FACTS

A person is considered dually eligible if he or she qualifies for both Medicare and Medicaid coverage.

Program for All-Inclusive Care of the Elderly (PACE)

PACE is program that covers comprehensive services for community-based adults who are dually eligible and who meet the requirements for nursing home admission. To qualify, a person must:

- Be 55 years of age or older
- Live in a service area in which a PACE organization is located
- Need a nursing home level of care (as certified by the state)
- Be able to live safely in the community with help from PACE

  Some of the services PACE covers include:

- Adult day primary care (including physician and recreational therapy nursing services)
- Dentistry

- Emergency services
- Home care
- Hospital care
- Laboratory and x-ray services
- Meals
- Medical specialty services
- Nursing home care
- Nutritional counseling
- Occupational therapy, physical therapy
- Prescription drugs
- Preventive care
- Social services, including counseling, caregiver training, support groups, and respite care
- Transportation to a PACE center for activities or medical appointments, if medically necessary, and to some medical appointments in the community

Application for PACE is made through the state's Medicaid program. People without Medicaid and Medicare are able to enroll in PACE and pay privately. A listing of PACE organizations can be found at: www.cms.hhs.gov/pace/pacesite.asp.

Long-Term Care Insurance

A minority of individuals have private long-term care policies. These plans vary as to conditions that must be met, types of services covered, and length of time covered.

4

Regulations

Regulations are administrative laws established to protect the public. These regulations must be met in order for a facility to be licensed and receive reimbursement from the Medicare and Medicaid programs. Nursing homes and assisted living communities face consequences for violations of regulations, ranging from fines to closure of the facility.

The federal government has established regulations for nursing homes that are consistent in every state. State governments are given the responsibility of monitoring and enforcing federal regulations; in addition, state and local governments can establish additional regulations.

Although nursing homes must adhere to numerous regulations, assisted living communities are governed by fewer regulations, and most of those exist on the state level. Thus, there can be considerable differences in assisted living standards among the states.

This chapter should enable you to:

1. List major regulatory requirements for nursing homes
2. Describe the areas that will be evaluated during a nursing home survey
3. List the quality indicators that will be noted during a nursing home survey
4. Describe the meaning of an F-tag
5. Identify the significance of various levels of deficiencies
6. Describe federal and state responsibilities for assisted living community regulation

NURSING HOME REGULATIONS

ESSENTIAL FACTS

> It is important to remember that regulations state the **minimum** standards that must be met.

The first federal nursing home regulations were authorized by the U.S. Congress in 1967 in response to the new Medicare and Medicaid reimbursement for nursing home care. Updates have occurred periodically since then, with the most significant being the Omnibus Budget Reconciliation Act (OBRA) of 1987, which was passed in 1989. Minor revisions to the regulations are made periodically.

Federal regulations for nursing homes are developed by the Centers for Medicare and Medicaid Services (CMS), which describe the various standards that must be met to be in compliance. State agencies conduct surveys to determine if the nursing home is satisfactorily complying. Surveyors only evaluate the facility's compliance with stated regulations and cannot impose additional conditions.

ESSENTIAL FACTS

> The federal government publishes the rules and regulations in the Federal Register under the title Code of Federal Regulations (CFR). Descriptions of regulations that nursing homes must meet are cited by a CFR number. For example, 42 CFR 483.20 refers to Title 42, which is the code for Public Health, Part 483 within that code, and the specific section under that, 483.20.

Among the federal regulations for nursing homes are requirements that they must:

- Promote each resident's quality of life (42 CFR 483.15)
- Maintain the dignity and respect of each resident (42 CFR 483.15)
- Conduct a comprehensive and accurate assessment of each resident's functional capacity upon admission (42 CFR 483.20)
- Develop a comprehensive care plan for each resident (42 CFR 483.20)
- Prevent the deterioration of a resident's ability to bathe, dress, groom, transfer and ambulate, toilet, eat, and communicate (42 CFR 483.25)
- Provide the necessary services to maintain good nutrition, grooming, and personal oral hygiene if a resident is unable to independently carry out activities of daily living (42 CFR 483.25)

- Ensure that residents receive proper treatment and assistive devices to maintain vision and hearing abilities (42 CFR 483.25)
- Ensure that residents do not develop pressure sores and, if a resident has pressure sores, provide the necessary treatment and services to promote healing, prevent infection, and prevent new sores from developing (42 CFR 483.25)
- Provide appropriate treatment and services to incontinent residents to restore as much normal bladder functioning as possible (42 CFR 483.25)
- Ensure that the resident receives adequate supervision and assistive devices to prevent accidents (42 CFR 483.25)
- Maintain acceptable parameters of a resident's nutritional status (42 CFR 483.25)
- Provide each resident with sufficient fluid intake to maintain proper hydration and health (42 CFR 483.25)
- Ensure that residents are free of any significant medication errors (42 CFR 483.25)
- Have sufficient nursing staff (42 CFR 483.30)
- Ensure that residents have the right to choose activities, schedules, and health care (42 CFR 483.40)
- Provide pharmaceutical services to meet the needs of each resident (42 CFR 483.60)
- Be administered in a manner that enables the nursing home to use its resources effectively and efficiently (42 CFR 483.75)
- Maintain accurate, complete, and easily accessible clinical records on each resident (42 CFR 483.75)

To receive Medicare reimbursement, nursing homes must meet additional regulations, such as higher staffing requirements.

ESSENTIAL FACTS

A nursing home can be licensed to operate but not certified for Medicare reimbursement.

NURSING HOME SURVEYS

Anticipated and actual surveys often cause some anxiety within nursing homes. Knowledge of and consistent compliance with the regulatory conditions that must be met can assure a positive survey experience and eliminate much of the anxiety. CMS has established interpretive guidelines for surveyors to ensure they are objective and evaluate all facilities with the same criteria.

When the survey team arrives in the nursing home, they will:

- Conduct a general tour to note the status of the physical facility and residents

- Ask the nursing administrator for general information about the residents, which they will document
- Identify residents who are capable of participating in interviews and select a sample of these residents to interview; areas reviewed in the interview include:
  - Satisfaction with their rooms and the general environment
  - Privacy afforded
  - Quality of meals
  - Activities
  - Satisfaction with staff
  - Activities of daily living
  - Degree to which they can make decisions affecting their care
  - Respect of their rights
  - Views pertaining to being treated with dignity
  - Presence of abuse and neglect
  - Handling of personal property
  - Satisfaction with medical services
  - Costs
  - Availability and participation in resident council

Surveyors will be present at mealtime to evaluate the appropriateness, quality, and temperature of meals and the assistance given to residents.

The process of medication preparation and administration will be observed for a sampling of residents. Specific areas that will be noted include:

- Appropriateness of prescriptions and dosages
- Storage of medications
- Drug pass procedure
- Documentation of medication administration
- Medication errors
- Knowledge of the person administering the medications of the purpose, interactions, and adverse effects of medications administered
- Procedures related to the use of antipsychotics, antidepressants, and PRN (as-needed) medication orders

Except for resident interviews, nursing home staff members can accompany the surveyors during their inspection. While the survey is conducted, staff should perform their routine activities in a normal manner. If asked questions by the surveyors, staff should answer to the best of their ability; if they do not know the answer to a question they should seek the assistance of their supervisor. Any problems that are discovered can be corrected while the surveyors are present.

ESSENTIAL FACTS

Staff should report any problems that arise during the survey to their supervisors.

Quality indicators are reviewed in the survey process (Table 4.1). Further investigation will be done if the nursing home is:

- At or above the 50th percentile for weight loss or pressure sores among residents
- At or above the 75th percentile for any of the other quality indicators

TABLE 4.1 Quality Indicators Noted During a Nursing Home Survey

Accidents	Incidence of new fractures Falls
Behavioral/Emotional Patterns	Prevalence of behavioral symptoms affecting others Prevalence of symptoms of depression Prevalence of symptoms of depression without antidepressant therapy
Clinical Management	Use of 9 or more medications
Cognitive Patterns	Incidence of cognitive impairment
Elimination/Incontinence	Prevalence of bladder or bowel incontinence Prevalence of occasional or frequent bladder or bowel incontinence without a toileting plan Prevalence of indwelling catheter Prevalence of fecal impaction
Infection Control	Presence of urinary tract infection
Nutrition/Eating	Presence of weight loss Presence of tube feeding Prevalence of dehydration
Physical Functioning	Prevalence of bedfast residents Incidence of decline in later-loss activities of daily living Incidence of decline in range of motion
Psychotropic Drug Use	Prevalence of antipsychotic use, in the absence of psychotic or related conditions Prevalence of antianxiety/hypnotic drug use Prevalence of hypnotic use more than 2 times in last week
Quality of Life	Prevalence of daily physical restraints Prevalence of little or no activity
Skin Care	Prevalence of stage 1–4 pressure ulcers

Among the quality indicators that CMS considers are several of such a serious nature that if found to affect more than a few residents the surveyors will conduct further investigation. These are:

- A pressure ulcer in a low-risk resident
- Prevalence of fecal impaction
- Dehydration

Typically, surveys last several days. If significant deficiencies are identified, surveyors can extend the survey or return to conduct an additional investigation.

Following the survey, an exit interview will be conducted and the nursing home will receive a report describing any deficiencies in meeting regulatory requirements. It is acceptable for staff to question findings and provide evidence of the inappropriateness of a cited deficiency. The nursing home will respond to the report of deficiencies with a written description of the actions they intend to take to correct the problems.

ESSENTIAL FACTS

When deficiencies are found during a survey, the surveyors will cite the specific standard not met using a federal-tag, commonly referred to as an F-tag. F-tags correspond to the section of the regulations involved; for example F-240 relates to section 483.15 Quality of Life, F-309 relates to 483.25 Quality of Care, and F-314 relates to section 483.25(c) Pressure Ulcers.

The surveyors also will rate the deficiency in terms of how severe it is in relation to causing harm to residents and the scope in terms of being an isolated finding, reflective of a pattern, or a widespread occurrence (Table 4.2). When the deficiency citations are serious,

TABLE 4.2 Survey Deficiency Rating System

Severity of Deficiency	Scope of Deficiency		
	Isolated	Pattern	Widespread
Immediate jeopardy to resident health or safety	J	K	L
Actual harm that is not immediate jeopardy	G	H	I
No actual harm but with potential for more than minimal harm that is not immediate jeopardy	D	E	F
No actual harm but with potential for more than minimal harm	A	B	C

CMS requires that the surveyors revisit the nursing home to ensure that the condition has been corrected and the nursing home is in compliance with the regulations. Sanctions also can be placed on the nursing home when deficiencies are serious. These include:

- Suspension or denial of Medicare or Medicaid payment
- Financial penalty
- Appointment of an outside agency to manage or monitor the nursing home
- Termination of the nursing home's ability to receive Medicare or Medicaid reimbursement

ESSENTIAL FACTS

CMS posts the survey results of all nursing homes on the website Nursing Home Compare, at: www.medicare.gov/nursing homecompare/search.html.

ASSISTED LIVING REGULATIONS

Currently, the regulation of assisted living communities occurs on the state level. Each state has its own set of regulations and process for inspections. (See "Assisted Living Regulations" in the "Resources" listing at the back of this book for a description of each state's regulations.)

Although the federal government does not regulate assisted living communities, it does ensure that regulations pertaining to the provision of Medicare services are adhered to for individuals receiving Medicare services who reside in assisted living communities. In addition, assisted living communities must abide by federal laws affecting work environments in general, such as those described in the Occupational Safety and Health Administration (OSHA) regulations.

NURSE PRACTICE ACTS

In many long-term care settings, registered nurses (RNs) are not available at all times and most direct care is performed by unlicensed personnel. These conditions heighten the risk that nursing employees may perform tasks that are beyond their legal scope of practice. For example, a licensed practical nurse (LPN) may perform a resident assessment in a nursing home because no RN is present at that time; doing so places the LPN in the position of functioning outside his or her legal scope of practice.

Each state has developed rules and regulations governing nursing practice, known as nurse practice acts. It is important that nurses be familiar with and adhere to their state's nurse practice act to ensure they are not performing functions that exceed their legal scope of practice or delegating functions to others that are not within their scope of practice. The National Council of State Boards of Nursing provides a listing of each state's Nurse Practice Act (see "Resources" at the end of this book).

5

Long-Term Care Nursing Responsibilities

There is a misconception among some individuals that long-term care nursing is less complex and demanding than nursing in acute care settings; however, the reality is quite different. Nurses in long-term care settings care for residents with a wide range of conditions and often do so without the regular presence of medical staff on the premises. In addition to clinical responsibilities, these nurses may carry considerable managerial functions. Additionally, the fact that fewer licensed nurses are available places heavy demands on each nurse to ensure that acceptable standards of nursing practice are maintained and that employees to whom tasks are delegated are performing satisfactorily. To deliver high-quality services, long-term care nurses must possess a wide range of competencies and assume responsibility for sustaining and improving them.

This chapter should enable you to:

1. Describe the key elements of long-term care nursing
2. Identify differences between long-term care nursing and acute care nursing
3. List major nursing responsibilities in long-term care settings
4. Identify acceptable responsibilities for registered nurses (RNs) and licensed practical nurses (LPNs) based on legal scope of practice

UNIQUE ASPECTS OF LONG-TERM CARE NURSING

Long-term care (LTC) nursing is a specialized branch of nursing that differs from other clinical specialties. The American Association for Long Term Care Nursing (2014) offers the following definition:

Long term care nursing provides holistic physical, emotional, mental, cultural, and psychosocial care to maximize independence and optimal functioning to people who have chronic illness and/or disability for which assistance is needed over extended periods of time. Long term care can be provided to persons of any age in the community, assisted living, or nursing home settings.

Several key elements to this definition highlight the essence of LTC nursing:

- *Care is holistic.* LTC nurses are concerned with every facet of the individual—body, mind, and spirit.
- *Chronic conditions are the major focus.* Although LTC residents experience acute conditions, the majority of their conditions are chronic ones. Often, LTC residents have multiple chronic conditions that must be cared for.
- *Care is needed for an extended period of time.* Most patients receiving acute care have conditions that will improve and, in many cases, be eliminated. Most LTC residents have conditions that will remain with them for life and will require ongoing care. This presents challenges to LTC nurses as they are tasked to not only provide a high quality of care, but also assist residents in achieving the highest possible quality of life.

For many individuals, the LTC facility becomes a long-term or permanent residence, causing nurses to be engaged in residents' quality of life concerns that may not be present in the acute care setting. LTC nurses assist residents in adjusting to new roles and relationships with loved ones and establishing a meaningful lifestyle, and in some circumstances, adapting to life in a health care facility.

ESSENTIAL FACTS

For many LTC residents, the health care facility also serves as a home. Nurses are challenged to create a homelike environment for residents while delivering complex care.

Unlike hospital settings, in which the professionals and medical staff are readily available, in LTC settings these individuals visit occasionally and rely on nurses to advise them of needs. LTC nurses must regularly assess residents and identify needs and changes in status that require the attention of other members of the interdisciplinary team. Plans developed by the interdisciplinary team are coordinated by nurses.

LTC nurses commonly are engaged with residents' family members who present their own set of needs. Family members may feel depression, guilt, anger, and other feelings related to their loved one being admitted to a nursing home or an assisted living community and displace their feelings to staff. Nurses need to assist families in adjusting to the new situation and developing a new style of relationship. They may be faced with questions related to consent, power of attorney, appropriateness of life-sustaining measures, and protection of assets.

In addition to clinical issues, nurses face many managerial challenges. Most LTC employees are unlicensed personnel whom nurses must supervise. This demands that LTC nurses:

- Know the residents and the care they require
- Understand the competencies and scope of practice of staff to whom tasks are delegated
- Effectively communicate the care plan to caregivers
- Ensure that care is provided consistent with accepted standards
- Obtain input from staff regarding signs, symptoms, and changes that require further attention
- Guide, coach, and teach staff to ensure their provision of appropriate care
- Evaluate staff's performance and correct performance problems

In a given day, an LTC nurse may have to guide a nursing assistant in calming the behavior of an agitated resident, provide emergency care for a resident who has fallen and is suspected of fracturing her femur, comfort the daughter of a resident who has just died, help the resident recovering from knee surgery to ambulate as instructed by physical therapy, determine the most appropriate pain control measures for a resident with pneumonia, and interact with surveyors who are doing an inspection. The situations faced by the LTC nurse are diverse and challenging.

ESSENTIAL FACTS

A majority of the population served in LTC settings is vulnerable due to their physical or cognitive impairments or advanced age. For this reason, LTC nurses must advocate for their residents, protect their rights, and ensure they are treated with fairness and dignity.

RESPONSIBILITIES OF LTC NURSES

Although nursing activities can vary among clinical sites, there are some basic responsibilities that nurses fulfill in LTC settings (Box 5.1). These responsibilities require that, in addition to basic nursing competencies, LTC nurses have knowledge and skills in areas related to their responsibilities in the LTC practice setting, such as age-related

Box 5.1 Responsibilities of Long-Term Care Nurses

- Assess residents (if registered nurse [RN]) or participate in the assessment process (if licensed practical nurse [LPN]), incorporating knowledge of age-related changes and norms
- Develop the care/service plan (if RN) or participate in development of the care/service plan (if LPN)
- Communicate the care plan to caregivers, residents, and residents' significant others
- Review, transcribe, communicate, and implement physicians' orders.
- Coordinate and participate in admissions, transfers, and discharges of residents
- Direct, supervise, and assist staff in delivering nursing care
- Actively engage residents in their care
- Address the unique caregiving requirements of residents with dementias
- Ensure that residents with dementias have activities and interventions appropriate to their function and needs
- Monitor and oversee immunizations and other health promotion activities
- Document according to required regulations and standards of care; supervise employees under direction in documenting resident care
- Communicate and coordinate care with residents and their families or significant others
- Administer treatments and other direct care
- Participate in medication management to promote optimal safety and effectiveness for residents by:
  - Preparing and administering medications as prescribed
  - Observing and evaluating residents' responses to medications
  - Evaluating effectiveness of timing, route, and form of drug
  - Identifying and promptly communicating adverse drug reactions
  - Maintaining narcotic records accurately
  - Ordering or arranging for ordering of pharmaceuticals
  - Notifying physicians of automatic stop orders
  - Notifying supervisor of discrepancies in drug inventories

(continued)

Box 5.1 *(continued)*

- Collect specimens as ordered
- Communicate abnormal laboratory data and x-ray findings to the physician or advanced practice nurse (APN) and document this information
- Identify restorative and rehabilitative nursing needs for residents; participate in developing and implementing restorative and rehabilitative nursing programs
- Actively prevent risks that can impair function and health
- Respect residents' rights
- Protect residents from abuse and neglect
- Determine residents' capacity to make informed decisions; encourage and provide opportunities for residents to make decisions concerning care
- Adjust care to accommodate cultural and religious preferences
- Communicate with residents' physicians
- Make rounds to assess residents' status and evaluate care
- Implement, practice, and ensure that staff adhere to infection control policies and procedures
- Prepare staff for resident admissions; ensure rooms are prepared for resident admissions
- Assist with emergencies; administer cardiopulmonary resuscitation
- Ensure that residents have documented advance directives and that residents' preferences are respected
- Accept and give shift reports
- Communicate unit needs to appropriate personnel
- Ensure that adequate and appropriate information is communicated to other sites to which residents may be transferred
- Prepare residents for discharge
- Support and participate in the facility's quality assurance program
- Participate on committees as assigned
- Complete records and reports as needed
- Adhere to professional codes of ethics
- Demonstrate positive customer service
- Ensure that problems and complaints are managed and resolved in a timely, appropriate manner, and reported to administrative staff
- Maintain positive working relationships between nursing and other departments' staff
- Protect the privacy of residents and employees
- Adhere to regulatory standards governing practice setting

changes, principles of geriatric nursing, geriatric syndromes, care of persons with dementias, management principles, regulations governing the setting, and resident-directed and resident-centered care.

ESSENTIAL FACTS

Competencies consist of the knowledge and skills required to effectively fulfill one's responsibilities.

Nurses have a responsibility to ensure that they are competent to practice. Having completed a nursing education program and successfully passed state boards are basic to competency but not sufficient. Nurses must ensure that they have the unique knowledge and skills to fulfill their roles in their specialty.

ESSENTIAL FACTS

One means of keeping current with new practices is to use PubMed, a government site that offers a listing of citations for biomedical literature from MEDLINE, life science journals, and online books that can be searched by topic, and the Cumulative Index of Nursing and Allied Health Literature, which contains a database of nursing and allied health journals, evidence-based care sheets, quick lessons, books, dissertations, conference proceedings, and standards of practice (see the "Resources" at the end of this book).

There are differences in expected competencies between RNs and LPNs based on their legal scope of practice(Boxes 5.2 and 5.3). It is important that nurses adhere to their scope of practice, remain competent to perform the functions within their scope of practice, and only delegate tasks to others that are appropriate within their scope of practice.

LTC nurses often assume responsibilities beyond basic nursing as they function in expanded roles, such as director of nursing, staff development director, infection control coordinator, and nurse manager. As the responsibilities exceed basic nursing functions, nurses must acquire additional skills to ensure competent performance. There are associations for LTC nurses that offer education and certification programs for specialized roles (see listing in the end-of-book "Resources" section). LTC nurses should assume personal responsibilities for gaining the additional competencies they need to fulfill their roles.

Box 5.2 Acceptable Responsibilities Within the Registered Nurses' (RNs') Scope of Practice

- Perform comprehensive nursing assessment of individuals or groups
- Compare data to normal values
- Determine nursing diagnoses
- Develop and coordinate care plans
- Implement and evaluate nursing care
- Delegate nursing actions to all levels of licensed and unlicensed nursing personnel
- Coordinate care with interdisciplinary team members
- Evaluate outcomes and effectiveness of care plan
- Identify changes in residents' status
- Communicate and collaborate with other team members
- Teach and counsel residents, families, groups, or nursing staff
- Manage, supervise, and evaluate those to whom tasks are delegated
- Ensure that safe care is delivered by self or others to whom tasks are delegated
- Assist in the development of policies and procedures
- Administer nursing services

Box 5.3 Acceptable Responsibilities Within the Licensed Practical Nurses' (LPNs') Scope of Practice

- Collect data to contribute to nursing assessment
- Identify changes in residents' status
- Compare data to normal values
- Implement and evaluate nursing care
- Participate in the development of the care plan
- Participate in the evaluation of the care plan
- Provide care within the scope of LPN practice
- Communicate and collaborate with other team members
- Delegate and supervise tasks to nursing assistants and other LPNs

(continued)

Box 5.3 (*continued*)

- Ensure that safe care is delivered by self or others to whom tasks are delegated
- Participate in teaching and counseling to residents, families, and groups
- Provide input into the development of policies and procedures
- Practice under the supervision of an RN, a physician, a dentist, or another person authorized by state law

ESSENTIAL FACTS

In addition to ensuring that residents receive the best quality of care and quality of life, LTC nursing administrators also must ensure the nursing department functions in compliance with regulatory, professional, and organizational standards and with fiscal accountability. This requires advanced management and leadership competencies.

Knowledge and skills related to nursing practice are not static. Nurses need to assume personal responsibility for maintaining and improving competencies to ensure that they are fulfilling their responsibilities safely and effectively. This requires nurses to regularly assess their competencies to identify areas in need of improvement. Figure 5.1 describes this process.

Assess professional and personal practices that affect competencies
- Use of evidence-based practices
- Effective interpersonal skills
- Use of critical thinking skills
- Adherence to standards
- Positive self-care practices

Identify indicators of need for improvement
- Errors
- Complaints
- Poor surveys or evaluations
- Negative feedback
- Relationship problems
- Poor health or physical condition
- Frustration
- Disorganization

Develop plans to improve
- Participating in continuing education
- Reading journals, texts
- Networking with peers
- Asking for mentoring or coaching
- Establishing positive health practices

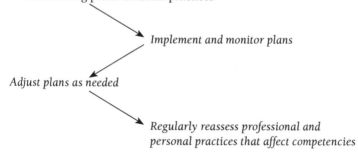

Implement and monitor plans

Adjust plans as needed

Regularly reassess professional and personal practices that affect competencies

FIGURE 5.1   Process for nurses to ensure continued competence in fulfilling responsibilities.

6

Culture Change

Dissatisfaction with the institutional style of nursing homes led to a movement known as culture change that was launched in the 1990s to transform these facilities. Basic to culture change is the belief that the nursing home should provide a high quality of life for its residents. This result is fostered when residents have control over their lives, such as choices about care, meals, activities, and schedules. The change affects direct care staff, too, as it encourages greater input into caregiving plans and active participation in decision making. A homelike environment is promoted by individualization of residents' rooms, attractive decor, the presence of pets, connection to nature, and comfortable areas for visitors of all ages to enjoy. The result is a more meaningful, satisfying life experience for residents and a more meaningful, satisfying work experience for staff.

This chapter should enable you to:

1. Describe signs of "institutionalization"
2. List risks associated with individuals becoming institutionalized
3. Identify similarities between institutional life and homelessness
4. Describe core elements of culture change
5. List positive outcomes associated with culture change
6. Describe the four stages of culture change
7. Describe actions nurses can take to support culture change

ELIMINATING THE INSTITUTIONAL MODEL

Today's culture change movement is the result of an effort to change the impersonal nature of the nursing home environment and the "institutionalization" of individuals who reside in this setting. The term *institutionalization,* coined more than a half century ago, refers to a "condition characterized by impaired social interaction, decision-making and independent living skills resulting from long-term care in an institutional setting," reflected by signs that included the following (Sommer, 1961):

- Deindividualization—increased dependence, lack of assertiveness, inability to make independent decisions, and reliance on the institution
- Disculturation—acquisition of institutional values and attitudes unsuited to general society
- Biopsychosocial damage from loss of status and security
- Estrangement from technological and other changes in the outside world
- Stimulus deprivation resulting from senses being deadened by prolonged institutionalization

Nursing home residents who become institutionalized risk having:

- *Regression of physical, mental, and social function:* Insufficient opportunity to use skills can cause them to be lost.
- *Adoption of atypical behaviors:* Residents may acquire behaviors that enable them to have their needs met, such as hoarding food if snacks are not readily available or screaming to get staff's attention because call lights are ignored.
- *Erosion of personal identity:* Labels are used to describe residents (e.g., "the total care in room 212," "the diabetic," "the screamer").
- *Separation from society:* As their behaviors become increasingly inappropriate, residents will have less in common with people who reside outside the facility, who may withdraw from the residents.

Concern about the institutional nature of nursing home care continued to grow over the next four decades. Research began to appear highlighting the sense of hopelessness and decreased sense of power felt by nursing home residents. One such study (Carboni, 1991) compared institutional life to homelessness in which there is:

- Nonpersonhood—loss of identity, not belonging
- Disconnectedness—distancing, loss of memories, feeling of no future
- Meaningless space—communal space with intrusion by others
- Insufficient boundaries—lack of privacy, which causes retreat into inner world

- Powerlessness and dependency—no choices, helplessness leading to dependency
- Insecurity and uncertainty—vulnerability, feeling of being in danger at all times
- Placelessness—no journeying to meaningful experiences, institution is just a structure

By the beginning of the 1990s the need to transform the nursing home culture was apparent, giving rise to the culture change movement.

ESSENTIAL FACTS

When people consider the meaning of home they think about a place where they can feel safe and comfortable, experience privacy, bond with other people who are significant to them, have items present that are meaningful to them, and be free to act as they desire.

Growth of the Culture Change Movement

One of the first programs to promote culture change was the *Eden Alternative*, founded by geriatrician Bill Thomas in 1991. The basic theme of the program was that nursing home residents should have a life worth living. The Eden Alternative provides training and consultation to assist nursing homes in effecting culture change. Core principles of the program include the following (Eden Alternative, 2014):

- The nursing home should create an elder-centered community that affords residents a purposeful life to combat feelings of helplessness and meaninglessness.
- The environment should offer close contact with plants, animals, and children.
- Maximum decision-making authority should be given to residents and those closest to them.
- Medical treatment should support and serve human caring rather than dictate it.
- Loving companionship through easy access to other people and animals should be provided as it is important to combat loneliness.
- Variety and spontaneity should be part of daily life to avoid boredom.

The concept of deinstitutionalizing the nursing home was further advanced by the Eden Alternative in the development of the *Green House Project,* which promotes a design accommodating 10 to 12 residents on a unit that is designed as a homelike environment. There are private bedrooms and bathrooms, many meals are prepared in a kitchen on the unit, and typical facility features such as the nursing station and medication carts are removed. Roles are redesigned, as well, to afford closer contact between staff and residents.

The *Wellspring Program*, launched in 1994, offered a model of culture change in which a focus on quality care was integrated with the emphasis on quality of life. Wellspring placed a greater emphasis on training staff to offer high-quality care that incorporated elements such as resident choice and empowerment. In 2012, Wellspring became part of the Eden Alternative family.

The *Pioneer Network*, formed in 1997, is an organization that has brought together stakeholders in long-term care to advance the culture change movement. They work with various groups to educate and promote culture change, develop resources to assist nursing homes in transforming their practice, and host a national conference that highlights innovative practices and promotes networking.

Although the models and physical structures in which they are carried out can vary, culture change principles and practices are expanding to growing numbers of nursing homes. Research reflects positive outcomes, such as the following (Pioneer Network, 2011):

- Lower rates of staff turnover and absenteeism (some even report having waiting lists of prospective employees)
- Higher resident census
- Less reliance on medication
- Fewer pressure sores
- Better performance on inspection surveys
- Improved quality of life for residents

COMPONENTS OF CULTURE CHANGE

The basic elements of culture change include:

- *Emphasis on the resident*. Rather than the physical environment and care activities being driven by the most efficient means for staff to organize work, they are based on what is best for the resident.
- *Resident-directed care*. Residents determine such things as when they arise, go to sleep, and eat. They can choose to stay in their bedroom and read a book rather than joining in a group activity. The emphasis is on what residents desire rather than what staff thinks is best for them.
- *Meaningful relationships*. Because the quality of relationships influences the quality of life, staff are encouraged to develop meaningful relationships with residents. This is fostered by consistent assignment of staff.
- *Homelike environment*. Consideration is given to creating an experience for residents that is as similar to living in a home as possible.

This includes decorating residents' rooms with their personal items, having snacks and drinks readily available, offering pleasant areas for visitation, including pets and plants, and keeping supplies and equipment out of sight as much as possible.

- *High-quality care.* A homelike environment and positive relationships mean little if poor care is offered. Ongoing assessment for identification of needs and changes in status, relevant care plans, competent caregiving, and active prevention of complications are essential components that foster the best possible quality of life for residents.

ESSENTIAL FACTS

Essential to culture change is an enlightened approach to management that fosters a high quality of work experience for staff. This approach is supported by including direct care staff in care planning meetings, asking for staff input into decisions, recognizing their efforts, and treating staff with dignity.

STAGES OF CULTURE CHANGE

Leslie Grant and LaVerne Norton, leaders in the culture change movement, developed a conceptual model of culture change that identifies four basic stages (Commonwealth Foundation, 2014):

- Stage One—The *institutional* model:
  - Organized around traditional and often large (30 to 60 residents) nursing units
  - Traditional organizational chart with administration on the top and direct care workers on the bottom
  - Decisions made by top managers with little input by direct care workers
  - Nursing staff not permanently assigned to the same group of residents
  - Kitchen off limits
- Stage Two—The *transformational* model:
  - Direct care workers and administrative staff aware of culture change
  - Group processes (e.g., learning circles) may be used but final decisions occur at the top
  - Nursing staff consistently assigned to the same unit or group of residents
  - Low-cost changes in décor; introduction of plants and animals
  - Residents' rooms personalized
  - More mealtime choices offered to residents
  - Direct care staff participate in decision making

- Stage Three—The *neighborhood* model:
  - Traditional units broken into smaller functional areas
  - Direct-care staff involved in making more decisions
  - Nursing staff permanently assigned to one or more neighborhoods within the same unit
  - Cross-training of workers; other direct care workers encouraged to become certified as certified nursing assistants (CNAs)
  - More choice given to residents
  - Decentralized dining without a full kitchen; small appliances used in dining area
  - Neighborhood coordinator role formalized
  - Decentralized leadership; decisions made by consensus in neighborhood teams
- Stage Four—The *household* model:
  - Residents live in self-contained living units (usually 16 to 24 residents) and share a common dining room and living area
  - Each household has a "nurse leader" who reports to the "clinical mentor" (i.e., director of nursing) and a household or community coordinator who reports to the "community mentor" (i.e., administrator or designee)
  - Nursing station and medication carts eliminated
  - Staff work in self-directed teams that are permanently assigned to a given household
  - Household teams plan their own work schedules
  - Residents determine daily routines, schedules, and activities
  - Residents have increased choice and accessibility to food
  - Traditional departments eliminated

ESSENTIAL FACTS

The **Artifacts of Culture Change tool**, developed for the Centers for Medicare and Medicaid Services (CMS), offers an objective means to assess where the nursing home is on its journey of culture change and to benchmark progress. The tool can be viewed on the Pioneer Network website at *www.pioneernetwork.net/Providers/Artifacts/*.

THE NURSE'S ROLE IN CULTURE CHANGE

Nurses play a critical role in facilitating culture change by:

- Assessing the extent to which the core elements are present in the facility:
  - Emphasis on resident-centered and resident-directed care
  - Existence of meaningful relationships between residents and staff

- Presence of homelike environment
- High-quality care
- Active engagement and empowerment of direct care workers
- Guiding the development of plans to strengthen core elements and foster practices that support culture change
- Teaching and guiding staff in practices that support culture change practices and principles
- Providing residents with sufficient information to make sound decisions
- Providing opportunities and encouraging residents to make decisions affecting their life and care
- Assisting in the implementation of best practices
- Implementing and supporting consistent assignments of staff to residents
- Identifying opportunities for families and significant others to be actively involved in residents' lives
- Ensuring that care plans and actions address holistic needs
- Encouraging active participation of direct care workers in care planning and evaluation activities (Box 6.1)
- Fostering a homelike environment (Box 6.2)

Box 6.1 Learning Circles

A learning circle is a style of discussion of a topic in which all group participants have an equal opportunity to contribute and be heard. The learning circle typically consists of 5 to 15 people who have an interest in or knowledge of the issue. It is led by a person designated to facilitate the process without influencing it. The basic process is as follows:

1. Participants are selected to participate in the learning circle. They can be employees, residents, or visitors; the determining factor is that they are stakeholders in the issue.
2. Participants meet in a room and sit in a circle in which they can easily view each other.
3. A question or issue is presented to the group by the facilitator (e.g., How could work schedules be changed to accommodate the large number of residents who prefer to sleep later? What are some ways that we can encourage residents' visitors to be more involved in activities?).
4. A participant sitting closest to the facilitator offers a response followed by the participant sitting next to that person; the process continues until everyone in the circle has had a chance to respond.

(continued)

Box 6.1 *(continued)*

5. Responses are not reacted to or discussed by other participants when contributed.
6. A participant can pass if he or she has nothing to contribute at the time.
7. The facilitator lists key points or summary of each participant's contribution on a flip chart or board.
8. Participants continue to go around the circle contributing until they have nothing more to add.
9. The facilitator invites open discussion.
10. The group reaches consensus on a response or recommendations.

Box 6.2 Elements of a Homelike Care Environment

- Is welcoming to visitors of all ages
- Allows personalization of bedrooms to reflect individual preferences and history
- Affords and respects privacy
- Incorporates pets, plants, and other elements of nature
- Offers opportunities for visual, auditory, olfactory, and tactile stimulation
- Allows easy access to snacks and beverages
- Has various areas that support periods of social engagement and solitude
- Is clean and odor-free
- Limits paging and the presence of equipment and supplies
- Allows for easy communication with outside community

Heightened interest in creating a different style of nursing home life is driving a transformation in this setting. There will be challenges as concerns such as addressing therapeutic needs and assuring safety are balanced against issues such as offering a more homelike environment and offering residents the ability to make choices that could increase their risks for injuries and complications. Nurses need to be actively engaged in this process to ensure that change occurs thoughtfully and is based on sound evidence.

PART

The Nursing Process in Long-Term Care

7

The Minimum Data Set (MDS)

The Minimum Data Set (MDS) is a standardized comprehensive assessment tool developed by the Centers for Medicare and Medicaid Services (CMS) that is the foundation of the Resident Assessment Instrument. Information collected on the MDS reflects the resident's acuity level and is used to classify Medicare residents into Resource Utilization Groups (RUGs) for reimbursement purposes. The MDS must be completed for all residents in Medicare- and Medicaid-certified nursing homes. Nursing homes forward the completed MDS tools electronically to their state agency. Data collected enable CMS to monitor the quality of care in nursing homes throughout the nation and provide information that can be accessed by consumers to learn about the characteristics and quality of nursing homes.

This chapter should enable you to:

1. Identify the times when an MDS assessment must be completed
2. Describe the data that are collected in the MDS assessment tool
3. Describe the Care Areas and their purpose
4. Describe the time period for which MDS assessments must be maintained by the nursing home

REGULATORY REQUIREMENTS RELATED TO THE MDS

As a result of the Omnibus Budget Reconciliation Act (OBRA), all nursing homes that receive Medicare and Medicaid reimbursement must complete the MDS tool for all of their residents. The MDS provides a uniform approach to conducting a comprehensive assessment that is recorded on a standardized tool.

OBRA requires a comprehensive assessment to be completed:

- Within 14 days of admission (date of admission is day 1)
- Annually
- Within 14 days of recognition of a significant change in clinical status
- When a significant error to the resident's prior assessment is identified
- Upon electing (and start of coverage) or declining (and end off coverage) of hospice benefits

ESSENTIAL FACTS

A resident who is discharged and then readmitted will need to have an MDS assessment completed (similar to the situation of a resident who is new to the facility) if the resident was discharged before the completion of the admission MDS assessment or if the discharge occurred more than 30 days before the current admission.

In addition, a specific subset of MDS items must be assessed quarterly. A comprehensive care plan must be developed within 7 days following the completion of the assessment. A registered nurse (RN) must conduct or coordinate the assessment with the input of other health team members and the resident. The RN coordinating the assessment must sign the MDS, verifying that it is complete.

Upon completion, the MDS is electronically transmitted to the quality improvement evaluation system assessment submission and processing system designated by CMS.

COMPONENTS OF THE MDS

The sections of the MDS 3.0 include:

A. Identification Information
B. Hearing, Speech, Vision

C. Cognitive Patterns
D. Mood
E. Behavior
F. Preferences for Customary and Routine Activities
G. Functional Status
H. Bladder and Bowel
I. Active Diagnoses
J. Health Conditions (includes Pain Management and Falls)
K. Swallowing/Nutritional Status
L. Oral/Dental Status
M. Skin Conditions
N. Medications
O. Special Treatments and Procedures
P. Restraints
Q. Participation in Assessment and Goal Setting
V. Care Area Assessment (CAA) Summary
X. Correction Request
Z. Assessment Administration

Table 7.1 lists the major information collected within each section. Chapter 9 offers guidance to specific skills that nurses can use when assessing the various areas.

ESSENTIAL FACTS

A copy of the *Resident Assessment Instrument Manual,* including the full MDS tool, can be obtained from the CMS website, at www.cms.gov.

Certain scores on the MDS will trigger the need for greater assessment of the area; these triggers are called Care Area Triggers (CATs). There are 20 major Care Areas that represent common problems in nursing home residents. Section V of the MDS is dedicated to the Care Area Assessment Summary. The Care Areas include:

1. Delirium
2. Cognitive Loss/Dementia
3. Visual Function
4. Communication
5. ADL (Activities of Daily Living) Functional/Rehabilitation Potential
6. Urinary Incontinence and Indwelling Catheter
7. Psychosocial Well-Being
8. Mood State
9. Behavioral Symptoms
10. Activities
11. Falls

12. Nutritional Status
13. Feeding Tube
14. Dehydration/Fluid Maintenance
15. Dental Care
16. Pressure Ulcer
17. Psychotropic Drug Use
18. Physical Restraints
19. Pain
20. Return to Community Referral

TABLE 7.1 Major Data Collected in Each Section of the Minimum Data Set

Section	Related Data Collected
A. Identification Information	Facility identifying information Type and reason for assessment Resident's name, Social Security number, Medicaid number, gender, birth date, race/ethnicity, language marital status Presence of developmental disabilities Location being admitted from, discharge date, discharge status Previous Medicare stay
B. Hearing, Speech, Vision	Persistent vegetative state/no discernible consciousness Ability to hear Hearing aid or other hearing appliance used Speech pattern Ability to express ideas and wants Ability to understand others Vision Use of corrective lenses
C. Cognitive Patterns	Complete mental status examination Signs and symptoms of delirium Evidence of acute change in mental status
D. Mood	Presence of feelings of depression, hopelessness, low energy; inability to concentrate; short tempered; suicidal thoughts Potential to harm self
E. Behavior	Presence of hallucinations or delusions Physical or verbal behavioral symptoms and their impact Rejection of care Presence and frequency of wandering

(continued)

TABLE 7.1 Major Data Collected in Each Section of the Minimum Data Set (*continued*)

Section	Related Data Collected
F. Preferences for Customary and Routine Activities	Daily preferences related to clothing, bathing, care of personal belongings, snacking, bedtime, use of phone, care of personal possessions, family involvement in care Activity preferences
G. Functional Status	Independence in performing each of the activities of daily living; type of assistance required
H. Bladder and Bowel	Presence of indwelling catheter, external catheter, ostomy, intermittent catheterization Toileting program Urinary and bowel continence; pattern of incontinence Bowel patterns
I. Active Diagnoses	Specific diagnoses present
J. Health Conditions	Pain (presence, frequency, intensity, management, effect on function) Shortness of breath Current tobacco use Conditions that could result in life expectancy less than 6 months Presence of fever, vomiting, dehydration, internal bleeding History of falls
K. Swallowing/ Nutritional Status	Presence and characteristics of swallowing disorder Height and weight Use of parenteral/intravenous (IV) feeding, feeding tube, mechanically altered diet, therapeutic diet Percentage intake by artificial route
L. Oral/Dental Status	Presence of broken or loose-fitting dentures, no natural teeth, abnormal mouth tissue, cavity, broken teeth, inflamed or loose teeth, bleeding gums, mouth or facial pain

(continued)

TABLE 7.1 Major Data Collected in Each Section of the Minimum Data Set (*continued*)

Section	Related Data Collected
M. Skin Conditions	Risk for developing pressure ulcers Presence of unhealed pressure ulcers, stages, dimensions Presence of healed pressure ulcers Presence of venous or arterial ulcers, wounds, other skin problems Skin and ulcer treatments
N. Medications	Number and type of injections Use of antipsychotic, antianxiety, antidepressant, hypnotic, anticoagulant, antibiotic, or diuretic medications
O. Special Treatments and Procedures	Treatments while a resident and within 14-day period before becoming a resident (chemotherapy, radiation, oxygen therapy, suctioning, tracheostomy care, ventilator or respirator, bilevel positive airway pressure (BiPAP)/continuous positive airway pressure (CPAP), IV medications, transfusions, dialysis, hospice, respite, isolation for infectious disease) Vaccines received (influenza, pneumococcal) Speech-language pathology and audiology services provided Occupational therapy services provided Physical therapy services provided Respiratory therapy services provided Psychological therapy services provided Recreational therapy services provided Type of restorative nursing programs provided Physical examinations and physician orders in last 14 days
P. Restraints	Use of bed rails, trunk restraint, limb restraint, other restraint
Q. Participation in Assessment and Goal Setting	Resident's participation in assessment Family's/legal guardian's participation in assessment Resident's goal Presence of active discharge plan Resident's/family's view on resident returning to community

For each Care Area triggered, staff must indicate whether a new care plan was initiated or an existing one revised or continued for the Care Area. The overall goals to be considered in developing plans for triggered Care Areas are to promote maximum independent function in the resident and prevent decline as possible.

ESSENTIAL FACTS

Based on the MDS data, residents are placed into RUGs, which are categories based on diagnoses, treatments, and services. RUGs are a means that the government uses to determine payment to the nursing home.

MDS RECORD MANAGEMENT

Federal regulations require that the nursing home maintain all resident assessments completed within the previous 15 months in the resident's active clinical record (regardless of whether the form is an electronic or a hard copy). If a resident is transferred to a new facility, the transferring facility must send the MDS assessments with the other necessary medical records to support continuity of care. If a resident is admitted from another facility, the existing MDS assessment should be reviewed; however, the nursing home admitting the resident needs to initiate a new MDS assessment.

The MDS offers a standardized approach for collecting assessment data. Although the information collected is valuable for obtaining an overall understanding of the resident and initiating a care plan, nurses should understand that it is not complete. Other areas, such as spirituality and family dynamics, also offer useful insights that enable nurses to provide holistic care. Chapter 8 reviews other areas that offer useful assessment data beyond the MDS.

8

Assessing Needs Beyond the Minimum Data Set (MDS)

The Minimum Data Set (MDS) is an assessment tool that is required for use in nursing homes certified to receive Medicare and Medicaid reimbursement. It guides nurses in collecting a wide range of information about residents. As comprehensive as it seems, the MDS assessment does not capture some aspects of residents' health status, personal preferences, and needs. Further, assisted living communities are not required to use the MDS tool and have other considerations that drive their assessment process for residents. To provide holistic care and address the needs of long-term care residents who are not in nursing homes, nurses must assess other resident needs that are not included on the MDS tool.

This chapter should enable you to identify methods to assess:

1. Psychosocial well-being
2. Preferred activities
3. Sleep patterns
4. Spiritual and religious needs
5. Family dynamics and needs
6. Ethnic practices
7. Decision-making capacity

HOLISTIC ASSESSMENT

The MDS provides a standardized approach to assessing many aspects of residents' status that influence the need for nursing care. While rich in the data it generates, the MDS does not address some of the psychosocial and spiritual aspects of residents that are necessary to foster an understanding of their holistic needs. Thus, nurses must supplement the MDS assessment with other factors to gain an understanding of the complete individual.

ESSENTIAL FACTS

A holistic assessment refers to assessment of the whole person: body, mind, and spirit.

PSYCHOSOCIAL WELL-BEING

Although dementias and other conditions can have an impact on an individual's psychological state, for most residents personality and psychological profiles have been consistent throughout their adult lives. To put residents' current function into perspective, it is useful to gain an understanding of what their lifelong patterns of psychosocial function have been. For example, staff may think that a resident who spends most of her time in her room and rejects participation in group activities is depressed, whereas it could be the resident was an independent or introverted person who preferred solitary to group activities her entire life. To gain insights into psychosocial function:

- Ask the resident about his or her past work history, interests, and social activities.
- Ask the resident to describe how being in the facility affects his or her ability to continue relationships and interests; discuss the losses that may have been experienced with admission to the facility (e.g., home, pet).
- Observe the ease with which the resident interacts with other residents and participates in activities.
- Ask the resident to describe any losses that he or she may have recently experienced.

PREFERRED ACTIVITIES

Exploring established patterns of activities can aid in gaining insights into the best activities for the resident while in the facility. To assess this area:

- Ask about activities or hobbies that the resident enjoyed in the past (e.g., games, art, crafts, sports, music, reading, gardening, pets, Bible studies, exercise).
- Review the resident's record and level of function to determine if there are factors that could interfere with the resident engaging in activities that were enjoyed in the past; determine ability to compensate for any factors that interfere with activities.
- Consider external factors that could impair the resident's ability to enjoy preferred activities (e.g., inadequate staffing, lack of peers with whom to engage in activities, scheduling conflicts).

SLEEP PATTERN

There can be considerable variation among residents in terms of sleep and rest patterns, ranging from those who need 9 to 10 hours of sleep each night to those who obtain 6 hours of nighttime sleep and take a few short naps during the day. To assess sleep pattern:

- Ask the resident about his or her typical times for going to sleep and awakening.
- Record the resident's sleep, rest, and awakening pattern to determine the pattern that is evident. Ask the resident if these reflect his or her usual pattern and the degree to which these are satisfactory.
- Ask the resident to describe factors that promote and interfere with sleep.
- Ask the night shift staff to note factors that could interfere with sleep (e.g., pain, nocturia, respiratory difficulties, nightmares).

SPIRITUAL AND RELIGIOUS NEEDS

Knowing the religious affiliation or lack thereof of residents is beneficial but does not provide insight into how this affects faith-related outlook, attitudes, or practices.

Spirituality and religion are not synonymous. Spirituality transcends the physical and refers to our connection with something greater than ourselves, such as God, the universe, and all living things. Religion is an expression of spirituality and refers to a structure of symbols, rituals, and beliefs created by humans.

People can be highly spiritual without having any specific religious affiliation; spiritual needs can exist separately from religion. Spiritual needs can include:

- Feeling loved and loving others
- Seeing a purpose to one's life
- Having hope
- Forgiving others and self, accepting forgiveness from others
- Showing gratitude
- Feeling part of something greater than oneself
- Holding beliefs and practicing one's faith

The fulfillment of spiritual needs helps people to achieve a sense of integrity and wholeness in late life that is important to their psychological well-being.

Observation can offer clues to residents' spiritual and religious needs. For example, a resident may wear a cross around his or her neck, read inspirational books, carry a Bible, or have a picture of a saint on the bedside table. Sometimes comments can give clues to spiritual needs, as when a resident says, "I really miss attending temple," or, "I don't know why God has allowed this to happen to me." There are some specific questions that can assist in assessing spiritual needs, such as:

- How did you practice your faith before your admission?
- Have you been involved with a church, temple, or faith community? If so, what is it and would you like us to contact them to visit you?
- Do you read the Bible or other religious text? Do you have one available to you now? If not, would you like us to obtain one for you?
- Would you like a visit from clergy?
- Is there anything related to your faith that is causing you distress or conflict?
- What is most meaningful to you? What gives you purpose?
- What is your source of strength?
- From whom do you receive love? What opportunities do you have to show love to others?

- Is there anything that causes you fear or spiritual pain? If so, please describe it.
- How can we best support your spiritual and religious practices while you are here?

  When spiritual needs and spiritual distress are identified, it is useful to discuss this with clergy affiliated with the facility.

FAMILY DYNAMICS AND NEEDS

Although nurses are formally responsible for the resident, the resident's family members can play an important role in his or her care and well-being; therefore, it is useful to consider them in the assessment process. In addition to information offered by family members to supplement that contributed by the resident, the family's relationship with the resident and reaction to his or her admission to the facility affect the resident and are important to consider in his or her care. Discharge planning, reinforcement of plans to the resident, and prevention of complaints are among the issues that can be aided by understanding family dynamics and needs. Information that is useful to obtain in assessing the family includes:

- *Family composition:* Identify the family members who are most engaged in the resident's life; keep in mind that there can be significant others who are not formally relatives but who are considered family by the resident and fulfill certain family functions.
- *Roles of family members:* Various family members may fill different roles in the family. Questions that can aid in revealing family roles include:
  - Who helps you make decisions?
  - Who helps you with bathing, care, chores?
  - Who assists you in managing finances?
  - Are there any family members who cause you distress? Who has mistreated you?
  - What is the health of your spouse?
- *Family's perspective on the resident's admission:* If the family has determined that regardless of what it takes, they want to have the resident return to the community, the plan of care will differ from that for the resident whose stay is viewed as a permanent one.
- *Relationships:* Even in families who love and are committed to each other, relationships are not always smooth and healthy. Listening to the resident's description of frustrations and observing interactions can yield insights into problematic areas in the relationship.
- *Family's needs:* Asking a simple question such as "How do you feel about your parent (or spouse) being here?" can disclose feelings that individual family members may have. For example, a spouse

may admit to being so depressed about her husband's admission to the facility that she cannot eat or sleep; a daughter may express frustration and anger that she is doing more than her siblings; a son may question whether the family home must be sold to pay for care. Family members may benefit from a listening ear, information, referral to counseling, or a facility-initiated family meeting in which issues can be discussed with the guidance of an objective staff member.

ESSENTIAL FACTS

Assessing family dynamics often is best done after the resident and family have had a chance to adjust to the facility and establish trusting relationships with staff.

ETHNIC PRACTICES

Although the MDS has a checklist to indicate a resident's ethnicity, knowing the ethnicity alone does not offer insights into practices related to ethnic identity. To learn about specific ethnic practices, ask the resident:

- Are there practices related to being ___[ethnic group]___ that you would like to engage in while here?
- Are there special foods or dietary restrictions that we need to know about related to your ethnicity?
- Are there any special holidays that members of ___[ethnic group]___ celebrate? If so, what can we do to help you celebrate them while you are here?

DECISION-MAKING CAPACITY

The physical and mental status of residents can offer insights into their ability to make reasonable decisions. For example, a person with advanced dementia or who is heavily medicated for pain can be expected to have challenges making decisions. However, there are situations in which residents' decision-making capacities cannot be determined through their medical status alone.

Observing residents over time can aid in assessing decision-making capacity. This can include noting their ability to make simple decisions (e.g., coffee or tea, sitting in their room or the dining room) and the appropriateness of their responses. Residents also can be asked to describe something that was just explained to them or their understanding of the reason for certain procedures.

Preferences related to caregiving activities should be respected for residents who have the ability to make good basic decisions. When residents lack decision-making capacity, efforts should be made through medical record review and interviews with family members to determine what the preferences of these residents could have been anticipated to be.

ESSENTIAL FACTS

A person's competency to make financial or legal decisions is determined by a court of law. The fact that a resident is not legally competent to make financial or legal decisions does not mean that he or she does not have the ability to make decisions concerning care preferences, such as those related to when to bathe, what to eat, and the type of activities he or she desires.

Nurses should encourage all members of the team to share any information they have gained from residents that could assist in individualizing care and identifying needs. Such findings should be documented and incorporated into care planning activities.

9

Assessment Skills

The multiple conditions that typically affect residents of long-term care facilities and the infrequency with which medical staff are on the premises place heavy burdens on nurses to monitor residents' status and identify changes and signs of new problems in a timely manner. Sharp assessment skills become crucial to that effort. Long-term care nurses can have a significant impact on the health and well-being of residents by incorporating assessment into every resident–nurse interaction.

This chapter should enable you to:

1. Describe the basic skills used in assessment
2. Outline the components and skills used in conducting a comprehensive physical assessment
3. Describe the method of conducting a mental status assessment

GENERAL ASSESSMENT SKILLS

Basic assessment skills of observation, interview, and examination can aid in differentiating normal from abnormal findings and identifying changes. In addition to using these skills when completing the

Minimum Data Set (MDS), nurses can incorporate them into general nursing activities so that every nurse–resident interaction provides an opportunity for assessment.

Observation

This is the deliberate use of the senses to gather information. Items to observe include:

- General level of consciousness, alertness
- General appearance, cleanliness, grooming, appropriateness of clothing
- Body language
- Quality and appropriateness of speech and language
- Skin coloring, discoloration, cuts, bruises, sores, growths
- Unusual sounds (e.g., wheezes, gurgling)
- Odors
- Reaction to touch
- Reaction to conversation and questions (e.g., Is there little or no change in resident's facial expression? Are directions and questions understood? Are appropriate responses and behaviors displayed?)

Interview

This is structured questioning and discussion. The collection of standardized information may be required for completion of the MDS and other assessment tools. In addition, other issues or problems may arise that may require further investigation through interview techniques. When interviewing a resident it is useful to:

- Ensure that the resident is comfortable and is able to dedicate the time for the interview.
- Be aware of any hearing or vision deficits that could interfere with the interview; ensure that hearing aids and eyeglasses are worn; compensate for deficits by using appropriateness loudness of voice.
- Use language that is appropriate for the resident.
- Provide sufficient time for responses, recognizing that older adults may need more time to process information and formulate responses.
- Listen carefully to responses.
- Validate information obtained to assure an appropriate understanding.
- Use different styles of questions based on the information being sought.

When direct, short responses are desired, closed-ended questions are effective, such as "How old are you?", "What type of work did you do?", and "How long have you used a hearing aid?" More lengthy responses that yield greater information and insights into the resident's cognitive status are supported by open-ended questions. Examples of open-ended questions include "Will you tell me about your problems with your son?", "How would you describe the pain you are having?", and "What types of things would you want your caregivers to know about you?"

Examination

Both mental and physical status are assessed through examination. Mental status is examined by:

- Observations of general attention to grooming, appropriateness of dress, body language, and general behavior
- Language and speech
- Affect
- Responses to questions
- The use of standardized assessment tools

Physical examination utilizes several major skills:

- Inspection—visually surveying the body for normality of structure and function
- Auscultation—listening to sounds within the body with the use of a stethoscope
- Percussion—tapping on the body surface to determine the underlying structure, size, and consistency of organs and the presence of fluid
- Palpation—touching various parts of the body to determine the size and location of organs, temperature, presence of unusual growths or fluids, and tender or painful areas

ESSENTIAL FACTS

Different sides of the stethoscope are used to hear different sounds. The diaphragm side is used to hear higher pitched sounds, such as the bowel sounds, normal heart sounds, and lung sounds. Lower pitched sounds, such as heart murmurs, are best heard with the bell side of the stethoscope.

Areas to assess as part of the physical examination include:

- Hearing and vision
- Speech and language
- Oral cavity
- Nutritional status
- Quality of circulation
- Respiration
- Bowel and bladder elimination
- Skin status
- Functional status
- Mobility
- Presence of pain
- Laboratory values

Table 9.1, at the end of this chapter, outlines factors to consider in conducting various parts of the physical assessment and describes the significance of key findings.

ASSESSING COGNITIVE FUNCTION

Cognitive function is an important component of the mental status examination, particularly given the high prevalence of dementia among residents of long-term care facilities. Tests of cognitive function typically include:

- *Orientation:* This includes the person's knowledge of his or her own name, current location, date, time of day, and season.
- *Language:* Spontaneous speech and appropriateness of responses throughout the interview assist in assessing language function. In addition, the person can be asked to name various objects that the examiner points to or repeat phrases.
- *Memory:* At the start of the examination the person is given three unrelated words (e.g., dog, cup, bed) and asked to repeat the words and remember them. Midway through the examination and again at the end, the person is asked to repeat the words.
- *Attention and concentration:* The person is asked to spell the word *world* backward or to count backward from 100 by 7s.
- *Executive function:* The person is asked to indicate what the items in a given two-word sequence have in common (e.g., apple and banana, shoe and sock, coffee and tea) or, within the span of 1 minute, to list as many words as he or she can that start with a particular letter, for example, "h".
- *Ability to follow a three-stage command:* The person is given instructions to follow three basic commands, such as pick up a piece of paper, fold it in half, and hand it to the examiner.

- *Judgment:* A situation that requires simple problem solving is presented to the person, such as asking what actions he or she would take if fire was seen coming out of the bathroom. As an alternative, the person can be asked to explain the meaning of a saying such as *an ounce of prevention is worth a pound of cure.*
- *Visuospatial functioning:* The person is asked to draw the face of a clock or copy a simple diagram.

ESSENTIAL FACTS

The Hartford Institute for Geriatric Nursing's website offers a comprehensive listing of assessment tools at www.consultgerirn .org/resources.

Developing competency in assessment skills is essential for long-term care nurses. Through identification of changes in status and deviations from normal, nurses can spare residents significant complications and ensure that appropriate care is provided in a timely manner.

TABLE 9.1 Physical Assessment: Techniques and Factors to Consider

Area of Assessment	Assessment Techniques	Factors to Consider
Hearing	• Observe capacity to hear during first contact. Note if resident has a tendency to cock the head to one side, rely on lip-reading and visual cues, ignore questions and comments, or asks to have things repeated. • Ask resident if a hearing aid is or ever has been used. • If a hearing aid is used, instruct resident to use it during the assessment. • During the interview assess resident's ability to hear speech at various levels by: ■ Asking a question in a whisper	Two general types of hearing problems could be present: • *Conductive* hearing loss stems from problems in passage of sound through canal, ossicles of middle ear, or tympanic membrane. • *Sensorineural* hearing loss involves dysfunction of inner ear receptors or nerve itself. With aging, some degree of sensorineural loss often occurs; this is known as *presbycusis.*

(continued)

TABLE 9.1 Physical Assessment: Techniques and Factors to Consider   (continued)

Area of Assessment	Assessment Techniques	Factors to Consider

	▪ Placing your hand over your mouth while asking a questions
	▪ Standing behind resident or turning your back and asking a question
	• Hold a watch to each of resident's ears and determine his or her ability to hear ticking.
	• If a hearing aid is used by resident examine it for condition, cleanliness, function and ask:
	  ▪ How long have you used the hearing aid?
	  ▪ Where did you obtain the hearing aide/who prescribed it?
	  ▪ How do you care for the hearing aid?
	  ▪ What problems do you have using the hearing aid?
	  ▪ Are you able to hear speech and environmental sounds clearly with the aid?
	• Inspect resident's ears for cerumen accumulation and foreign matter.
	• If hearing deficit is noted, review record to determine date of last audiometric examination; consult with physician to arrange audiometric examination if one has not been conducted in past year.
	• Ask resident how hearing deficit has impacted activities of daily living, social activities, role.
		With age, keratin in the cerumen is of a harder consistency and easily can form a cerumen impaction that can interfere with adequate hearing.

(continued)

TABLE 9.1 Physical Assessment: Techniques and Factors to Consider   (_continued_)

Area of Assessment	Assessment Techniques	Factors to Consider
	• Ask resident to describe effective means of communicating with him or her.	
Vision	• Inspect eyes for redness, tearing, dryness, turning in (_entropion_) or out (_ectropion_) of eyelid, yellow sclera, infection, lesions, and drooping of eyelid over pupillary area (_ptosis_). • If resident has eyeglasses or contact lenses, ensure that they are worn during the assessment. • Ask about date of last eye examination and where eyeglasses were obtained; review medical record for information concerning date of last eye exam. Refer resident for ophthalmological exam if one has not been performed in more than 1 year. • Ask about use of eye medications. If resident has been using drops for glaucoma management, ensure that they are ordered and continued without interruption (abrupt discontinuation could cause an increase in intraocular pressure). • Ask about sensitivity to glare, problems with certain types of lighting, difficulty with vision in dark areas or at night.	Age-related changes to eyes include: • _Presbyopia_—reduction in accommodation that causes difficulty in seeing small objects closely • Increased lens opacity—due to cataracts, this can cause vision to appear hazy and increase sensitivity to glare • Reduction in peripheral vision • Yellowing of lens, causing difficulty discriminating among various shades in color groups of blues, greens and violets • Reduced corneal sensitivity, thereby decreasing older resident's ability to detect irritation and infection in a timely manner • _Arcus senilis_, a grayish ring at outer border of cornea, can be seen; this does not affect vision

(_continued_)

TABLE 9.1 Physical Assessment: Techniques and Factors to Consider *(continued)*

Area of Assessment	Assessment Techniques	Factors to Consider
	• Ask resident about symptoms, changes, and problems related to eyes and vision. For example: Has your ability to read/see things at a distance/see things clearly changed? Are your glasses strong enough? Do you have any blind areas in your vision? Do your eyes ache or pain? Do you ever see flashes of light or halos or rainbows around lights? Have you been bumping into things lately? • Use a newspaper to obtain a gross assessment of resident's visual acuity. Ask resident to read the headlines and progressively move to smallest print; describe specific size of newsprint that resident is able to see (e.g., "Can see only headline-size print matter"; "Able to read small newsprint using eyeglasses"). • If resident is unable to read headlines in newspaper, determine if resident can see and follow your finger; if resident cannot do this, determine gross visual capacity (e.g., "Can make out shapes"; "Able to differentiate dark and light, but cannot see objects"; "No vision").	• More time is required for adaptation from dark to light, and vice versa *Homonymous hemianopsia,* reduction in same half of visual field of both eyes, may be present in residents who have had a stroke. People with *macular degeneration* have loss of central vision. *Vitreous floaters* can cause person to complain of seeing spots floating across visual field. Weakening of structures around orbit can cause eyelids to turn in (*entropion*) or turn out (*ectropion*).

(continued)

TABLE 9.1 Physical Assessment: Techniques and Factors to Consider (continued)

Area of Assessment	Assessment Techniques	Factors to Consider
	• Determine peripheral vision: Seat resident and position yourself at eye level with resident, approximately 3 feet away. Extend your arm and point your index finger so that it is outside your visual field. Instruct resident to look into your eyes and to tell you when he/she first sees your finger. Gradually bring your index finger into visual field; note when you first see your finger and compare it to when resident first describes seeing your finger. Repeat at different points along a 360-degree area for both eyes. • Review with resident measures used to compensate for visual deficits, e.g., use of large-print books and magnifying glasses, wearing sunglasses when in bright areas, placing objects on right side to compensate for poor left-sided vision.	Seeing flashes of light, or halos or rings around light, is an abnormality that could be associated with various pathologies (e.g., glaucoma, digitalis toxicity).
Speech and language	• Observe resident's reaction to conversation and questions: Does resident have little or no change in facial expression? Are directions and questions understood? Are appropriate responses and behaviors displayed? • Ask resident to perform a simple task (e.g., "Please pick up that glass of water") to determine if a receptive problem exists.	Communication problems can stem from neurological conditions, altered mental status, adverse drug reactions, and disease of the ears, nose, and throat. During the assessment, attention should be paid to the phase of communication that is impaired as problems can be:

(continued)

TABLE 9.1 Physical Assessment: Techniques and Factors to Consider (*continued*)

Area of Assessment	Assessment Techniques	Factors to Consider
	• Write a simple question on a piece of paper, give it to resident, and ask him/her to answer it (e.g., "What is your first name?"); if a problem exists, determine if it is a result of resident not understanding written question or inability to form or articulate answer. *Dyslexia* is the term used to describe problems in reading material. • Ask resident to write his/her name and a short sentence on paper. *Dysgraphia* is the term used to describe inability to write words or sentences. • Ask resident to repeat the sounds "me, me, me," "la, la, la," and "ga, ga, ga" to assess presence of articulation problems related to motor problems. ("Me" sounds involve motor control of the lips; "la" sounds require tongue control; "ga" sounds demand control of pharynx.) *Dysarthria* is the term used to describe articulation problems related to poor motor control. • Point to familiar objects (e.g., watch, pencil, cup) and ask resident to state name of the objects. Note inability to name objects or substitution of the name for a close, although different object's name for that presented (e.g., calling a watch a clock, a pencil a crayon, or a cup a bowl). *Paraphasia* is substitution of one word for another and frequently accompanies dementias.	• *Receptive:* Difficulty hearing, seeing, interpreting, understanding • *Expressive:* Difficulty selecting appropriate word, forming sentences, forming words, writing, and using nonverbal means of expression • *Global:* Total inability to understand, formulate words or express self Throughout assessment of communication ability, consideration must be given to resident's education level and competency in using the English language.

(*continued*)

TABLE 9.1 Physical Assessment: Techniques and Factors to Consider *(continued)*

Area of Assessment	Assessment Techniques	Factors to Consider
	• Ask resident and family members or significant others if there have been any changes in resident's communication pattern over the past few months. If problems have been noted, ask about other symptoms that may be present or factors that may have contributed to the problem (e.g., new medication, recent infection, mood change).	
	• When comprehension problems are apparent, determine to what extent they are present (e.g., understands most of the time, understands if instructions are broken into simple steps, does not understand at all). Ask family members and significant others for their assessment of resident's level of understanding.	
	• Inquire about mechanisms resident has used to facilitate communication, such as communication boards, pad and pencil, synthesizers.	
Oral cavity	• Ask resident about status of teeth and oral cavity (e.g., Do your teeth or gums every hurt? . . . If so, please describe the type of pain an factors that cause it. Do your teeth feel loose to you? Do your gums bleed? . . . how often? Are you able to bite and chew all foods? . . . If not, describe the problems you have? How do you care for your teeth? When was the last examination from a dentist?)	Although not a normal outcome of aging, tooth loss is common in older persons and dentures are commonly present.

(continued)

TABLE 9.1 Physical Assessment: Techniques and Factors to Consider *(continued)*

Area of Assessment	Assessment Techniques	Factors to Consider
	• If dentures are present, ask resident how long they have been used, where they were obtained, how they are worn (e.g., only for meals, during daytime only), how well they fit, if there are any problems with them, if/when they were adjusted or replaced.	Teeth that are present often are found to be brittle due to increased calcification; pieces of teeth can break off while residents eat and lead to aspiration, as a result. Reabsorption of gum tissue at the base of the teeth may occur. Poor dental care, a high carbohydrate diet, and insufficient intake of calcium can influence the development of caries.
	• Inspect oral cavity (wearing gloves); use a flashlight and tongue depressor to assist. Note presence of debris and general cleanliness. Observe condition of mucous membrane; note color, moisture, and integrity of membrane. If irritation or sores are present ask resident how long the problem has been there and try to determine causative/contributing factor (e.g., friction from poor-fitting denture).	
		White patches on tongue resembling dried beads of mold could indicate moniliasis infection; brown pigmentation in light-skinned persons can occur with Addison's disease; bright red spots encased by hyperkeratotic epithelium, on hard palate, may be nicotine stomatitis; dryness can reflect dehydration.
	• Detect unusual breath odors; describe as precisely as possible.	
	• If dentures are present, examine for proper fit; ask resident to remove dentures and note condition.	
	• Inspect gums; note discoloration, inflammation, bleeding.	Sweet, fruity breath occurs with ketoacidosis; urine odor to breath can be associated with uremic acidosis; clover-like breath may accompany liver failure; and an extremely foul odor to breath can reflect halitosis or a lung abscess.
	• Ask resident to extend his/her tongue and observe color, symmetry, papillae, and movement. Examine undersurface for varicosities (a common finding) and lesions	

(continued)

TABLE 9.1 Physical Assessment: Techniques and Factors to Consider (*continued*)

Area of Assessment	Assessment Techniques	Factors to Consider
	(cancerous lesions occur more often on undersurface than on top of tongue). • Review resident's cognitive patterns and physical functioning for disabilities that could interfere with independent oral hygiene; arrange for special oral hygiene assistive devices if necessary.	Swollen gums can be associated with phenytoin (Dilantin) therapy or leukemia; red, bleeding, swollen gums can occur with periodontal disease; a bluish-black line along gumline can develop from lead, mercury, or arsenic poisoning. A coated tongue may be due to poor hygienic practices or dehydration; a smooth, red tongue can be associated with deficiency of iron, vitamin B_{12}, or niacin; unremovable white patches can be leukoplakia.

Nutritional status	• Ask resident or family/significant others about resident's lifelong weight range, dietary habits, and changes noted.
	• Review resident's food and eating likes and dislikes; discuss how they can be accommodated in the facility.
	• Explore factors that could interfere with adequate food and fluid intake by examining oral cavity and reviewing cognitive patterns, functional status, and disease diagnoses and health conditions.
	• Examine body for clinical signs of malnutrition, such as:
	  ▪ Weight loss
	  ▪ Dull, dry hair; hair loss
		Age-related changes to gastrointestinal system that can that can affect nutritional status include:
		
		• Altered taste sensations due to reduction in number of functioning taste buds (the most significant losses involve buds for sweet and salty flavors)
		• Slower movement of food down esophagus and delayed emptying of food from stomach, which gives a sense of fullness after meals and increases risk for aspiration

(continued)

TABLE 9.1 Physical Assessment: Techniques and Factors to Consider   (*continued*)

Area of Assessment	Assessment Techniques	Factors to Consider
	■ Dark circles under eyes ■ Dry, flaky, or scaling skin ■ Poor skin turgor (since skin turgor can be poor in many older residents due to reduced skin elasticity, this can be an unreliable sign; however, skin turgor is best maintained over the sternum and forehead areas, thus testing over these areas may yield more usable data) ■ Swollen face ■ Pale, dry eyes ■ Red, swollen lips; fissures at corner of mouth ■ Tongue that is swollen, raw, bright red, smooth, or "hairy" looking; fissures, sores or white patches on tongue ■ Bleeding gums ■ Dry, rough, flaking, broken, or swollen skin ■ Hypo- or hyperpigmented skin; petechiae ■ Brittle, ridged, or spoon-shaped nails ■ Muscle atrophy ■ Weakness; confusion ● Assess vital signs. (Decreased blood pressure and increased pulse and temperature can be associated with dehydration). ● Obtain height and weight. Be sure to take weight consistently each time (i.e., same time in relation to meals, same amount of clothing on resident). Report weight loss of at least 5% in past 30 days or 10% in past 180 days.	● Increased indigestion problems due to poorer food breakdown, intolerances to fatty and fried foods, delayed gastric emptying ● Higher risk for constipation due to slower peristalsis, low fiber intake, and inactivity ● Reduced sense of thirst, which can interfere with adequate fluid intake ● Less total body fluid, thereby reducing safety margin for dehydration Although tooth loss is *not* a normal consequence of aging, most of today's older adults wear dentures, thereby affecting chewing and taste of foods.

(continued)

TABLE 9.1 Physical Assessment: Techniques and Factors to Consider *(continued)*

Area of Assessment	Assessment Techniques	Factors to Consider

	• Ask resident about symptoms that could affect nutritional intake or indicate nutritional problems (e.g., nausea, vomiting, indigestion, excessive flatus, mouth pain, bleeding gums).
	• Review nutritionist's assessment; discuss and consult as necessary.
	• Review laboratory values for indications of nutritional problems; for example:
	  ▪ *Albumin:* Decreased with malnutrition
	  ▪ *Sodium:* Increased with low fluid intake; decreased with dehydration, diabetic acidosis, diarrhea, overhydration
	  ▪ *Potassium:* Decreased with diarrhea, vomiting, diabetic acidosis
	  ▪ *Blood urea nitrogen (BUN):* Increased with dehydration, high protein intake, intestinal obstruction; decreased with low protein intake, starvation, cirrhosis
	  ▪ *Uric acid:* Increased in fasting states
	  ▪ *Glucose:* Increased with diabetes mellitus; decreased with starvation
	  ▪ *Creatinine:* Increased with dehydration
	  ▪ *Fibrinogen:* Decreased with malnutrition
	• Maintain a 24-hour record of resident's fluid and food intake for several days if resident is a new admission or is suspected of having a	

(continued)

TABLE 9.1 Physical Assessment: Techniques and Factors to Consider *(continued)*

Area of Assessment	Assessment Techniques	Factors to Consider
	nutritional problem. (This may be a useful measure to perform periodically for all residents in order to gain data for reassessment.) • Review medications resident is taking for those that may be or could potentially affect nutritional status (e.g., diuretics, analgesics, antipsychotics). • Observe resident during mealtime. Note ability to feed self, chew, swallow. • If special nutritional approaches are necessary (e.g., feeding tube, modified utensils) evaluate effectiveness of these measures and appropriateness of use	
Circulation	• Observe: ■ General coloring: Note pallor. ■ Energy level: Note posture, speed of responses, activity level, evidence of fatigue. ■ Nail condition: Inspect for clubbing (associated with advanced cardiac disease), thickness, dryness, response to blanching (circulatory insufficiency can delay return of pink color to nails after blanching). ■ Extremities: Note varicosities, discoloration, edema, hair loss (which can indicate poor circulation).	Age-related changes to cardiovascular system include: • Slight left ventricular hypertrophy • Enlargement of left atrium • Dilation and elongation of aorta • Thickening and rigidity of atrioventricular valves interfering with contraction of heart • Systolic and diastolic murmurs associated with incomplete valve closure • Irritability of myocardium leading to sinus arrhythmia and extrasystolic sinus bradycardia

(continued)

TABLE 9.1 Physical Assessment: Techniques and Factors to Consider (continued)

Area of Assessment	Assessment Techniques	Factors to Consider

	• Ask:
	  ▪ How often do you exercise and what type of exercises do you do?
	  ▪ What vitamin and herbal supplements do you take?
	  ▪ Could you give me an example of your typical daily diet?
	  ▪ Do you drink alcoholic beverages? If so, how much and how often?
	  ▪ What type of things do you do to promote health?
	  ▪ What medications, prescribed and over-the-counter, are you taking?
	  ▪ Do you have any difficulty or have you had any changes in your ability to walk or stand?
	  ▪ Are you able to bathe and dress yourself?
	  ▪ Are you able to get out and shop, attend church/temple, engage in social activities?
	  ▪ Do you ever feel dizzy or lightheaded?*
	  ▪ Do you ever have pain or strange feelings in your chest, shoulder, or arms?*
	  ▪ Do you have dull head-aches or nosebleeds?* (These may be indicative of hypertension)
	  ▪ Have you noticed any changes in your thinking, memory, or mental clearness?*
	  ▪ Does exercise or activity cause you to become extremely tired, short of breath, or have palpitations?*
		• Changes in resting ECG due to reduction in pacemaker and conduction cells
		• High prevalence of extra heart sound due to atrial contractions in diastole, S4
		• Prolonged isometric contraction phase and relaxation time of left ventricle
		• More time needed for completion of diastolic filling and systolic emptying cycle
		• Increased systolic blood pressure due to impaired baroreceptor function and increased peripheral resistance
		• Impaired regulation of blood pressure due to impaired baroreceptor function leading to postural hypotension

(continued)

TABLE 9.1 Physical Assessment: Techniques and Factors to Consider   (*continued*)

Area of Assessment	Assessment Techniques	Factors to Consider

	▪ Do your feet and ankles swell as the day goes on? Do you find that your fingers swell as the day goes on?*
	▪ Do you bruise easily?*
	
	(*If positive response is given, ask about onset, frequency, duration, management, and characteristic of symptom.)
	
	• Perform a physical assessment:
	  ▪ Starting at head, inspect the body. Note distended vessels, varicosities, areas of redness, pallor, cyanosis, lesions, edema, and bruises.
	  ▪ Assess apical and radial pulse. Normal rate should range between 60 and 100 beats per minute. Keep in mind that some tachycardia can be present due to activity that the patient engaged in hours before examination and stress of examination. If tachycardia is detected, reassess at a later time.
	  ▪ Measure blood pressure with patient seated comfortably with both feet on floor. It should be measured at least twice with a 5-minute rest period between each measurement. Obtaining blood pressure in lying, sitting, and standing positions is useful to detect postural
		For the most part, daily activities typically are not significantly affected by these changes. However, when added demands are placed on heart (e.g., during exercise), changes become more apparent. It takes older adults longer to recover from tachycardia so activities prior to time of assessment should be considered when tachycardia is identified.

(continued)

TABLE 9.1 Physical Assessment: Techniques and Factors to Consider *(continued)*

Area of Assessment	Assessment Techniques	Factors to Consider
	hypotension. Postural drops greater than 20 mmHg are significant. ■ Auscultate heart. Note thrills and bruits. ● Review medical record to determine if resident has had a recent ECG and blood work, including C-reactive protein (CRP) screening. (CRP is a marker of inflammation that is a stronger predictor of cardiovascular events than low-density lipoprotein [LDL] cholesterol.)	
Respiration	● Observe: ■ Coloring ■ Ease of breathing ■ Fullness of lung expansion ■ Symptoms related to respiratory conditions (e.g., wheezes, cough, shortness of breath) ● Ask about: ■ Dyspnea ■ Shortness of breath ■ Coughing ■ Expectoration of mucus ■ Bloody mucus ■ Chest pain or tightness ■ Runny nose ■ Wheezing ● If symptoms are present ask about frequency, characteristics, and factors that trigger them. ● Inspect chest: ■ Look for equal expansion of both sides during respirations, scars, discoloration, structural abnormalities.	Age-related changes include: ● Less supporting connective tissue in nose that can lead to nasal septum deviations that interfere with passage of air ● Thicker mucus in nasopharynx due to reduced submucosal gland secretions; greater difficulty expelling mucus ● Rigidity of trachea and rib cage due to calcification of cartilage ● Blunting of laryngeal and coughing reflexes leading to reduced coughing ● Reduction in elastic collagen and elastin in lungs causing less elastic recoil during expiration

(continued)

TABLE 9.1 Physical Assessment: Techniques and Factors to Consider   (continued)

Area of Assessment	Assessment Techniques	Factors to Consider

	■ There may be some barreling of chest as a result of aging, but anterior–posterior chest diameter normally should not be greater than lateral diameter.
	■ A ruddy complexion of face, neck, and chest can be associated with emphysema; a bluish-gray coloring can occur with chronic bronchitis.
	• Auscultate lungs:
	  ■ Close door to room and turn off televisions and radios to create as quiet an environment as possible.
	• Assist resident in sitting upright.
	• Rub diaphragm of stethoscope to warm it prior to placing it on resident's bare chest.
	• Begin at base of lungs and work up back. Listen for at least two full respirations.
	• Abnormal breath sounds include:
	  ■ *Rales* or *crackles:* A crackling sound heard at end of inspiration, indicating extra interstitial fluid
	  ■ *Rhonchi:* A rattling sound heard at end of expiration, indicating increased mucus production and partial airway obstruction
	  ■ *Wheezes:* A groaning sound, indicating presence of large amounts of mucus
		• Greater use of accessory muscles during expiration
		• Fewer functional capillaries, development of fibrous tissue, and less elasticity of alveoli
		• Increase in anterior-posterior chest diameter
		
		These changes result in:
		
		• Reduced lung expansion during respiration
		• Poor inflation of base of lung
		• Increased difficulty expelling foreign or accumulated matter from lungs
		• Less effective exhalation, leading to increased residual volume

(continued)

TABLE 9.1 Physical Assessment: Techniques and Factors to Consider (*continued*)

Area of Assessment	Assessment Techniques	Factors to Consider

	• Palpate chest:
	  ■ Using ulnar surface of hands, place hands on both sides of chest at area at top of lungs, and ask resident to say "99."
	  ■ Move hands down along other areas of lungs and repeat.
	  ■ Fremitus is normally best felt in upper lobes. Reduced fremitus in upper lobes can be associated with chronic obstructive pulmonary disease (COPD) or pneumothorax; increased fremitus in lower lobe can occur with pneumonia or a mass.
	  ■ Percuss lungs over intercostal spaces:
	   – Start at from top of lungs and move to bases, comparing sides.
	   – Place middle finger of your nondominant hand firmly on chest over an intercostal space and using middle finger of opposite hand, tap over distal interphalangeal joint of finger that is on chest several times (tapping motion should come from the wrist, not movement of the whole arm).
	  ■ Note sound produced.
	  ■ Repeat for opposite side.
		Normally, percussion of lung field reveals *resonance*—a clear, low pitched sound. A *dull* sound indicates filling of a space, as in consolidation or pleural effusion. *Hyperresonance*, a high-pitched, drumlike sound, can reveal an overinflated organ, as may occur with COPD.

(*continued*)

TABLE 9.1 Physical Assessment: Techniques and Factors to Consider *(continued)*

Area of Assessment	Assessment Techniques	Factors to Consider

Elimination	• Review medical history for problems that could contribute to incontinence (e.g., delirium, dementia, depression, cerebrovascular [CVA], diabetes mellitus, congestive heart failure, and urinary tract infection).
	• Review assessment data related to resident's cognitive patterns and physical functioning and structural problems for problems that could contribute to incontinence or affect bladder and bowel training efforts.
	• Review medications resident is taking for those that can affect continence, including:
	  ▪ Diuretics—particularly furosemide, bumetanide, metolazone
	  ▪ Antianxiety drugs
	  ▪ Sedatives
	  ▪ Antipsychotics
	  ▪ Antidepressants
	  ▪ Narcotics
	  ▪ Antiparkinsonism agents
	  ▪ Antispasmodics
	  ▪ Antihistamines
	  ▪ Calcium channel blockers
	  ▪ Alpha blockers and alpha stimulants
	• Note odors, stained clothing, and other indicators of incontinence.
	• Ask resident about presence of incontinence by using questions such as:
	  ▪ Do you have any problem with bladder or bowel control?
		Age-related changes affecting elimination include:
		
		• Urinary frequency due to reduced bladder capacity
		• Reduced muscle tone leading to some residual urine after voiding
		• Slower peristalsis, contributing to constipation
		
		Incontinence of bladder or bowel is not normal.

(continued)

TABLE 9.1 Physical Assessment: Techniques and Factors to Consider (*continued*)

Area of Assessment	Assessment Techniques	Factors to Consider
	<ul><li>Do you ever dribble urine?</li><li>Do you leak urine when you cough or sneeze?</li><li>Do you ever wet during the night?</li><li>Do you have problems reaching the toilet in time?</li><li>Can you sense the urge to void?</li><li>Do you ever need to wear a pad or special undergarment to contain urine?</li></ul><ul><li>Inspect, percuss, and palpate abdomen for bladder fullness, pain, or abnormalities.</li><li>Test female resident for *stress incontinence:* Give resident some fluids to drink and wait until she has a full bladder. Have resident stand (if this is not possible, have her assume as upright a sitting position as possible). Ask her to hold a 4-by-4 gauze between her legs; if necessary, hold it in place for her at perineum. Instruct her to vigorously cough. The test is negative if there is no leakage or if there is leakage of only a few drops.</li><li>If an incontinence problem exists, ask resident:<ul><li>How long has incontinence been present? When did it begin?</li><li>Did incontinence accompany another problem or event, such as start of a new medication, relocation, constipation?</li></ul></li></ul>	

(continued)

TABLE 9.1 Physical Assessment: Techniques and Factors to Consider (*continued*)

Area of Assessment	Assessment Techniques	Factors to Consider
	■ How often does it occur? Every time? Only at night? ■ What amount is released? A large amount? A few drops? ■ Does it occur in relationship to other factors or events (e.g., after meals, when excited?) ■ Do you feel the urge to void or is urine just released with no notice? ■ Do you have enough time to reach the toilet after sensing the need to void? ■ Can you toilet independently? What type of help do you need? ■ How does incontinence affect your activities, your lifestyle? • Assess resident's reaction to incontinence (e.g., does he/she accept it under belief that it is normal with advanced age; is he/she socially isolated due to embarrassment over the condition?). • Check resident who has bowel incontinence for fecal impaction (unless contraindicated or not allowed by your nursing home): inset a gloved finger into rectum and note palpation of a hard mass or the presence of a large amount of stool on your finger when it is withdrawn.	

(continued)

TABLE 9.1 Physical Assessment: Techniques and Factors to Consider (continued)

Area of Assessment	Assessment Techniques	Factors to Consider
	• A postvoid residual (PVR) may be ordered to assist in resident's evaluation: After resident has voided normally, measure urine. Within 15 minutes of voiding, catheterize (with a non–indwelling catheter) and measure residual urine. Maintain sterile technique throughout procedure. If resident is incontinent, observe when voiding occurs and catheterize within 15 minutes.	
	• If resident is incontinent, ensure that a recent clean catch or sterile urine specimen has been sent to the laboratory for evaluation.	
	• Discuss positive findings for incontinence with physician to determine need for further diagnostic evaluation. Obtain physician's opinion as to potential for continence.	
	• Establish resident's normal pattern of bladder and bowel elimination by asking resident about normal pattern or by maintaining an elimination record (flow sheet) for several days.	
	• Identify factors that could interfere with resident's continence, such as inability to ambulate independently or not remembering location of bathroom.	

(continued)

TABLE 9.1 Physical Assessment: Techniques and Factors to Consider   (*continued*)

Area of Assessment	Assessment Techniques	Factors to Consider
	• Ask resident or family/caregivers for information regarding incontinence control products or approaches that have been effectively used. • Ask resident or family/caregivers if any change in continence has been noted in the past 90 days; describe the change.	

Skin	• Review record for history of resolved/cured pressure ulcers, descriptions of skin care measures, special treatments, etc.
	• Review resident's diagnoses and assessment data for factors that make resident high risk for skin problems (e.g., infection, diabetes mellitus, CVA, dementia, poor sensations).
	• Observe:
	  ▪ Ask resident to remove clothing and examine all surfaces of body. Observe general status of skin.
	  ▪ Note color, cleanliness, moisture, temperature and abnormalities. (Dry, flaky skin, known as *ash*, can be a normal finding in black-skinned individuals and may be assisted by moisturizers.)
	• Ask:
	  ▪ Question resident about itching, burning or other symptoms. If symptoms are present, ask how long and about pattern (e.g., all the time, worsens at night).
		Age-related changes to skin make it more fragile and sensitive; these include:
		
		• Loss of papillae, causing flattening (thinning) of epidermis
		• Reduction in contact area between dermis and epidermis, causing an increased risk of peeling of epidermis from a shearing force
		• Decreased strength, vascularity, and elasticity of epidermis
		• Decreased amount, flexibility, and solubility of collagen
		
		Benign and malignant dermatological problems increase with age.

TABLE 9.1 Physical Assessment: Techniques and Factors to Consider (continued)

Area of Assessment	Assessment Techniques	Factors to Consider
	■ Review history to determine factors that could be associated with symptoms (e.g., exposure to pet, use of new soap, stress).	
	• Examine:	
	■ Using the back of your hands, touch cheeks and extremities of resident to obtain a gross assessment of skin temperature. Note inequalities between sides. (*With stasis ulcer, the affected extremity will feel cool, although it may look red and inflamed; poor circulation can cause coolness of skin surface.*)	
	■ Test skin turgor by gently pinching various areas of skin. (Since many older persons have decreased turgor due to age-related changes, poor turgor is a common finding. However, skin over sternum and forehead areas tends to lose less turgor than other areas, thus these are good areas to test.)	
	■ If lesions are present, describe them in as much detail as possible in relation to color, type, and distribution.	
	■ If a pressure ulcer is present, describe exact location, size (measure diameter and depth), stage, and drainage. A photograph may be useful as a means to accurately record ulcer status and evaluate progress.	*(continued)*

(continued)

TABLE 9.1 Physical Assessment: Techniques and Factors to Consider (*continued*)

Area of Assessment	Assessment Techniques	Factors to Consider
	• Stage pressure ulcers based on the following criteria (National Pressure Ulcer Advisory Panel [2007]):	

- **Stage 1:** Intact skin with nonblanchable redness of a localized area usually over a bony prominence. Darkly pigmented skin may not have a visible blanching; in dark skin tones only it may appear with persistent blue or purple hues.
- **Stage 2:** Partial-thickness loss of dermis presenting as a shallow open ulcer with a red or pink wound bed, without slough. May also present as an intact or open/ruptured blister.
- **Stage 3:** Full-thickness tissue loss. Subcutaneous fat may be visible but bone, tendon, or muscle is not exposed. Slough may be present but does not obscure depth of tissue loss. May include undermining and tunneling.
- **Stage 4:** Full-thickness tissue loss with exposed bone, tendon or muscle. Slough or eschar may be present on some parts of the wound bed. Often includes undermining and tunneling.

(*continued*)

TABLE 9.1 Physical Assessment: Techniques and Factors to Consider (*continued*)

Area of Assessment	Assessment Techniques	Factors to Consider

	• **Unstageable/Unclassified:** Full-thickness skin or tissue loss—depth unknown. Full-thickness tissue loss in which the presence of slough or eschar obscures depth
	• **Unclassified/Suspected deep tissue injury—depth unknown:** An area of discolored intact skin or a blood-filled blister resulting from damage to underlying soft tissue as a result of pressure or shear, or both
	Reverse staging is not appropriate
	
	• Select best description of type of tissue present in any pressure ulcer bed:
	  ▪ **Epithelial tissue:** New skin growing in superficial ulcer; can be light pink and shiny, even in persons with darkly pigmented skin
	  ▪ **Granulation tissue:** Pink or red tissue with shiny, moist, granular appearance
	  ▪ **Slough:** Yellow or white tissue that adheres to ulcer bed in strings or thick clumps, or is mucinous
	  ▪ **Necrotic tissue (eschar):** Black, brown, or tan tissue that adheres firmly to wound bed or ulcer edges, may be softer or harder than surrounding skin.	

(*continued*)

TABLE 9.1 Physical Assessment: Techniques and Factors to Consider (*continued*)

Area of Assessment	Assessment Techniques	Factors to Consider

Functional status	• Determine resident's ability to understand and follow instructions; review findings from mental status evaluation.
	• Observe:
	  ▪ Inspect resident's entire body for deformities, inflammation, etc.
	  ▪ Note resident's use of handrails, energy level, breathing pattern, and use of walls or furniture for support during ambulation.
	  ▪ Observe for and question resident about use of cane, walker, wheelchair, brace, or prosthesis. If these devices are used, ask:
	    – How long it has been used
	    – Where/how obtained
	    – Understanding of how to use
	    – If there are any problems in use
	  ▪ Observe resident during a meal; note ability to:
	    – Arrange items on tray
	    – Open containers (e.g., salt, sugar, cream, mustard, milk)
	    – Spread butter on bread
	    – Hold utensils
	    – Coordinate use of utensils
	    – Cut food
	    – Hold bread or finger foods
		Activities of daily living (ADLs) consist of bed mobility, transfer, locomotion, dressing, eating, toilet use, personal hygiene, and bathing.
		ADL function can be affected by paralysis, weakness, shortness of breath, missing limbs, pain, and other physical conditions, as well as dementia, depression, and other mental status alterations. Consideration also must be given to other factors that limit ADL performance, such as adjustment to a new environment, lack of knowledge of facility's routine, and inability to locate materials needed to perform self-care tasks.

(*continued*)

TABLE 9.1 Physical Assessment: Techniques and Factors to Consider   (*continued*)

Area of Assessment	Assessment Techniques	Factors to Consider
	– Put food in mouth – Hold and drink from cup – Chew, drink, swallow – Use napkin, clean food spills from self – Complete meal without supervision or reminders ■ Observe resident during performance of the following activities and note ability: – Washing and drying face – Washing and drying hands – Combing hair – Brushing teeth or cleansing dentures – Applying makeup – Shaving – Cleansing perineum ■ Review medical history for problems that could threaten independence in hygienic practices (e.g., limited range of motion, arthritis, paralysis, poor vision, dementia). ■ Observe resident's ability to: – Travel to tub/shower room – Transfer in/out tub or shower stall – Maneuver washcloth and soap – Wash and rinse face, trunk, extremities – Use water faucets – Recognize water temperatures that are excessively cold or hot	

(*continued*)

TABLE 9.1 Physical Assessment: Techniques and Factors to Consider *(continued)*

Area of Assessment	Assessment Techniques	Factors to Consider
	<ul><li>Note resident's general mobility, energy level, responses during bath/shower.</li><li>Observe resident during toileting; note ability of resident to: – Travel to toilet – Remove/open clothing in preparation – Sit on/transfer to commode – Eliminate into commode – Reach, tear and use toilet paper – Flush commode – Replace/adjust clothing when completed – Wash hands</li><li>Observe resident's general performance of ADLs; note slowness, fatigue, confusion, forgetfulness, or other factors that impair function.</li></ul><ul><li>Ask:<ul><li>Question resident about pain, weakness, breathing difficulties or other problems that interfere with ability to move in bed.</li><li>Instruct resident to do the following and note ability to perform: – Sit up – Swing legs to side of bed while in sitting position – Lie down – Turn side to side</li></ul></li></ul>	

(continued)

TABLE 9.1 Physical Assessment: Techniques and Factors to Consider (continued)

Area of Assessment	Assessment Techniques	Factors to Consider

	– Turn from supine to prone position
	– Reach for item on bedside table while in bed
	■ Ask resident if prosthetic devices, canes or walkers are used for ambulation; have resident use them during assessment; ask where device was obtained/ who prescribed; check for appropriate fit and correct use.
	■ Ask resident if assistive devices are used for eating; obtain these for resident, if necessary.
	■ Ask resident if assistive devices are used for personal hygiene (e.g., large handled toothbrush or comb) and obtain the devices as necessary.
	■ Ask resident what type of assistance he/she has required in the past.
	■ Ask resident:
	  – "Do you believe your function can improve/ that you can do more by yourself?"
	  – "What would enable you to do more for yourself?"
	  – "Would you like to be more independent, increase your ability to feed/toilet/ dress/bathe/walk independently?"	

(continued)

TABLE 9.1 Physical Assessment: Techniques and Factors to Consider   (*continued*)

Area of Assessment	Assessment Techniques	Factors to Consider

	– "Do you believe others are incorrect in how much they believe you can do for yourself? How?"
	
	 – "Do you feel staff do too much for you? Not enough?"
	
	 – "What would you like to achieve in regard to your function?"
	
	 • Examine:
	 ▪ Place all joints through active and passive range of motion; note limitations.
	 ▪ Instruct resident to do the following and note ability to perform:
	    – Sit on edge of bed and rise to standing position
	    – From standing position, sit on bed and raise legs into bed
	    – Approach and sit in a chair
	    – Position self in chair
	    – Raise from seated position in chair
	 ▪ If resident uses a wheelchair, instruct him/her to do the following and note ability to perform:
	    – Transfer from bed to wheelchair and wheelchair to bed
	    – Adjust brakes and footrests of wheelchair
	 ▪ Observe balance and coordination during transfers.	

(*continued*)

TABLE 9.1 Physical Assessment: Techniques and Factors to Consider *(continued)*

Area of Assessment	Assessment Techniques	Factors to Consider

	• Ask resident to walk at least 50 yards on level surface. Note balance, gait abnormalities (e.g., ataxic, flat-footed, scissors, spastic, hemiplegic).
	• Check condition of mobility appliance/device.
	• Observe resident while he/she is using mobility appliance/device; note:
	  ▪ Appropriateness of application/placement (e.g., use of can on stronger side)
	  ▪ Appropriateness of use (e.g., advancement of can with weaker leg, braking wheelchair during transfers)
	  ▪ Appropriateness of fit to resident's size and disability
	• Determine and describe the amount of assistance resident requires (e.g., needs to have prosthesis put on, one-person assist required during ambulation, completely independent).
	• If resident uses wheelchair, evaluate ability to:
	  ▪ Propel wheelchair at least 50 yards
	  ▪ Make turns in wheelchair
	  ▪ Position self at table in wheelchair	

(continued)

TABLE 9.1 Physical Assessment: Techniques and Factors to Consider *(continued)*

Area of Assessment	Assessment Techniques	Factors to Consider

	• Instruct resident to do the following and note ability to perform:
	  ▪ Locate clothes closet/dresser
	  ▪ Select a complete change of clothing
	  ▪ Remove all clothing
	  ▪ Put on clothing (note dexterity with snaps, buttons, zippers)
	  ▪ Put on stockings and shoes (note ability to tie laces)
	• Ask resident if assistive devices are used for dressing; obtain these devices if necessary.
	• Observe appropriateness of actions, understanding of order of removing and replacing clothing, judgment in clothing selection.
	• If resident is unable to use commode, note ability to:
	  ▪ Reach for bedpan/urinal
	  ▪ Position bedpan/urinal
	  ▪ Adjust clothing
	  ▪ Eliminate into bedpan/urinal
	  ▪ Reach, tear, and use toilet paper
	  ▪ Remove bedpan/urinal without spilling contents
	  ▪ Wash hands
	• If appliances such as ostomy and catheters are used, note ability of resident to appropriately care for these appliances and handle eliminated wastes.	

(continued)

TABLE 9.1 Physical Assessment: Techniques and Factors to Consider *(continued)*

Area of Assessment	Assessment Techniques	Factors to Consider
	• Review medical history for problems that could threaten toileting independence, such as paralysis, arthritis, hypotension, limited range of motion, dementia.	
	• If resident is not able to use bathtub or shower, determine the degree to which resident can participate in bed bath	
	• Review resident's medical history for diagnoses and factors that impact rehabilitation potential.	
	• Ask physical therapist, occupational therapist, and other team members for their assessment of resident's rehabilitation potential.	
	• Ask each shift to record resident's level of independence in performing ADLs; review documentation to identify differences among the shifts.	
Mobility	• Review medical history for problems that could increase potential for body control problems (e.g., Parkinson's disease, CVA, seizure disorder, arthritis, osteoporosis, dizziness, hypotension, multiple sclerosis, dementia, depression).	An increase in postural sway, and slower myoneural transmission, can delay an older adult's ability to regain balance if it is lost.

(continued)

TABLE 9.1 Physical Assessment: Techniques and Factors to Consider (*continued*)

Area of Assessment	Assessment Techniques	Factors to Consider

	• Review medications resident is taking for those drugs that could alter body control (e.g., cardiac drugs, diuretics, psychotropics, analgesics).
	• Observe:
	  ▪ Determine resident's general mobility status by requesting resident (unless he/she is known to be unable) to get out of bed, walk approximately 50 feet, and sit.
	  ▪ Inspect resident's body; note deformities, amputations, contractures, tremors.
	  ▪ Observe resident changing positions; note unsteadiness, need for support, inability to properly position body.
	• Ask:
	  ▪ Question resident about changes in ability to walk and move, coordination, and balance. Review length of time problem has existed and impact on ADLs.
	• Examine:
	  ▪ Place the resident's joints through active and passive range of motion; note limitations.
	  ▪ Test resident's strength in both hands by asking him/her to grab and squeeze your hands; note weakness, differences between hands.
		People with a history of inactivity can be expected to have reduced muscle strength, atrophy of proximal muscles of lower extremity with neuropathic changes of distal portion of leg, a replacement of muscles with fibrotic tissue, and a decrease of skeletal mass.

(*continued*)

TABLE 9.1 Physical Assessment: Techniques and Factors to Consider *(continued)*

Area of Assessment	Assessment Techniques	Factors to Consider
	■ Have resident assume an upright position and ask him/her to close eyes and hold arms out straight, perpendicular to body, for approximately 20 seconds; note weakness, inability to maintain position (could be associated with hemiparesis).	
	■ Ask resident to hold arms straight and resist your efforts to push them down; ask resident to raise arms over head with palms forward and hold that position for approximately 20 seconds. (Weakness or swaying of arms could be associated with hemiparesis or shoulder girdle disease.)	
	■ Test hip abduction by having resident lie in bed, placing your hands against outer sides of his/her knees, and ask resident to spread his/her legs and push them against your hand. Test hip adduction by repeating this test with your hands placed between the resident's knees and asking him/her to move the legs together. Test hip flexion by placing your hand on resident's thigh and asking him/her to raise the leg against your hand's resistance (test both legs). (Weakness could be associated with neuropathies, muscle disease.)	

(continued)

TABLE 9.1 Physical Assessment: Techniques and Factors
to Consider (*continued*)

Area of Assessment	Assessment Techniques	Factors to Consider
	■ Test plantar flexion by placing your hand on undersurface of resident's foot and asking him/her to push down. Test dorsiflexion at the ankle by placing your hand in front of foot and asking him/her to pull toes up against your hand. (Weakness could be associated with neuropathies, muscle disease.)	
	■ Test hand coordination by asking resident to rapidly tap hand on leg, turn hand over and back approximately 6 times, touching his/her thumb against each finger on the same hand. (Inability to perform these tasks could be associated with cerebellar disease.)	
	■ If resident is ambulatory, ask him/her to walk length of a hallway, or at least 50 feet. Look for ability to initiate and stop gait, coordination of movements, toe and foot lift, base of gait, smoothness and steadiness of gait, movement of legs, position and swing of arms, and ease of ambulation. Describe abnormalities.	

(*continued*)

TABLE 9.1 Physical Assessment: Techniques and Factors to Consider (*continued*)

Area of Assessment	Assessment Techniques	Factors to Consider
	▪ Test coordination by asking resident to walk touching heel of one foot to toe of the other as he/she steps. Hold resident's hand if he/she appears unsteady. (This test is referred to as *tandem walking*.) ▪ Review and discuss physical therapy and medical evaluations to obtain realistic appraisal of resident's rehabilitative potential.	

Pain	• Observe for:
	  ▪ Grimacing, crying, moaning, clutching fists
	  ▪ Limitations of movement
	  ▪ Favoring or rubbing of specific body part
	  ▪ Discoloration
	  ▪ Swelling
	• If resident indicates pain is present, ask:
	  ▪ Where is the pain located? Does it stay in one place or travel to other locations?
	  ▪ What does it feel like? Stabbing? Throbbing? Aching? Dull? Sharp?
	  ▪ On a scale of 0 to 10, with 0 being no pain and 10 being unbearable pain, how would you rate it as typically being? How would you rate it when it is at its best? At its worst?
		Pain is classified according to its pathophysiological mechanism as either nociceptive or neuropathic pain. *Nociceptive pain* arises from mechanical, thermal, or chemical noxious stimuli to A delta and C afferent nociceptors. These nociceptors are found in fasciae, muscles, joints, and other deep structures, and their activation causes a transduction of painful stimuli along the primary afferent fiber of the dorsal horn of the spinal column. Common forms of nociceptive pain include:

(*continued*)

TABLE 9.1 Physical Assessment: Techniques and Factors to Consider (*continued*)

Area of Assessment	Assessment Techniques	Factors to Consider
	■ How frequently does it occur? Several times a day? Daily? A few times a week? Every few weeks? ■ How long does it last? A few seconds? A few hours? All day? ■ Is the pain related to any medical problems, injuries, or unusual events? ■ What factors seem to bring it on? ■ What factors worsen it? Activity? Weather? Stress? ■ Is it worse at certain times of the day? ■ What helps to relieve the pain? Medications? Positions? Special treatments? ■ If medications are used, what are they, what is their dosage, how are they taken, and what effects do they produce? ■ Are any complementary or alternative therapies used? If so, what, how, and with what results? ■ How does the pain affect your life? Sleep? Appetite? Activity? Socialization? Self-care? Home responsibilities? Relationships? • Examine for: ■ Range of motion ■ Sensitivity to touch ■ Temperature of affected area as compared to adjacent areas	• Somatic pain: Characteristic of pain in bone and soft tissue masses; the pain is well localized and described as throbbing or aching • Visceral pain: Associated with disorders that can cause generalized or referred pain; the pain is described as deep and aching *Neuropathic pain* is associated with diabetic neuropathies, postherpetic neuralgias, and other insults to nervous system. The pain is sharp, stabbing, tingling, or burning, with a sudden onset of high intensity. It can last a few seconds or linger for a longer period. *Acute pain* has an abrupt onset, can be severe, but lasts only a short time *Chronic pain* is that which has persisted for 3 months or longer and can be of mild to severe intensity.

10

Identifying Changes in Status

The population served in long-term care settings has become increasingly complex as people are being admitted with multiple conditions and, sometimes, with acute conditions that continue to require management after hospitalization. In addition, the advanced age of many residents heightens the risk for changes in status and complications to develop. Monitoring of residents' conditions is essential to identifying and addressing problems early and ensuring treatment to avoid serious consequences.

This chapter should enable you to:

1. List observations that unlicensed personnel can be instructed to report
2. Identify changes that could be detected in residents and their possible causes
3. Describe information that should be communicated to the medical provider when a change in status is identified

MEANS OF IDENTIFYING CHANGES

ESSENTIAL FACTS

Because nurses often must rely on unlicensed direct caregivers to bring changes in residents' status to their attention, it is beneficial for nurses to regularly do rounds and specifically ask direct caregivers if any changes or new problems have been noted. Regularly reinforcing to caregivers the importance of observing for and reporting changes to nurses can also be helpful.

In most long-term care settings, nurses must rely on unlicensed personnel who have the most direct contact with residents to recognize changes and properly report them. This requires that nurses ensure that unlicensed staff have the knowledge to recognize these changes and understand the importance of properly reporting them. If it is determined that the direct caregivers may not fully understand the type of observations that should be brought to nurses' attention, educational programs can be offered, as well as resource materials. Figure 10.1 shows a sample resource sheet that can be provided to caregivers and posted at the nursing station to remind staff of observations to note.

As nurses often have limited direct contact with residents, maximizing the contact that does occur to identify changes in status can prove useful. For example when administering medications, nurses can:

- Inspect for changes in coloring, signs of pain, impairment of skin integrity, difficulty moving
- Note changes in mental clarity, speech, appropriateness of behavior
- Listen for abnormal sounds during respiration, abdominal gurgling
- Ask specific questions (e.g., "How has the pain in your knee been since you've been taking this new medication?" "You seem a little tired. Did you sleep well last night?" "Are you holding your head because it hurts?" "How did you get that bruise on your arm?")

Rather than requiring more time, these actions depend on using the time required to administer medications more strategically.

CHANGES TO IDENTIFY

Any change in physical or mental status requires attention. Table 10.1 offers examples of changes and possible causes for them.

Change in mental function
Problems understanding speech
Problems speaking
Changes in alertness

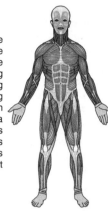

Report of unusual taste
Change in food or fluid intake
Change in appetite
Choking
Trouble swallowing
Nausea, vomiting
Complaints of indigestion
Constipation, diarrhea
Blood or mucus in feces
Discharge from vagina or penis
Reduced ability to bend joints
Swelling of any body part

Change in ability to hear
Blurred or decreased vision
Red or watery eyes
Blood or discharge from nose
Difficulty breathing
Unusual breath sounds
Coughing
Chest pain
Change in voiding frequency
New incontinence
Burning when voiding
Blood or pus in urine or feces

Change in vital signs
Change in weight
Change in activity level
Complaints of pain

Change in sleep pattern
Rash, skin breaks, bruise
Reduced energy
Body warm to touch

FIGURE 10.1   Observations to report.

ACTIONS TO TAKE WHEN CHANGES ARE IDENTIFIED

In most long-term care settings, medical staff are not on site at all times; therefore, nurses carry the responsibility of identifying and appropriately communicating changes in status. The quality of the information that is communicated to the medical providers by nurses can have a significant impact on the timeliness and appropriateness of the actions taken and, consequently, on the well-being of residents.

When changes in status are identified it is important for the nurse to assess and gather as much information as possible, such as current:

- Vital signs
- Level of consciousness
- Cognitive function
- Coloring
- General physical function
- New signs, symptoms, and complaints
- Recent events (e.g., fall, physical activity, consumption of food, administration of new medication)

Findings should be compared with the resident's usual status. The information collected should be readily available when the medical provider is called.

TABLE 10.1 Examples of Changes in Physical or Mental Status and Possible Causes for Them

Change	Possible Cause
Mild to severe pain at middle to upper portion of sternum radiating to arms, neck, back, and jaw; numbness in arms and hands	Angina
Dyspnea, moist pale skin, angina symptoms, substernal pressure, decreased blood pressure, arrhythmias, chest pain (although not always present), low-grade fever, elevated sedimentation rate	Myocardial infarction
Shortness of breath, orthopnea, edema, sudden weight gain, weakness, mental status changes, dyspnea, fatigue	Congestive heart failure
Chest pain during inspiration, fever, malaise, anorexia, productive cough, abnormal breath sounds, delirium	Pneumonia
Shortness of breath, increased respirations, chest discomfort, tachycardia, low blood oxygen, ECG and x-ray changes	Pulmonary embolism
Severe pain around eye, blurred vision, perception of halos around lights, nausea, vomiting	Acute glaucoma
Sudden or gradual blurred vision, feeling of coating over eye, blank areas of vision progressing to complete loss of vision	Detached retina
White patches on tongue	Moniliasis infection
Swelling, redness, bleeding gums	Periodontal disease
Disruption in neurological function lasting minutes to hours; can include falling, aphasia, diplopia, hemiparesis, motor weakness, ataxia, unilateral loss of vision	Transient ischemic attack
Altered or worsened cognitive function with altered level of consciousness	Delirium
Cloudy urine, odorous urine, hematuria, new incontinence, urinary frequency	Urinary tract infection
Itching, redness, and discomfort along a nerve pathway followed by appearance of painful vesicles; local lymph glands can be tender and palpable	Herpes zoster
White specks in hair with itching; crusts may be present on scalp	Pediculosis capitis (head lice)

(continued)

TABLE 10.1 Examples of Changes in Physical or Mental Status and Possible Causes for Them *(continued)*

Change	Possible Cause
Small red macular lesions on body with severe itching	Pediculosis corporis (body lice)
Severe itching, linear whitish-gray pattern with dark dot at end (commonly on digital web spaces, flexor surface of wrists, axilla, nipples, genitalia)	Scabies
Abnormal position of limb, inability to move limb, one limb longer than the other, swelling of limb, pain	Fracture

ESSENTIAL FACTS

When communicating changes in status to the medical provider it is important to include not only current assessment findings, but also previous vital signs, recent laboratory reports, and medications and treatments being administered. It should not be assumed that the medical provider recalls or has knowledge of all of the resident's history.

The content of the communication should be documented. If the medical provider prescribes a medication, treatment, or transfer to a hospital the facility's policy for communicating medical orders of this nature should be followed.

With the increasing acuity levels of residents being admitted to long-term care facilities and the complexities of conditions they possess, it is not unusual to have residents experience changes in physical and mental status. Prompt attention and correction of the cause of the change not only may spare residents unnecessary complications, but also may save their lives.

Creating Care Plans

Each resident who enters a long-term care facility will have unique needs that drive the care that will be required. To ensure that comprehensive needs are addressed in an individualized manner and that all staff members have the same understanding of the care that is required to do so, care plans are developed. It is essential that care plans be based on the individual resident's holistic needs and risks, provide measurable goals for addressing those needs and risks, offer specific approaches, actively engage the resident, and be regularly evaluated.

This chapter should enable you to:

1. Describe the care planning process
2. Identify characteristics of well-developed goals and interventions
3. List regulatory requirements related to care plans
4. Describe measures to encourage residents' participation in the care planning process

CARE PLANNING PROCESS

Care planning begins with the assessment process in which physical, emotional, and psychosocial needs are identified. Not only problems related to needs, but also potential problems must be considered.

From this initial survey a list of problems is developed and validated with the resident and other members of the interdisciplinary team.

A *goal* is developed for each major problem that has been identified, describing the specific outcome the resident will achieve. A goal states the desired outcome for the resident, not the actions of the staff. For example, stating that *Staff will offer 5 glasses of fluid to the resident* does not reflect an outcome for the resident; a properly stated goal would be: *Resident will consume at least 5 glasses of liquids during waking hours.* The goal needs to be specific and measurable so that any individual can determine if it has been achieved. Examples of correctly stated goals are listed in Table 11.1.

ESSENTIAL FACTS

Goals need to describe desired resident outcomes in a measurable manner that can be objectively evaluated by anyone. For example, a goal stating that *Resident will increase ambulation* can be difficult to evaluate as one person may view the goal as fulfilled if the resident walks across the bedroom twice daily while another may expect the resident to ambulate the distance of the hallway several times daily to fulfill the goal. An appropriate way to state the goal would be "By the end of 1 month resident walks from his bedroom to the dining room independently at least three times daily"; this clearly provides the desired outcome against which the goal will be evaluated.

Specific *interventions* are developed for each goal. Interventions are the approaches, actions, and procedures that support the resident in meeting the goal. They should be realistic, achievable, and tailored to the individual resident. As the care plan provides instructions for caregivers, to ensure that all caregivers have the same understanding of the actions to take it is useful for the interventions to include:

- The type of staff who should perform the activity
- How often the activity is to be performed
- The type of specific equipment or supplies that are used

All members of the interdisciplinary team who are involved with the resident, as well as the resident himself or herself, contribute to the care plan and participate in the care planning conference. If the resident is not competent and has a guardian appointed to act on his or her behalf, that individual is included in the care planning conference. The resident or representative of the resident needs to fully understand the goals and actions and be afforded the opportunity to react to and offer changes to the plans.

TABLE 11.1 Examples of Correctly Stated Goals

Problem	Possible Goals
Poor nutritional status	Resident will increase food intake to ____ calories per day Resident will consume at least 75% of each meal Resident maintains weight between ____ and ____ pounds Resident is free from signs of malnutrition
Constipation	Resident has a bowel movement at least q2d without use of laxatives or enemas Resident is free from signs of constipation and fecal impaction Resident consumes one glass of fruit juice with each meal
Urinary incontinence	Resident has cause of incontinence identified Resident restores bladder control within 30 days Resident is free from skin irritation and breakdown
Impaired mobility	Resident increases ambulation to ____ feet twice daily Resident maintains full range of motion in all joints Resident uses cane/walker/wheelchair correctly Resident is free from contractures and skin breakdown
Pain	Resident is free from pain Resident rates pain at 3 or less (on scale of 10) Resident achieves level of pain control that allows maximum participation in activities of daily living
Pressure ulcer	Resident's sacral ulcer improves from stage 4 to stage 3 Resident is free from infection secondary to pressure ulcer Resident is free from new pressure ulcer development

ESSENTIAL FACTS

Care plan goals and interventions should be realistic and achievable. Goals or actions copied from a text may look impressive on paper but if they state actions that are not individualized for the resident or that the facility cannot realistically implement, they do little to direct care. Further, if care is not provided according to the stated plan, legal problems could arise as staff are accountable for following the care plan.

An important part of the care planning process is the communication of the plan to all members of the team involved with the resident. As it can be challenging to review the care plan with all staff who provide care on every shift, care plans should be easily accessible and staff should be reminded to review them regularly. Placing the highlights of the care plan on cards that are kept at the nursing station and distributed to caregivers at the beginning of the shift can serve to remind caregivers of goals and interventions for residents to whom they are assigned. Changes in care plans should be communicated to staff for several days to ensure that all team members are aware of changes.

As the care plan is implemented, feedback should be sought from the resident and staff to determine the effectiveness of the plan. Interventions that may have seemed appropriate when discussed in the care plan conference may prove to be ineffective when implemented. The care plan should be revised as needed to reflect current goals and interventions.

ESSENTIAL FACTS

When changes are made in care plans, the revised items should not be obliterated. The care plan is part of the legal record and must be legible, including items that are no longer active or that have been changed.

REGULATORY REQUIREMENTS

Because care planning is viewed as a crucial component of resident care, specific regulations address the process. Among them are the following:

- Care plans must be developed within 7 days of the completion of the resident assessment instrument.
- The comprehensive care plan must include services that aid the resident in attaining and maintaining the highest level of physical, mental, and psychosocial well-being.
- Information about interests and preferences should be obtained from residents and included in the care plan.
- Residents have the right to make decisions and choices about their care.
- Residents have the right to refuse treatment and interventions. Residents' concerns related to treatments and interventions must be addressed and relevant alternatives offered.

- Care plans must be adjusted when residents have had a change in health status.

When surveyors inspect care plans for compliance with regulations they will consider the needs of the individual resident, the resident's specific choices, the facility's education of the resident, attempts to prevent negative outcomes through the care plan, documentation of the process, and monitoring of the outcomes.

ENCOURAGING RESIDENT PARTICIPATION

Residents are more likely to comply with the care plan if they have actively participated in its development and if it reflects their desires and preferences. Developing relationships with residents facilitates their participation.

Efforts should be made to identify a resident's priorities. For example, a female resident may have a history of chronic obstructive pulmonary disease, poor nutritional intake, weakness, and fatigue. A high risk for pneumonia, falls, malnutrition, and pressure ulcers may be top-priority problems that staff view as needing to be addressed. While understanding the importance of these problems, the resident's primary concerns may be how she can continue to have contact with her children and her church community. The problems identified by the resident also should be included in the care plan.

Goals and actions that staff believe to be beneficial should be reviewed with the resident. It is important that the resident understand the care that is planned and his or her role in it; this is facilitated by:

- Explaining goals and actions in a manner and on a level that the resident can understand
- Asking the resident for his or her thoughts about the plan
- Encouraging the resident to offer suggestions on other issues that need to be addressed or preferences and views on how care activities should be implemented
- Asking the resident if there is anything about the plan that is not clear or that the resident is uncomfortable with

The care plan provides a map to care that ensures the resident's physical, mental, and psychosocial needs are met in a manner that addresses the unique characteristics of that individual. In addition to benefiting the resident, a well-developed care plan benefits staff in assuring the care they provide is appropriate and effective, thereby preventing wasted time and efforts.

12

Ensuring Person-Centered Care

The culture change movement brought about many positive changes in nursing home care, one of which was an emphasis on person-centered care. Every aspect of resident–staff interaction affects the degree to which person-centered care is present.

This chapter should enable you to:

1. Describe basic features of person-centered care
2. Describe benefits and factors to consider with consistent assignments
3. Describe how staff can use communication to foster person-centered care
4. List the benefits of empowering residents
5. Describe measures that can enhance a meaningful life and optimal function for residents

COMPONENTS OF PERSON-CENTERED CARE

An essential element of culture change is person-centered care that:

- Views the resident holistically so that the highest level of physical, mental, and psychosocial well-being that is possible is achieved
- Promotes maximum resident choice
- Offers the resident purpose and meaning in daily life

A variety of factors contributes to person-centered care, including consistent assignment of staff, effective communication, empowerment of residents, and promotion of a meaningful life for residents.

ESSENTIAL FACTS

Core person-directed values are choice, dignity, respect, self-determination, and purposeful living (Pioneer Network, 2014).

CONSISTENT ASSIGNMENTS

Being cared for by the same staff on a regular basis fosters residents' ability to receive person-centered care. By being consistently assigned to residents, caregivers become familiar with residents' norms, required care, and preferences, and can develop strong relationships with residents and their families. There can be greater staff satisfaction as caregivers can better plan their work activities and anticipate residents' needs; they also benefit from having closer relationships with residents.

There are some considerations when caregivers are consistently assigned to the same group of residents. The needs and caregiving demands of each resident must be considered to ensure fairness of workload. The experience of caregivers should be matched with the care needs of residents. In addition, compatibility of the caregiver and resident should be considered. Rather than managers assigning residents to caregivers, input should be obtained from the caregivers involved as to resident assignments.

COMMUNICATION

Communication is a key element of person-centered care and involves many aspects, such as:

- *The way in which residents' preferences are learned.* Trusting relationships foster open, honest sharing. Residents need to know that their caregivers truly are interested in knowing what is important to them and will incorporate that knowledge into caregiving activities. Caregivers need to ask residents about preferences and pay attention to residents' reactions and comments. For example, if during a morning bath a resident shares that she always enjoyed a bath before bedtime, the caregiver could ask if the resident would prefer to be bathed at night. It must be remembered that a resident may not directly state a preference but could offer it if asked.

In addition, having residents participate in care planning conferences provides an opportunity for them to react to plans and state their preferences.

- *The way in which residents' preferences are shared.* Knowing preferences means little if the information is not communicated to others involved in the resident's care. Preferences should be documented and included in the care plan.
- *The way in which staff react to residents' preferences.* Staff must be sensitive to the fact that their reactions can foster or inhibit residents' expressions of preferences. For example, if a resident states that he would prefer to eat breakfast at 11 a.m. rather than 8 a.m. when it is typically served, and the staff member rolls her eyes and sighs, the resident may feel he is creating a burden for staff and withdraw his preference. Reactions to residents' preferences also include respect for residents' sexual orientation and religion.

ESSENTIAL FACTS

It can be difficult for residents with cognitive impairments to express their preferences. Asking their family members about past practices and observing reactions to care and activities are useful ways to determine some preferences for these residents.

EMPOWERMENT

The ability to choose when and how care will occur and the type of activities that they wish to engage in fosters an active role for residents in their care, respects them as adults, and enhances quality of life. When care and activities reflect residents' desires, compliance is heightened, which offers benefits to staff. Resident and staff satisfaction can be positive as a result.

It is important to equip residents to make sound decisions by ensuring they have the information they need. For example, a resident may state that she would like to spend the weekend in bed watching television rather than getting out of bed and following her daily walking schedule as recommended. By explaining to the resident the risk for pressure ulcers, pneumonia, loss of muscle strength, and other complications that could result from prolonged inactivity, she may make the decision to continue adhering to the ambulation schedule every day.

In addition to empowering residents, it is beneficial to empower direct care staff. Those caregivers who work most closely with residents often know best what residents' needs are and the likelihood of plans being effective. Their input and feedback should be sought and used.

ESSENTIAL FACTS ≡≡≡

> As residents' preferences may change it is useful to regularly validate their preferences and inquire about changes they would like.

MEANINGFUL LIFE

Living in a long-term care facility and being dependent on others for assistance with care certainly impacts one's life. Residents will not have the fullness of life that they may have enjoyed previously when they lived independently in the community. However, people thrive on having a purpose and something to look forward to, and therefore helping residents experience a meaningful life within the facility is an important part of person-centered care.

Residents should be assisted to participate in activities that can offer stimulation and socialization opportunities. This includes such considerations as:

- Assisting residents in getting bathed, groomed, and dressed in time to attend activities
- Making residents aware of the schedule of activities
- Helping to create a comfortable environment for visitors
- Providing privacy for residents' visits with family, friends, and other residents

Some residents may prefer solitary activities rather than group activities. As part of the assessment, residents should be asked about their previous interests and hobbies and, as possible, plans should be developed to afford residents the opportunity to participate in these activities in the facility.

The fulfillment of spiritual needs offers purpose and satisfaction to many individuals' lives. In addition to asking residents about their religion, it is beneficial to inquire about spiritual practices. The same resident who responds "none" for religion, may have a daily practice of meditation, inspirational reading, and prayer that fulfills spiritual needs.

ESSENTIAL FACTS ≡≡≡

> Although religion can be a component of one's spirituality, religion and spirituality are not synonymous. Spirituality refers to that which transcends the physical and connects a person to God or another higher power and other living organisms. Religion encompasses the symbols, rules, and rituals created by humans that offer a means of expressing an aspect of spirituality. A person can be highly spiritual without identifying with or practicing any specific religion.

Spiritual needs can include giving and receiving love, hope, dignity, forgiveness, expressing and receiving gratitude, and expressing one's faith. There are a variety of ways in which a resident can be helped to fulfill spiritual needs, such as:

- Respecting the resident's personal spiritual and religious beliefs
- Assisting the resident in obtaining books, artifacts, and materials that assist in meeting spiritual and religious needs
- Providing privacy for personal prayer time and visits with clergy
- Treating the resident in a manner that reflects the resident's value as a human being

Life review offers a means for residents to reflect on their purpose and achieve satisfaction from the life they have lived. For residents who are impaired and have limited opportunities for new experiences and activities, this can be a highly therapeutic activity. Activities that can facilitate life review include:

- Discussions on specific topics, such as differences in childrearing practices between residents and their children, the ways people entertained themselves before cable television and the Internet, and the type of music they enjoyed as teenagers
- Oral histories in which residents are asked to share their life stories from birth to present
- Written histories in which residents write the highlights of their lives or dictate it to others who will write if for them
- A review of old magazines that can spark a discussion of topics related to their earlier years

Reflection on their lives can aid residents in understanding the purpose of their entire lives and contribute to their psychosocial well-being.

PROMOTING HIGHEST LEVEL OF WELL-BEING

Helping residents achieve the highest possible level of physical, mental, and psychosocial function and well-being are crucial elements of person-centered care. Promoting physical activity not only carries many benefits for physical health, but also enhances residents' confidence and independence, which influences quality of life. Residents' health conditions and assessment findings will provide insights into the level of physical activity that is realistic. In addition to discussing plans for physical activity during the care planning conference, encouragement of physical activity can be incorporated into routine care activities. Staff should provide the support that could facilitate activity, such as reducing environmental obstacles, ensuring that mobility aids are readily available, and assisting with transfers and ambulation.

Pain, dizziness, and other symptoms that can reduce activity should be noted and addressed to reduce barriers to activity and exercise. Encouragement and recognition of efforts to be active can aid in promoting and sustaining positive actions.

Hearing and vision deficits are common among older adults and can contribute to injuries, reduced participation in care, and a poor quality of life. When these deficits are present, ensure that they have been properly evaluated. If eyeglasses or hearing aids have been prescribed, assess their condition and ensure they are used. Some tips for communicating with residents who have hearing and vision impairments are offered in Box 12.1.

Box 12.1 Communication Tips for Residents With Hearing and Vision Impairments

Hearing Impairments

- Control environmental noise
- Face the person when speaking
- Speak in loud, low-pitched voice
- Use short sentences, pronouncing all syllables clearly
- Supplement verbal communication with body language and written communication
- If the resident has difficulty hearing particular words, substitute other words that may have different types of sounds
- Assure the resident that it is fine to ask to have things repeated

Vision Impairments

- Ensure that the resident wears prescribed eyeglasses
- Provide adequate lighting, avoiding glare
- Avoid drastic changes in environmental lighting (e.g., going from a dark bedroom into a brightly lit bathroom) as it takes older eyes longer to accommodate to these changes
- Position yourself in the resident's visual field (remember that older residents have reduced peripheral vision and may not see you if you are to the far side)
- If the resident has difficulty reading printed instructions, menus, schedules, and so on, request large-print versions for the resident or read the content to the resident

Vision and hearing deficits can reduce a resident's ability to fully participate in care and express preferences. Correcting and compensating for these deficits contribute to resident empowerment.

Person-centered care respects the individuality and fosters the dignity of residents. Residents are supported in enjoying a meaningful life in which they can achieve a sense of worth and connection with others. Staff also benefit by providing individualized care with which residents are more likely to comply, developing more positive relationships with residents, and working more efficiently. Person-centered care contributes to improved outcomes and higher levels of resident, family, and staff satisfaction.

13

Caring for Families

Most individuals have been part of families that have played a role in their lives. Together they have shared many joys, struggles, and challenges. Relationships among family members can display various degrees of healthy function and have positive and negative impacts.

In long-term care settings, family members are extensions of the residents. They often are interested and involved in care. Their continued involvement in residents' lives can contribute to a high quality of life for residents; it also can be a source of stress for residents and staff. Understanding families and effective ways of relating to and involving them are important elements of long-term care nursing.

This chapter should enable you to:

1. List diverse family structures to which residents may belong
2. Describe the losses that families experience when their relatives are admitted to a long-term care facility
3. List possible reactions of families to having their loved ones in a long-term care facility
4. Describe actions that nurses can take to offer support to families

FAMILY STRUCTURES, ROLES, AND RESPONSIBILITIES

In today's society, the traditional nuclear family consisting of father, mother, and children can no longer be assumed to be the norm for all families. Residents may be part of family structures that include:

- Couples (married, unmarried, same sex, heterosexual)
- Couples with children
- Single parent and child or children
- Adult siblings living together
- Multiple generations
- Unrelated individuals living together

To ensure that persons significant to residents' lives are identified, it is important to have an open mind when asking residents about family members. In addition to asking about family with whom they have regular contact it is beneficial to ask questions such as:

- Do you live with anyone? If so, who?
- Are there any individuals who you would like to have involved in your care?

Family members vary in their roles and responsibilities within the family unit. Common roles that family members assume when they have an ill, disabled, or dependent relative include:

- *Caregiver:* This person, usually a wife or daughter, provides assistance to the resident with various aspects of personal care and management of medical conditions. As the caregiver will know the resident's history, care, and preferences well, suggesting to the resident that this person be included in care planning conferences (unless this person already is legally designated to do so) could prove beneficial.
- *Decision maker:* The responsibility for making important decisions is assumed by this person. This could be the same individual who serves as the caregiver but may not be in all situations. The decision maker may not be involved with the resident on a regular basis or be geographically near.

Asking residents about the relatives or other persons who have served or currently serve these roles can assist in identifying key individuals whom it could be important to involve in care.

ESSENTIAL FACTS

For some residents, persons who are not formally related may be serving roles traditionally assumed by relatives. It is important to identify these individuals during the assessment and involve them to the degree desired by residents.

In addition to serving in helpful roles to their loved one who is now a resident, family members may have depended on the resident for assistance. An example of this is the developmentally disabled child of the resident or an ill spouse for whom the resident has provided care. It also can be the adult child who has a troubled life, financial challenges, or is irresponsible and has depended on the resident for assistance. Despite his or her own condition and needs, the resident may be distressed at no longer being able to assist the relative, which could affect the resident's emotional health and willingness to remain in the facility. If it is discovered that a resident has concerns over the welfare of a relative, referral to the social worker for counseling and identification of resources to assist the family is beneficial.

ESSENTIAL FACTS

The dysfunction that may be identified in a resident's family often has existed for years and is not easily corrected. Referral to the social workers or counselors can aid in protecting the resident from the negative impact of this dysfunction. These professionals also can offer insights to staff as to effective ways of supporting the resident and working effectively with the family members.

FAMILY REACTIONS

The manner in which the family copes with having their loved one in a long-term care facility can have an impact on the health of the resident, as well as his or her relationship with staff. Identifying, planning for, and addressing the needs of the family should be considered as part of comprehensive care of the resident.

Families may display behaviors related to the changes and grief; a variety of losses could contribute to this, including the loss of:

- *Usual roles.* The resident may have been the matriarch or patriarch of the family who provided guidance to others and maintained traditions. With the resident no longer able to fully assume those roles, family members may lose the leadership the resident provided and find their lives upset.
- *Relationships.* Although relationships can continue among family members after the relative becomes a resident of a long-term care facility, they differ from those experienced when the relative lived in the community. The spouse can no longer experience intimacy in the same manner; grandchildren can no longer spend the night at their grandmother's home and awaken to her specially prepared

breakfast; a brother can no longer sit on the sofa with his sibling and enjoy a football game and beer in the privacy of his sibling's home. Dementias, pain, and other conditions can seriously alter the ability of the resident to engage in a meaningful relationship with family members.

- *Purpose.* A spouse or other family member who provided care in the home to the relative may feel a loss of purpose when the relative has care provided by the facility.
- *Finances.* Long-term care can be very expensive and deplete the savings and investments of the family. In some situations, a wife or other family members who resided in the home owned by the resident may have to move if the equity in the home must be used to pay for care.

These losses can affect families deeply and cause them to react with behaviors that can be distressing or disruptive to the resident and staff, such as:

- Crying during visitation or upon leaving the resident's room
- Avoiding visitation
- Making unreasonable demands on staff
- Complaining about and making critical comments to staff

Staff need to understand that these behaviors are the result of the emotional pain and turmoil the family members are experiencing. Supporting family members as they adjust to the changes and losses associated with having their relative in a nursing home or assisted living community is necessary.

ESSENTIAL FACTS

The sadness and life changes that family members may experience as a result of having their loved enter a nursing home or an assisted living community can be responsible for negative behaviors that are displaced to staff. Rather than become defensive or angry, staff need to show patience, understanding, and support as the family adjusts to this significant change in family roles and relationships.

OFFERING SUPPORT TO FAMILIES

A successful adjustment to having their relative in a facility and establishing new ways of maintaining a meaningful relationship with the relative benefits the family and the resident. Patience and support to family members, therefore, become an extension of holistic, individualized care of the resident. Beneficial actions to support family members include:

- *Orienting them to the facility and activities.* Show them the location of restrooms, vending machines, telephones, and offices of key staff with whom they may have to interact. Describe policies related to visiting and laundry. Instruct them on what they should do if the resident needs assistance or desires something to eat or drink. Explain the typical schedule of daily activities.
- *Suggesting activities they can do during their visits.* Nursing homes usually are not places with which most people have had experience. They may feel uncomfortable and unsure of how they are supposed to act. Describing facility activities that they can attend with the resident or activities that they can do with the resident (e.g., compiling a scrapbook, playing cards, wheeling to the outside patio, sharing a snack) could make their visits more comfortable and enjoyable.
- *Keeping them informed.* Learning that their loved one was moved to another room or experienced a fall can be unwelcomed surprises to family members. While respecting the resident's confidentiality by not sharing personal or health care–related information with those who are not privileged to receive this information, preparing family members for changes or unusual occurrences is beneficial.
- *Inviting feedback.* Let family members know that you welcome their suggestions and criticisms because you are interested in what is best for the resident.
- *Offering a listening ear.* Family members can experience many reactions to having their loved one in a facility, reacting with depression, anger, confusion, or denial. They need opportunities to vent their feelings and reassurance that you are available to assist them.

Most residents are members of family units. Assisting residents and their families in developing and sustaining meaningful relationships during the resident's stay in the facility can yield benefits to his or her health and quality of life. This also has benefits for family members' well-being and the facility's ability to promote customer satisfaction.

14

Documentation Essentials

Effective documentation serves several purposes in long-term care facilities. The response to care, current status, changes in status, and effectiveness of treatments can be determined through meaningful documentation. Staff can work more efficiently when guided by written care plans and activities. Documentation of incidents, complaints, and adverse reactions can assist in identifying problems that require education, supervision, different resources, or new policies and procedures. Reimbursement can depend on evidence of care provided through documentation. And importantly, in the event of allegations of negligence, the written record can support the staff and facility by confirming that appropriate assessment, monitoring, and care was provided.

This chapter should enable you to:

1. List items that are typically documented
2. Describe legal aspects of documentation
3. Describe safeguards in using electronic medical records
4. List guidelines for safe, effective documentation

ITEMS TO DOCUMENT

The typical resident has various care and treatment measures provided by several different members of the health care team. Documentation provides an important means for all team members to be informed of care that is planned and provided, as well as the resident's status, preferences, and response to care. Typically, the types of items that are documented include:

- Assessment information (including the Minimum Data Set tool as well as additional assessment data to supplement it)
- Plan of care
- Care provided, and response to care
- Implementation of special orders (e.g., intake and output, mental status checks, turning and repositioning) and resident response
- Medications and treatments administered
- PRN (as-needed) medications administered, reason for their administration, and resident response
- Laboratory and diagnostic tests
- Description of unusual occurrences or changes in status, along with actions taken
- Physician orders
- Communication with other providers related to resident care
- For Medicare residents, at least one notation every 24 hours

The facility should have policies and procedures related to documentation that include information such as the scope and limitations of documentation by various staff, acceptable forms, approved abbreviations, sequence of information in the record, length of time the records are maintained, and process to follow when requests for the medical record are received from individuals who are not part of the health care team.

ESSENTIAL FACTS

Staff may fail to use flow sheets and checklists that they believe are of no value or no longer relevant for residents due to improvements in residents' status. For this reason, special flow sheets, checklists, and documentation requirements should be implemented only when necessary, because once they are initiated they must be maintained accurately and consistently.

LEGAL ASPECTS OF DOCUMENTATION

ESSENTIAL FACTS

All persons who are involved with documentation must understand that the resident's record is a legal document that potentially could be examined in a court of law in the event of litigation. It also is a means to demonstrate the care provided for reimbursement purposes.

Although documentation may seem to be a simple task, several requirements must be met to ensure that the process is legally sound and fulfills its purpose.

Documenting Care Within Scope of Practice

In addition to regulations governing the care setting, each state has practice acts for various members of the health care team that state the approved scope of practice for those individuals. Documentation must comply with these laws. For example, assessment is beyond the scope of practice of nursing assistants. If a certified nursing assistant (CNA) signs an assessment tool or makes a notation such as "wheezes heard in lower left lung," the CNA is practicing outside the scope of practice and violating legal standards. Nurses need to review the documentation made by other team members to ensure that all members of the team are adhering to standards of practice for their position.

Accuracy and Appropriateness of Content

Documentation needs to be timely and correct. There is a risk when staff are busy that they will wait until the end of the shift to make their notations and sign off on treatments and care. This can create problems, especially if the resident experiences a change in status or needs to be transferred from the facility before the documentation is completed. In addition, the time lag increases the risk that relevant information could be forgotten. The appropriate standard is for documentation to occur as soon as possible after an observation is made, care is provided, or an incident or event has occurred.

The resident's record is not the place to express personal opinions or complaints. The record should not contain:

- Complaints about coworkers, residents, or visitors
- Comments about inadequate staffing
- Unsupported beliefs about the cause of a resident's condition or an incident

HIPAA

The Health Insurance Portability and Accountability Act (HIPAA) is a federal law that protects the privacy of health information and grants residents the right to see and obtain copies of their records. Care must be taken to ensure that only members of the health care team and outside providers who are treating the resident have access to resident's records and personal information. Violations of HIPAA could include actions such as:

- Leaving records and computer screens containing information about residents in view of the public
- Discussing a resident in an area where non–health care team members can hear the conversation
- Discarding without shredding documents that contain a resident's name
- Disposal in regular trash of supplies that show a resident's name
- Posting documents that contain information about the resident's care, vital signs, treatments, or condition in an area that can be viewed by the public
- Storing equipment and records showing the resident's name in areas where they are visible to the public
- Releasing records to banks, life insurance companies, and other entities without the resident's signed consent

ESSENTIAL FACTS

The U.S. Department of Health and Human Services can impose civil monetary penalties on facilities that violate HIPAA rules. In addition, the U.S. Department of Justice can enforce monetary and criminal penalties against individuals for the wrongful disclosure of resident information.

Electronic Medical Records

The use of electronic medical records (EMRs) adds a new dimension to documentation and its risks. As with the paper record, use of the EMR can result in inaccurate or fraudulent entries, inappropriate access to the record by unauthorized persons, and record loss due to environmental disasters. In addition, with EMRs, there can be the risk of system failures, hacking, and technology changes that make the system obsolete. Box 14.1 lists some of the safeguards to remember when using EMRs.

In addition to being a means to communicate care activities that can affect the quality of care provided, staff's documentation can be a significant proof of the care provided in the event of litigation. Box 14.2 offers general guidelines to promote safe documentation.

Box 14.1 Safeguards with Electronic Medical Records

- Use the user name and password that you have been assigned; do not share this with anyone.
- Ensure that all individuals documenting on the record have provided electronic signatures.
- Ensure that the correct record has been accessed.
- Be accurate with the date and time references entered as the computer typically will automatically document the date and time at which the entry was actually made.
- Do not open and use the record if unauthorized persons can view it.
- Log off and do not leave the record open after completing documentation.
- Ensure that a mechanism is in place for accessing and reconstructing the medical record if the system has a malfunction.
- Adhere to the facility's policies and procedures regarding electronic records.

Box 14.2 Guidelines for Documentation

- Ensure that the correct date, time, and person documenting are apparent.
- Medication and treatment records and flow sheets should be complete; omissions should be circled at the chronological place in the document where an entry was omitted and explained. (For electronic medical records, follow the instructions provided for correcting admissions.)
- Document all care that is provided in chronological order.
- Document all communication with providers.
- Maintain the record in proper order, according to facility policy.
- On forms that allow for initialing, ensure the a master legend is available that includes the full name, title, and initial of each person who documented on the form.
- Ensure that all entries are legible.
- Avoid subjective comments, criticisms, or judgments about other members of the health care team.

(continued)

Box 14.2 *(continued)*

- If corrections to documentation must be made, do not erase or obliterate the documentation that was incorrect. Draw a line through and write "documentation error" and make a notation of the correction. Ensure that the original entry remains visible. (For electronic medical records, follow the instructions provided for making corrections.)
- If a late entry is needed, document the actual date and time that the entry is made and mark the entry "late entry for [*date, time*]."
- Do not document care before it is provided or document care that was not provided.
- Ensure that documentation is ongoing and accessible to all members of the health care team.
- Maintain confidentiality of the record, protecting it from accessibility by people other than members of the health care team.
- Remember that the record is a legal document.

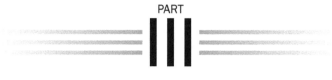

PART

III

Clinical Challenges

Clinical Challenges

15

Promoting Medication Safety

The wide range of health conditions that are present among persons residing in long-term care settings contributes to the high use of medications. In addition to interactions, the risks associated with the number of drugs used are heightened by the reality that most long-term care residents are of advanced age and often absorb, metabolize, distribute, and excrete medications differently than younger people. These realities reinforce the need for long-term care nurses to be knowledgeable about the principles of safe medication use and adhere to standards related to this significant area of practice.

This chapter should enable you to:

1. List nurses' responsibilities related to medications
2. Identify common medication errors
3. Describe the way in which aging can affect the action of drugs in an older adult
4. List federal regulations related to medications
5. Describe considerations associated with specific drugs that are commonly administered in long-term care settings

NURSES' RESPONSIBILITIES RELATED TO MEDICATIONS

Administering medications is a common nursing function in long-term care settings; however, that is just one component of the responsibilities related to medications. Nurses must be involved in:

- Discussing residents' conditions and related medication needs with physicians
- Accepting and transcribing medication orders
- Ensuring that medication orders are properly transferred to the pharmacy
- Transcribing medications on the facility's medication administration record
- Checking medication orders against contraindications (e.g., allergies, interactions)
- Accepting medications from the pharmacy and ensuring their accuracy against the order
- Educating residents about their medications
- Administering the medication
- Evaluating residents' responses to medications
- Identifying and informing the physician of adverse reactions
- Ensuring the competencies and safe function of unlicensed assistive personnel if they are involved in medication administration

ESSENTIAL FACTS

Some states allow the delegation of medication administration to unlicensed assistive personnel (UAP) such as certified medicine aides or technicians. Although these individuals are trained to administer drugs, the registered nurse (RN) or licensed practical nurse (LPN) to whom they are responsible is accountable for the UAP's management as this is considered a delegated responsibility. This accountability reinforces the importance of nurses ensuring the competencies of any UAP who administers medications and taking action to correct performance that does not meet standards.

As can be seen with the list of responsibilities, medication administration is a complex process that demands that nurses be competent and conscientious. Common errors that can occur related to medications include:

- Medication order not transcribed or implemented
- Medication not given as ordered
- Incorrect medication administered

- Medication administered despite an expired order
- Medication administered when it should have been held due to allergy, signs of adverse reaction, or a hold order related to vital signs or laboratory results
- Medication administered but not documented

Precautions should be taken to prevent these errors. It is important that errors be reported and that the facility's policy related to the type of error involved be followed.

MEDICATIONS AND OLDER ADULTS

Because most long-term care residents are of advanced age, consideration must be given to the impact of age on the way drugs behave. Age-related changes that can influence the effects of medications in older adults include:

- Reduced metabolism, cardiac output, and circulation, which can delay absorption
- Decreased circulation to the lower bowel, which can delay the melting and absorption of suppositories
- Less muscle mass and subcutaneous tissue, which can reduce the absorption of injected medications
- Changes in circulation, tissue structure, and membrane permeability that can affect drug distribution
- Slower metabolic rates, which can reduce drug metabolism
- A decline in central nervous system function, which can cause drugs that affect this system to have a more profound effect
- Reduced liver size, function, and blood flow that can affect the metabolism of antibiotics, cimetidine, chlordiazepoxide, digoxin, lithium, meperidine, nortriptyline, and quinidine
- Decreased glomerular filtration rate, causing drugs to take longer to be excreted from the body

ESSENTIAL FACTS

A reduction in serum albumin levels occurs with age in many people, which can affect the distribution of protein-bound drugs. If several protein-bound drugs are administered together, there is a risk that they will compete for the limited protein molecules, displace each other, and not be effective. Examples of protein-bound drugs include acetazolamide, amitriptyline, cefazolin, chlordiazepoxide, chlorpromazine, cloxacillin, digitoxin, furosemide, hydralazine, nortriptyline, phenylbutazone, phenytoin, propranolol, rifampin, salicylates, spironolactone, sulfisoxazole, and warfarin. Careful monitoring of these medications and their effects are needed when given concurrently.

Based on strong evidence, Dr. Mark Beers and other experts have identified drugs that should not be used with older adults due to their high risk for adverse reactions (American Geriatrics Society 2012 Beers Criteria Update Expert Panel, 2012). The list they have created is known as the *Beers Criteria for Potentially Inappropriate Medication Use in Older Adults*. Table 15.1, at the end of this chapter, highlights some of the medications identified as inappropriate for older adults. If these medications are prescribed, nurses should question their use with the prescribing physician and pharmacist.

TABLE 15.1 Inappropriate Drugs to Use in Older Adults, from the Beers List*

Antihistamines, first-generation (as single agent or as part of combination products)	Brompheniramine, carbinoxamine, chlorpheniramine, clemastine, cyproheptadine, dexbrompheniramine, dexchlorpheniramine, diphenhydramine (oral), doxylamine, hydroxyzine, promethazine, triprolidine
Anti-infective	Nitrofurantoin
Antiparkinson agents	Benztropine (oral), trihexyphenidyl
Antispasmodics	Belladonna alkaloids, clidinium–chlordiazepoxide, dicyclomine, hyoscyamine, propantheline, scopolamine
Antithrombotics	Dipyridamole (oral short-acting), ticlopidine
Cardiovascular	Digoxin (> 0.125 mg/day), disopyramide, dronedarone, nifedipine (immediate release), spironolactone (> 25 mg/day) *Alpha$_1$ blockers:* Doxazosin, prazosin, terazosin *Alpha blockers, central:* Clonidine, guanabenz, guanfacine, methyldopa, reserpine (> 0.1 mg/day) *Antiarrhythmic drugs (classes Ia, Ic, III):* Amiodarone, dofetilide, dronedarone, flecainide, ibutilide, procainamide, propafenone, quinidine, sotalol
Central nervous system	*Antidepressants—tertiary TCAs, alone or in combination:* Amitriptyline, chlordiazepoxide–amitriptyline, clomipramine, doxepin (> 6 mg/day), imipramine, perphenazine–amitriptyline, trimipramine

(continued)

TABLE 15.1 Inappropriate Drugs to Use in Older Adults, from the Beers List* *(continued)*

	Antipsychotics, first- (convention) and second- (atypical) generation: Mesoridazine, thioridazine *Barbiturates:* Amobarbital, butabarbital, butalbital, mephobarbital, pentobarbital, phenobarbital, secobarbital *Benzodiazepines, short- and intermediate acting:* Alprazolam, estazolam, lorazepam, oxazepam, temazepam, triazolam *Long-acting:* Chlorazepate, chlordiazepoxide, chlordiazepoxide–amitriptyline, clidinium–chlordiazepoxide, clonazepam, diazepam, flurazepam, quazepam Chloral hydrate Meprobamate *Nonbenzodiazepine hypnotics:* Eszopiclone, zolpidem, zaleplon *Other:* Ergot mesylates, isoxsuprine
Endocrine	*Androgens:* Methyltestosterone, testosterone Desiccated thyroid Estrogens (with or without progestins) Growth hormone Insulin (sliding scale) Megestrol *Sulfonylureas (long-duration):* Chlorpropamide, glyburide
Gastrointestinal	Metoclopramide Mineral oil (given orally) Trimethobenzamide
Pain medications	Meperidine *Non–COX-selective NSAIDs, oral:* Aspirin (> 325 mg/day), diclofenac, diflunisal, etodolac, fenoprofen, ibuprofen, ketoprofen meclofenamate, mefenamic acid, meloxicam, nabumetone, naproxen, oxaprozin, piroxicam, sulindac, tolmetin Indomethacin, ketorolac (includes parenteral) Pentazocine *Skeletal muscle relaxants:* Carisoprodol, chlorzoxazone, cyclobenzaprine, metaxalone, methocarbamol, orphenadrine

COX, cyclooxygenase; NSAID, nonsteroidal anti-inflammatory drug; TCA, tricyclic antidepressant.

*The listed drugs are identified as having a high risk for adverse reactions in older adults.

Adapted from the American Geriatric Society 2012 Beers Criteria Update Expert Panel (2012).

REGULATIONS RELATED TO MEDICATIONS

Regulations have been developed to ensure the safe use of medications in long-term care settings. Federal nursing home regulations (Centers for Medicare and Medicaid Services, 2014c) state that:

- Drugs cannot be used that are without adequate indication for use, in excessive dose, for excessive duration, without adequate monitoring, and for which there is the presence of adverse effects.
- Residents must be free from any significant medication error.
- The facility must have a medication error rate that is less than 5%.

These regulations also address antipsychotic therapy (Centers for Medicare and Medicaid, 2014c), stating that:

- Residents should not be given antipsychotic drugs unless this therapy is necessary to treat a specific condition that has been diagnosed and is documented in the record.
- When antipsychotic drugs are used, there must be gradual dosage reductions and behavioral interventions, unless contraindicated, in an effort to discontinue the use of these drugs.

In both nursing homes and assisted living communities, residents can self-administer medications if they so desire and if the team has determined that it is safe for the resident to do so. Box 15.1 offers a checklist of items that the nurse can use to assess the resident's ability to safely self-administer medications. The resident's continued ability to safely self-administer medications should be regularly reassessed.

ESSENTIAL FACTS

Antipsychotic medications have had a long history of use in long-term care facilities to manage challenging resident behavior. In many situations, the residents' diagnoses did not warrant the use of these drugs and doses were inappropriate. Because of the serious risks associated with antipsychotic use, there have been efforts to reduce antipsychotic medication use in long-term care residents. If antipsychotics are used, there must be documentation of a justified need, the targeted behavior for which they are prescribed, factors that trigger the behavior, and nonpharmacological interventions that have been attempted and their results.

Box 15.1 Checklist for Assessing a Resident's Ability to Safety Self-Administer Medications

For each drug that will be self-administered the resident is able to:

_____ Read the instructions on the medication container
_____ State the name of the drug
_____ State the dosage and administration times
_____ State any special administration instructions
_____ Describe common side effects
_____ Open and remove the correct dosage from the container
_____ Properly administer the drug
_____ Obtain and return the container to the secure storage cabinet
_____ Describe the conditions under which a PRN (as-needed) medication could be administered
_____ Describe reactions and situations that should be reported to the nurse
_____ Document that the drug was administered

RISKS ASSOCIATED WITH SPECIFIC DRUGS

Nurses need to be knowledgeable about the drugs they are administering in terms of dosage, intended effects, precautions, adverse effects, and special monitoring that may be needed. Table 15.2, which concludes this chapter, describes some of the considerations with commonly administered medications. It is useful for nurses to have drug reference resources readily available to obtain full information on all drugs administered.

TABLE 15.2 Considerations With Commonly Prescribed Medications

Analgesics
Acetaminophen
- Daily doses > 4 g increase risk of liver toxicity; if doses at this level are given, periodic liver function tests are useful to obtain

Nonsteroidal Anti-Inflammatory Drugs (NSAIDs)
- Include nonselective NSAIDs (e.g., aspirin, diclofenac, diflunisal, ibuprofen, indomethacin, meclofenamate, naproxen, salicylates, tolmetin), cyclooxygenase-II (COX-2) inhibitors
- Should not be used if lower risk analgesics (e.g., acetaminophen) can control symptoms
- Beers Criteria recommends that aspirin not be consumed in amounts greater than 325 mg/day (see Table 15.1)
- Signs of salicylate toxicity should be observed for; these include dizziness, vomiting, tinnitus, hearing loss, sweating, fever, confusion, burning in the mouth and throat, convulsions, and coma
- Aspirin can increase the effects of oral anticoagulants, oral antidiabetics, cortisone-like drugs, penicillins, and phenytoin, and decrease the effects of probenecid, spironolactone, and sulfinpyrazone
- Effects of aspirin can be increased by large doses of vitamin C and decreased by antacids, phenobarbital, propranolol, and reserpine
- Aspirin may increase the adverse effects of COX-2 inhibitors on the gastrointestinal (GI) tract
- Some NSAIDs (e.g., ibuprofen) may reduce the cardioprotective effect of aspirin
- NSAIDs may cause gastrointestinal bleeding in residents with a prior history of, or with increased risk for, GI bleeding, and those using anticoagulants
- NSAIDs may cause or worsen renal failure, increase blood pressure, or exacerbate heart failure

Opioids
- Increased risk for adverse effects requires that these drugs be used with caution in older adults
- Meperidine is viewed as an inappropriate drug for older adults due to its high risk for toxicity
- Older adults are at risk for developing opioid-induced urinary retention

Antacids
- Unless otherwise ordered, antacids should not be administered within 2 hours of other medications to avoid having them interfere with absorption
- Magnesium hydroxide can increase the effects of dicumarol
- Aluminum hydroxide can increase the effects of pseudoephedrine
- Most antacids can decrease the effects of barbiturates, chlorpromazine, digoxin, iron preparations, isoniazid, oral anticoagulants, penicillin, phenytoin, phenylbutazone, salicylates, sulfonamides, tetracycline, and vitamins A and C

(continued)

TABLE 15.2 Considerations With Commonly Prescribed Medications (*continued*)

- Sodium bicarbonate can cause hypernatremia and metabolic acidosis
- Sodium bicarbonate and magnesium-containing antacids can cause diarrhea leading to fluid and electrolyte imbalances
- Calcium carbonate can result in hypercalcemia
- Long-term use of calcium-based antacids can cause constipation and renal problems
- Long-term use of aluminum hydroxide can cause hyperphosphatemia

Antianxiety medications

- Can interact with anticonvulsants, antidepressants, diazepam, digoxin, diltiazem, erythromycin, grapefruit juice, haloperidol, levodopa, nefazodone, rifampin, ritonavir, some antifungal medicines (e.g. itraconazole, ketoconazole, and voriconazole), verapamil, and warfarin
- Regular grapefruit consumption can increase the concentration of these drugs
- Barbiturates and benzodiazepines are included on the Beers list of drugs that are inappropriate to use for older adults (see Table 15.1)

Antibiotics

- Should only be used when there is a confirmed or suspected bacterial infection
- Can cause diarrhea, nausea, vomiting, anorexia, and allergic reactions
- Can reduce beneficial microorganisms
- Oral thrush, colitis, and vaginitis can occur as secondary infections from antibiotic therapy, affecting comfort, intake, and general well-being
- Hearing loss and renal failure can occur with the use of parenteral vancomycin and aminoglycosides
- Fluoroquinolones increase the risk of hypoglycemia and hyperglycemia
- False results with urine testing for glucose can occur when cephalosporins are used

Anticoagulants

- Require monitoring of prothrombin time (PT)/international normalized ratio (INR)
- High rate of interaction with other medications
- Effects can be decreased by antacids, antithyroid agents, barbiturates, carbamazepine, chlorpromazine, cholestyramine, estrogens, rifampin, thiazide diuretics, and vitamin K

(*continued*)

TABLE 15.2 Considerations With Commonly Prescribed Medications (*continued*)

- Effects can be increased by acetaminophen, allopurinol, alteplase, amprenavir, androgens, aspirin and some other NSAIDs, azithromycin, bismuth subsalicylate, some calcium channel blockers, capsaicin, broad-spectrum antibiotics, chlorpromazine, colchicine, ethacrynic acid, mineral oil, phenylbutazone, phenytoin, probenecid, reserpine, thyroxine, tolbutamide, and tricyclic antidepressants
- Observe for signs of bleeding

Antidepressants

- Monitor for impact on symptoms; several weeks of therapy may be necessary before results are apparent
- Can be used for conditions other than depression, such as anxiety disorders, post-traumatic stress disorder, obsessive compulsive disorder, insomnia, neuropathic pain, and migraine headaches; assess recipient to determine if it is bringing about desired effect
- Tricyclic antidepressants are not antidepressants of choice for older adults unless used for neurogenic pain and the benefits are assessed to outweigh the risks
- Effects can be increased by alcohol and thiazide diuretics
- Can increase the effects of anticoagulants, atropine-like drugs, antihistamines, sedatives, tranquilizers, narcotics, and levodopa; decrease the effects of clonidine, phenytoin, and various antihypertensives
- Dizziness and drowsiness can occur, increasing the risk of falls
- When discontinuing, gradually taper dose to avoid withdrawal syndrome

Antidiabetic medications

- Monitoring of blood glucose is beneficial to evaluate effectiveness
- Continued use of sliding scale insulin is not recommended
- As hypoglycemia is a risk, monitor for symptoms which include tachycardia, palpitations, irritability, headache, hypothermia, visual disturbances, lethargy, confusion, seizures, and coma

Antiparkinson medications

- Confusion and restless can appear as adverse reactions

Antipsychotic medications

- Includes first-generation (conventional) agents (e.g., chlorpromazine, fluphenazine, haloperidol, loxapine, mesoridazine, molindone, perphenazine, promazine, thioridazine, thiothixene, trifluoperazine, triflupromazine) and second-generation (atypical) agents (e.g., aripiprazole, clozapine, olanzapine, quetiapine, risperidone, ziprasidone)
- Should be used only for the following conditions/diagnoses as documented in the record and as meets the definition(s) in the *Diagnostic and Statistical Manual of Mental Disorders, Fourth Edition, Training Revision (DSM-IV TR)* or subsequent editions): schizophrenia, schizo-affective disorder, delusional disorder, mood disorders, psychosis
- Close monitoring is essential

(*continued*)

TABLE 15.2 Considerations With Commonly Prescribed Medications (*continued*)

- Have a high risk for producing anticholinergic effects (signs include dry mouth, constipation, urinary retention, blurred vision, insomnia, restlessness, fever, confusion, disorientation, hallucinations, agitation, picking behavior), and extrapyramidal symptoms (signs include tardive dyskinesia, parkinsonism, akinesia, dystonia)
- Can increase the effects of sedatives and antihypertensives, and decrease the effects of levodopa
- Effects can be reduced by anticholinergic drugs, phenytoin, and antacids
- Should not be discontinued abruptly

Cardiovascular medications
- Antiarrhythmics can have serious adverse effects in older individuals, including impaired mental function, falls, appetite, behavior, and heart function
- Antihypertensives may cause dizziness, postural hypotension, fatigue, and an increased risk for falls; effects can be potentiated by interaction with other medications
- Antihypertensives can increase the effects of antidiabetic drugs, sedatives, and thiazide diuretics
- Doxazosin, prazosin, and terazosin can cause significant hypotension and syncope with initial doses; these medications should be initiated at bedtime with a slow titration of dose
- Prazosin can cause more central nervous system side effects and generally should be avoided in older individuals
- Beta-adrenergic blockers may cause or exacerbate bradycardia, dizziness, fatigue, depression, bronchospasm, or cardiac decompensation; they can mask tachycardia associated with symptomatic hypoglycemia
- Digoxin is indicated only for congestive heart failure, atrial fibrillation, paroxysmal supraventricular tachycardia, or atrial flutter; it should be used with caution in individuals with impaired renal function; it may interact with many other medications, possibly resulting in digoxin toxicity or elevated serum concentrations of other medications; signs of digoxin toxicity include fatigue, nausea, vomiting, anorexia, delirium, cardiac arrhythmia

Cholesterol-lowering medications
- Can impair liver function; liver function tests should be monitored
- Can cause muscle pain, myopathy, and rhabdomyolysis (breakdown of skeletal muscle) that can precipitate kidney failure especially in combination with other cholesterol lowering medications

Cognitive-enhancing drugs for dementia
- Include cholinesterase inhibitors (e.g., donepezil, galantamine, rivastigmine tartrate, tacrine), and N-methyl-D-aspartate (NMDA) receptor antagonists (e.g., memantine)

(*continued*)

TABLE 15.2 Considerations With Commonly Prescribed Medications (*continued*)

- Can cause nausea, vomiting, diarrhea, anorexia, weight loss, urinary frequency, muscle cramps, joint pain, swelling, or stiffness, fatigue, drowsiness, headache, dizziness, nervousness, depression, confusion, changes in behavior, abnormal dreams, difficulty falling asleep or staying asleep, discoloration or bruising of the skin, and red, scaling, itchy skin
- Should not be abruptly discontinued

Diuretics
- Can cause fluid and electrolyte balance; signs include dry oral cavity, confusion, thirst, weakness, lethargy, drowsiness, restlessness, muscle cramps, muscular fatigue, hypotension, reduced urinary output, slow pulse, and GI disturbances
- Can raise blood glucose in people with diabetes and worsen existing liver disease, renal disease, gout, and pancreatitis
- Can increase the effects of antihypertensives and decrease the effects of allopurinol, digoxin, oral anticoagulants, antidiabetic agents, and probenecid

Laxatives
- Stool softeners (e.g., docusate sodium) take effect in 24–48 hours
- Bulk formers (e.g., methylcellulose) usually take 12–24 hours to take effect; need to be mixed with large amounts of water; are contraindicated when there is any indication of intestinal obstruction
- Stimulants (e.g., cascara sagrada) take effect in 6–10 hours; can cause intestinal cramps and excessive fluid evacuation
- Hyperosmolars (e.g., glycerin) take effect in 1–3 hours; should not be used when there is the risk of fecal impaction
- Lubricants (e.g., mineral oil) take effect in 6–8 hours; are not recommended for older adults as they can cause serious problems if aspirated during administration and if used on a long-term basis can cause a depletion of fat-soluble vitamins (A,D, K, and E)

Sedatives/Hypnotics
- Effects can be increased by alcohol, antihistamines, and phenothiazines

Sedatives
- Slow activity and have a calming effect; at higher doses induce sleep and are considered hypnotics
- Nonbenzodiazepines (e.g., eszopiclone, ramelteon, zaleplon, zolpidem) are considered safer than benzodiazepines, although with the exception of eszopiclone, they are not approved for long-term use
- Carry the risk for serious adverse effects, including falls, sleepwalking, residual sedation, and memory and performance impairment

Hypnotics
- Can increase the effects of oral anticoagulants, antihistamines, and analgesics, and decrease the effects of cortisone and cortisone-like drugs

16

Reducing Common Risks

Individuals who are of advanced age, have multiple health conditions, use a wide range of medications, and have compromised physical or mental function—which describes most residents in long-term care settings—are at high risk of developing problems and complications. Each resident must be assessed for current and potential risks that may be present at admission and on an ongoing basis thereafter and have plans established to address them.

This chapter should enable you to identify causative factors, signs, and approaches to prevent and manage:

1. Falls
2. Infections
3. Pressure ulcers
4. Dehydration
5. Weight loss
6. Urinary incontinence
7. Delirium

PROACTIVE APPROACH TO RISKS

Long-term care residents not only are vulnerable to developing complications and new health problems, but also experience more challenges in recovering from them. This reinforces the need for nurses to actively identify and reduce risks. During the admission assessment factors that increase risks should be identified and plans developed to actively address them. In addition, risks should be reassessed and addressed on a regular basis, recognizing that advancing age, changes in condition, new diagnoses, and new medications or new adverse effects from medications long taken can create new risks. Plans developed to address risks should be reviewed on a regular basis to ensure their ongoing appropriateness and effectiveness.

Here are some common risks that occur in long-term care residents.

FALLS

Falls are a common risk among long-term care residents and have the potential for serious consequences.

ESSENTIAL FACTS

About half of all long-term care residents experience a fall each year. Although most falls result in minor soft-tissue injuries, the risk for dying from fall-related complications increases with age.

Some of the factors contributing to the high rate of falls in residents include:

- Advanced age
- Cognitive impairment
- Impaired vision
- Symptoms, such as fatigue, dizziness, generalized weakness, and edema
- Lower extremity weakness
- Foot disorders
- Gait disturbances
- Poor balance or coordination
- Medication side effects, especially those associated with sedatives, antipsychotics, and diuretics
- Improper use of canes, walkers, and wheelchairs
- Unsafe clothing

- Environmental hazards, such as wet or highly waxed surfaces, items left on the floor, and poor lighting
- History of falls

Upon admission and regularly thereafter, residents should be assessed for fall risk; this would include residents who are of advanced age, use multiple medications, are in a new environment, or have:

- Cognitive impairment
- Delirium
- Depression
- Mobility problems
- Hypotension
- Paralysis
- Muscle weakness or tremors
- Unsteady gait
- Seizure disorders
- Impaired vision
- Incontinence
- A history of falling

ESSENTIAL FACTS

The Beers criteria, described in Chapter 15, identify fall-risk medications as those that increase the risk of falling in older adults. Examples include anticholinergics, antipsychotics, barbiturates, benzodiazepines, muscle relaxants, clonidine, digoxin, doxazosin, and zolpidem. When these medications are prescribed with antithrombotics in residents older than 80 years of age, the risk of experiencing a postfall intracranial hemorrhage is 4 times greater (Hohmann, Hohmann, & Kruse, 2014). Caution and close monitoring of residents receiving these drugs are essential.

Interventions should be planned and implemented to prevent falls. These measures include:

- Offering assistance to residents with transfers, ambulation, and toileting as needed
- Reminding residents to use handrails and change positions slowly
- Avoiding leaving linens or objects on the floor
- Cleaning spills promptly
- Monitoring residents' status when new medications are administered
- Ensuring that residents wear safe shoes and pants that do not drag on the floor
- Having adequate lighting in areas in which residents ambulate

When a fall occurs:

- Keep the resident immobile until examined
- If there is any possibility of a fracture, make sure that the resident undergoes x-ray evaluation
- Even if the resident is believed to be free from injury, monitor carefully after the fall because some injuries are not apparent immediately
- Complete an incident and accident form according to your facility's procedure

INFECTIONS

Infections are a common and serious risk to residents. Factors that contribute to their occurrence include:

- Age-related alterations in the antigen–antibody response
- Presence of chronic conditions
- Immobility or inactivity
- Poor nutritional status
- Exposure to pathogens in the health care setting
- Use of catheters and invasive procedures
- Misuse or overuse of antibiotics

ESSENTIAL FACTS

Infections are a particular challenge to older residents because age-related factors cause them to develop more easily and to present atypical symptoms that can delay diagnosis.

Older residents may not present with high fevers and other signs of infection that are common in younger people with infections. Signs of infections could include:

- Delirium or worsening of existing behavioral problems
- Hypotension
- Increased pulse
- Increased respirations
- Chills
- Headache; pain in the affected area
- Malaise or weakness
- Anorexia or weight loss

- Vomiting
- Diarrhea
- Purulent drainage
- Lesions or pruritus
- With urinary tract infections—urinary frequency, incontinence, flank pain, dysuria, burning, hematuria, or pyuria
- With respiratory infections—cough, chest discomfort, rhinorrhea, purulent sputum, or nasal congestion
- White blood cell (WBC) count greater than 10,000
- Positive blood, wound, or sputum cultures

ESSENTIAL FACTS

Clostridium difficile (C. difficile) is a common cause of infectious diarrhea in long-term care settings and can be life threatening. This infection can be spread when the fecal matter of an infected person is transferred by contaminated hands or objects to another person. This scenario reinforces the importance of adhering to strict handwashing guidelines, properly cleaning environmental surfaces, and adhering to enteric or contact precautions.

Measures that can aid in reducing residents' risk for infections include:

- Following standard precautions and infection control practices
- Promoting good hydration and nutrition
- Avoiding immobile states
- Keeping skin intact
- Preventing exposure to people with actual or suspected infections
- Ensuring that pneumococcal and influenza vaccines have been administered

ESSENTIAL FACTS

The use of antibiotics in the treatment of infections creates new risks for residents. Many antibiotics can interact with antacids, antihypertensives, digoxin, lipid-lowering agents, oral hypoglycemic agents, and warfarin. Diarrhea can occur, which can lead to dehydration. Secondary infections also can occur. Observation for signs of these problems is essential.

PRESSURE ULCERS

A pressure ulcer involves damage to the skin and underlying soft tissue as a result of unrelieved pressure or the combination of pressure and a shearing force. The Centers for Medicare and Medicaid Services (CMS) have identified pressure ulcers as one of the primary markers of quality of care in long-term care settings.

Pressure ulcers can result from age-related changes to the skin that make the skin more fragile and sensitive. These include:

- Loss of papillae, causing a flattening (thinning) of the epidermis
- Reduction in contact area between the dermis and epidermis, causing an increased risk of peeling of the epidermis from a shearing force
- Decreased strength, vascularity, and elasticity of the epidermis
- Decreased amount, flexibility, and solubility of collagen

Other factors that contribute to pressure ulcer development include:

- Incontinence
- Poor nutritional status or dehydration
- Presence of diseases that compromise circulation and sensation, such as diabetes mellitus, cerebral vascular accident, or arterial disease
- Low body mass
- Immobility
- Altered mental status
- History of pressure ulcers

Several validated tools are available to assist in the objective assessment of pressure ulcer risk, such as the Braden scale (Bergstrom, Allman, & Carlson, 1994) and the Norton scale (Norton, McLaren, & Exton-Smith, 1962). Although helpful in identifying a resident's risk for pressure ulcers, they do not replace regular skin inspection.

Active prevention of pressure ulcers should be ongoing and consists of:

- Regular skin inspection with special attention to bony prominences, heels, and sacrum
- Promoting good nutrition and hydration; consulting with the facility's dietician for recommendations
- Correcting incontinence when possible; effectively containing incontinence and keeping skin dry; using absorbent pads and undergarments that take moisture away from the skin
- Using mild cleansing agents for bathing; applying moisturizers
- Preventing immobility
- Keeping pressure off heels by placing a pillow longitudinally beneath each calf to suspend the heels

- Using an alternating pressure mattress
- Avoiding friction and sheer (e.g., using lift sheets rather than sliding the resident across the surface of the bed)
- Changing the resident's position on a schedule frequent enough to prevent red areas from developing
- Repositioning and relieving pressure for residents who are chair bound
- Preventing extended times in bed with the head of the bed elevated more than 30 degrees
- Not massaging bony prominences and red area
- Consulting with the dietician regarding recommended daily protein intake
- Educating and encouraging the resident to frequently shift weight

ESSENTIAL FACTS

An every-2-hour (q2h) turning schedule may not provide sufficiently frequent position changes for some residents. An individualized turning schedule should be developed based on assessment of how long the resident can remain in the same position without red areas developing. For example, if redness develops after 1 hour in the same position, the resident needs to be turned more frequently than hourly.

Careful attention must be paid to existing pressure ulcers to prevent them from worsening and to promote healing. Pressure ulcers should be properly staged (Box 16.1), treated as ordered, and monitored. Follow your facility's procedures for specific treatments.

Box 16.1 Pressure Ulcer Staging

- *Stage 1: Nonblanchable erythema.* An area of nonblanchable redness without a break in the skin; the area may feel of different temperature or firmness from the surrounding skin and may be painful
- *Stage 2: Partial-thickness skin loss.* Partial-thickness loss of skin layers involving the epidermis, which can appear as an intact or open blister, or a shiny or dry shallow ulcer
- *Stage 3: Full-thickness skin loss.* Loss of skin through the epidermis to the subcutaneous tissue that can be deep on shallow; no muscle, tendon, or bone is visible
- *Stage 4: Full-thickness tissue loss.* Full-thickness loss of tissue exposing muscle, tendon, bone, or a combination of

(continued)

Box 16.1 *(continued)*

these structures, that presents as a deep crater; slough or eschar can be present, and tunneling can occur
- *Unstageable/Unclassified: Full-thickness skin or tissue loss—depth unknown.* Full-thickness tissue loss in which the presence of slough or eschar obscures depth
- *Suspected deep tissue injury—depth unknown.* An area of discolored intact skin or a blood-filled blister resulting from damage to underlying soft tissue as a result of pressure or shear, or both

Source: National Pressure Ulcer Advisory Panel. (2007).

DEHYDRATION

Dehydration is a common risk among long-term care residents due to:

- Age-related changes that can result in a reduced sense of thirst, decreased intracellular fluid, decrease in fluid-rich muscle tissue, and less efficient renal handling of water and sodium
  - These factors can affect adequate fluid intake and give a smaller margin of safety when there is fluid loss or reduced fluid intake. In addition, age-related urinary frequency can cause older residents to reduce fluid intake in an effort to decrease the need for voiding.
- The high prevalence of conditions that can cause:
  - Vomiting
  - Diarrhea
  - Polyuria
  - Profuse perspiration
  - Altered mental status leading to insufficient intake
  - Physical inability to consume fluids
- Medications that can increase fluid loss, such as diuretics and laxatives

Dehydration can occur rapidly; therefore, nurses must be alert to signs which can include:

- Dry oral mucosa and tongue (poor skin turgor may not be reliable sign of dehydration as age-related decreases in skin elasticity cause skin turgor to be poor in many older residents)
- Reduced saliva
- Decreased urine output

- Sunken eyes
- Weakness
- Tachycardia
- Increased body temperature
- Reduced urinary output; dark-colored urine
- Delirium or worsening of existing confusion

   Laboratory test results consistent with dehydration include:

- Blood urea nitrogen (BUN)/creatinine ratio greater than 25
- Serum sodium greater than 150 mEq/L
- Serum osmolality greater than 300 mmol/kg
- Urine specific gravity greater than 1.029
- Urine osmolality greater than 1050 mmol/kg

   Assessment should be performed to identify the underlying cause so that it can be corrected. As dehydration can be life-threatening, immediate replacement of fluids and restoration of fluid balance are essential. Nursing actions would include:

- Supporting the treatment plan to correct the underlying problem
- Strictly monitoring intake and output, vital signs, and mental status
- Obtaining and monitoring weights daily or as ordered
- Providing good skin care

   If the cause of dehydration is a problem that could predispose the resident to this risk again (e.g., newly prescribed diuretic, weakened state that interferes with ability to drink fluids), this risk should be addressed in the care plan.

WEIGHT LOSS

ESSENTIAL FACTS

A weight loss of at least 5% in the past 30 days or 10% in the past 180 days is considered significant. The underlying cause needs to be identified and addressed.

   Weight loss in residents can indicate underlying physical or mental conditions that require attention. Left uncorrected, weight loss can lead to serious complications and death. There are various causes of weight loss, such as:

- Pain (generalized, oral cavity, throat, gastric)
- Poor condition of teeth

- Swallowing difficulty
- Altered taste sensations
- Anorexia
- Altered cognition
- Emotional stress; depression
- Inability to feed self
- Food intolerance
- Fatigue or weakness
- Dislike of diet
- Diarrhea
- Medication side effects

Improving the condition requires addressing the underlying cause and could include:

- Correcting medical problems that have an impact on appetite and intake
- Improving dental problems; obtaining new dentures
- Assisting with feeding
- Offering appetite stimulants
- Providing dietary supplements
- Offering a diet that incorporates the resident's food preferences
- Promoting socialization during mealtimes
- Consulting with the physician and pharmacist about changing medications that negatively affect appetite

Close monitoring of the resident's weight is essential when unintended weight loss has occurred. It is useful to weigh the resident at the same time of day, with the resident wearing the same amount of clothing, and using the same scale.

URINARY INCONTINENCE

Urinary incontinence affects about half of all long-term care residents. Although common among this population, incontinence is not a normal finding. It can lead to many physical and psychosocial problems for residents; thus, prevention and, when present, correction of urinary incontinence as soon as possible are important.

ESSENTIAL FACTS

Urinary incontinence can lead to other health risks, such as pressure ulcers, falls, skin infections, reduced socialization, depression, sleep interruption, and reduced quality of life.

A variety of factors can cause incontinence, including:

- Weakened pelvic muscles due to obesity, trauma, or multiple pregnancies
- Urinary tract infection
- Compression of the urethra and bladder from prostatic hypertrophy or fecal impaction
- Cognitive impairment that causes the person to not recognize the signal to void
- Impaired mobility; inability to travel to the bathroom or use the toilet, bedpan, or urinal
- Inaccessible bathroom
- Medications, especially alpha-adrenergic agonists, alpha-adrenergic blockers, antispasmodics, cholinesterase inhibitors, diuretics, narcotic analgesics, and sedatives
- High caffeine or alcohol intake
- Diseases (e.g., Parkinson's disease, cerebrovascular accident, multiple sclerosis, diabetes mellitus, or bladder disease)
- Chronic cough

A comprehensive assessment to identify the underlying cause is warranted when incontinence develops. Like other geriatric syndromes, urinary incontinence can be associated with more than one factor and addressing all factors is necessary. The assessment should include:

- History of onset—date, time, relationship to other events or changes, precipitating factors
- Symptoms—urgency, burning, hesitancy, pain, edema, genital itching, or rash
- Pattern—dribbling, sudden expulsion of large amounts of urine
- Bowel function—constipation, diarrhea
- Fluid intake and type
- Condition of abdomen (e.g., ascites, tenderness)
- Status of urine—discolored, concentrated
- Resident's reaction and description

It is useful to obtain a urinalysis when urinary incontinence occurs to aid in identifying possible causes.

ESSENTIAL FACTS

Incontinence-associated dermatitis, previously referred to as diaper rash or peri-rash, describes painful skin inflammation without blistering, erosion, or loss of the skin due to repeated exposure of the skin to urine or fecal matter. This is a potential problem when the urine of incontinent individuals is not adequately cleansed from the skin. To prevent this condition, it is essential to keep the area clean and establish a means for keeping urine off the skin.

Interventions to assist the resident who is incontinent include:

- Ensuring that the cause of the incontinence has been properly identified
- Monitoring intake and output
- Ensuring that toileting facilities, bedpans, or urinals are easily accessible
- Providing assistance with toileting as needed
- Implementing a bladder retraining program if it has been determined that the resident can regain bladder control (Box 16.2)
- Implementing a prompted voiding program if the resident is unable to regain bladder control by:
  - Determining the resident's voiding pattern and anticipated time of voiding
  - Regularly asking or checking the resident for wetness or dryness
  - Instructing the resident to void or toileting the resident before anticipated time of voiding
  - Offering positive reinforcement for successful toileting

Box 16.2   Bladder Retraining Program

- Review the record and consult with the unit nurse, physician, or nurse practitioner to learn of the resident's potential to regain bladder control.
- Explain the procedure to the resident.
- Ensure that all caregivers are aware of the plan and are following it consistently.
- Encourage good fluid intake.
- Maintain a record of the resident's voiding pattern (time, amount, awareness of need to void, ability to reach commode in time, ability to control elimination, related factors).
- Determine the average time the resident can hold urine before becoming incontinent.
- Remind or assist the resident to toilet approximately 30 minutes before the anticipated time to void.
- Encourage voiding by running water, pouring a small amount of water over the vulva or penis, or massaging over the bladder.
- Offer praise for appropriate toileting.
- If the resident is incontinent between scheduled voiding times, evaluate the cause.
- Document outcomes.

- Providing adult briefs and other urine containment products as needed
- Ensuring that the skin is kept clean and dry (remind caregivers to cleanse the resident's skin thoroughly after each incontinent episode as urine salts that dry on skin can be irritating)
- Cleaning urine spills promptly to prevent falls, and keeping the path to the bathroom or commode obstacle-free
- Ensuring that the resident maintains sufficient fluid intake (fluid intake can be reduced in the evening but should not be eliminated entirely)
- Respecting the resident's privacy (do not discuss incontinence or check for wetness in presence of others)
- Avoiding indwelling catheter use if at all possible; if one must be used, follow the procedure for care of the catheter to prevent infections

DELIRIUM

Delirium is a sudden alteration in mental status accompanied by a change in level of consciousness that can range from stupor to hypervigilance. A variety of factors can cause delirium, including:

- Hypoxia
- Malnutrition or dehydration
- Hyper- or hypoglycemia
- Congestive heart failure or decreased cardiac function
- Infection
- Drug reaction
- Alcohol ingestion
- Sensory impairment
- Emotional stress
- Pain
- Trauma

Sudden confusion and disorientation accompany delirium; other signs could include:

- Combativeness, restlessness, agitation, irritability
- Disturbed intellectual function, altered attention span, poor memory, incoherence, disorganized speech, disorientation of time and place but usually not of identity
- Insomnia, nightmares
- Meaningless chatter
- Auditory or visual hallucinations, delusions
- Personality changes
- Tachycardia, increased blood pressure

- Altered level of consciousness (hyperalert, lethargic, stuporous, comatose)

These signs can fluctuate in severity and consistency of appearance.

Prompt action is needed when delirium develops. A thorough assessment is necessary to identify the cause and to develop an appropriate treatment plan to address it. A quiet, stable environment with consistent caregivers should be provided. Hearing aids and eyeglasses used by the resident should be worn to reduce impaired sensory perception. Close supervision of residents with delirium is essential to prevent injuries resulting from residents' poor judgment and abnormal behaviors.

ESSENTIAL FACTS

Residents with dementias can develop delirium if something has disrupted the body's balance. It is important that behavior changes in these residents be promptly identified to prevent new problems from going untreated and causing serious complications. Beneficial measures include obtaining good baseline data about residents' mental status and behaviors to serve as a basis for comparison, and consistently assigning staff to residents so that caregivers will recognize changes in norms.

ESSENTIAL FACTS

Nurses should assess residents for risks that could predispose them to delirium and provide interventions to reduce those risks. Prevention of delirium is the best strategy for managing it.

17

Identifying and Managing
Clinical Emergencies

Residents of long-term care facilities experience a range of emergency health conditions similar to those affecting nonresidents. However, their many coexisting conditions and the likelihood that they are frail or of advanced age heightens their risk for developing acute conditions. These conditions often present with atypical symptoms in older individuals, posing challenges for diagnosis. Long-term care nurses must have the clinical competencies to promptly identify emergencies and facilitate the provision of medical attention in a timely manner for residents with emergency conditions.

This chapter should enable you to:

1. Describe general changes that can indicate emergency conditions
2. List actions to take when an emergency condition occurs
3. Identify the signs of and nursing responses to possible:
   - Acute glaucoma
   - Angina pectoris
   - Congestive heart failure
   - Detached retina
   - Hypothermia
   - Myocardial infarction
   - Pneumonia
   - Pulmonary embolism
   - Transient ischemic attack

RECOGNIZING EMERGENCY CONDITIONS

Sudden changes in a resident's status may indicate a life-threatening health problem and need to be addressed promptly. It is essential that the resident's baseline status be known by staff so that changes can be identified. Areas useful in evaluating baseline function include:

- Ambulation
- Energy, strength
- Vital signs
- Mental status
- Level of consciousness
- Coloring
- Speech
- Sleep pattern
- Voiding and bowel pattern

Pain, nausea, vomiting, dyspnea, bleeding, and other signs and symptoms also need to be noted. Changes in status demand assessment. Unusual findings and symptoms reported by the resident should be explored and thoroughly described, as should recent relevant events, such as a fall or administration of a new medication. Table 17.1 summarizes several medical emergencies that can occur among residents and their accompanying signs and symptoms.

TABLE 17.1 Clinical Signs and Symptoms of Medical Emergencies

Emergency	Signs and Symptoms
Acute glaucoma Sudden increase in pressure within eyeball due to increased production or decreased outflow of aqueous humor, or both	• Severe pain in and around eye • Nausea, vomiting • Blurred vision • Dilated pupils • Perception of halos around eyes
Angina pectoris Ischemia of heart muscle	• Mild to severe pain at middle to upper portion of sternum, radiating to neck, jaws, and sternum • Tight, vicelike feeling around chest • Weakness • Numbness in arms and hands • Apprehension

(continued)

TABLE 17.1 Clinical Signs and Symptoms of Medical Emergencies (continued)

Emergency	Signs and Symptoms
Congestive heart failure Inability of heart to pump adequate amount of blood to meet metabolic needs of tissues	• Dyspnea at rest • Shortness of breath • Fatigue • Confusion • Rapid weight gain *Left-sided failure:* • Cough • Orthopnea, dyspnea on exertion • Nocturia, abnormal breath sounds *Right-sided failure:* • Distended neck veins • Symmetrical peripheral edema • Hepatic enlargement and tenderness • Abdominal distension, ascites • Gastrointestinal discomfort
Detached retina Condition in which retina separates from its attachment to underlying tissues in back of eye due to retinal breaks, tears, or holes	• Sudden or gradual onset of symptoms • Blurred vision • Floaters (small particles that float across field of vision) • Perception of flashes of light • Feeling of coating over eye • Blank areas to complete loss of vision
Hypothermia Core temperature of less than 95°F (35°C); older residents are at high risk due to their reduced ability to adjust to extreme environmental temperatures	*Early signs:* • Body temperature less than 95°F (35°C) • Confusion • Rectal temperature less than 95°F (35°C) • Slowed respirations • Gray skin color, cold skin • Shivering • Slurred speech *In later stage:* • Cyanosis • Bradycardia • Hypotension • Decreased level of consciousness • Slowed reflexes • Generalized edema
Myocardial infarction Lack of blood supply to myocardium resulting in tissue damage	• Confusion (can be the primary sign in an older adult) • Sudden dyspnea • Decreased blood pressure • Fluctuating pulse rate

(continued)

TABLE 17.1 Clinical Signs and Symptoms of Medical Emergencies (*continued*)

Emergency	Signs and Symptoms
	• Weakness • Pain radiating to arm, chest, neck, or abdomen (although pain may be absent) • Moist, pale skin • Low-grade fever • Elevated sedimentation rate
Pneumonia Inflammation of lung (Onset of symptoms varies with type [e.g., pneumococcal and klebsiella pneumonias have rapid onset with shaking and chills; staphylococcal pneumonia develops slowly with subtle signs])	• Fever (may not be of a high spiking nature) • Confusion • Increased respirations • Elevated pulse • Fatigue • Anorexia • Cough (may be less intense and nonproductive) • Chest pain (may be absent) • Abnormal breath sounds • Cyanosis • Elevated white blood cell count may not be present
Pulmonary embolism Blockage in a main artery of lung caused by a clot that has traveled from another location	• Shortness of breath • Increased respirations • Chest discomfort • Low blood oxygen • Dyspnea and hemoptysis may or may not be present • Tachycardia may be absent if resident is taking a beta-blocker or has a disease of cardiac conduction
Transient ischemic attack Impairment of cerebral blood flow that causes nervous system dysfunction lasting several minutes to hours; residual effects are seldom present	• Signs last minutes to hours • Confusion • Dizziness • Aphasia • Falling • Personality changes • Diplopia, hemiparesis • Amnesia • Motor weakness • Unilateral loss of vision • Ataxia • Headaches

All members of the health care team need to be aware of the importance of promptly identifying, reporting, and documenting changes in a resident's status.

TAKING ACTION

After assessing the situation action is needed to address the emergency. In some circumstances, this consists of providing emergency care (e.g., controlling bleeding, providing resuscitation). Depending on the emergency situation, the physician will be called for direction or 911 may be called to obtain emergency care and transfer the resident to an acute care (hospital) setting. (Check your facility's policies and procedures related to emergency care.) Information that is beneficial to share when communicating with a physician, emergency medical technician, or hospital includes:

- Resident's diagnoses and usual status
- Medications administered
- Usual and current vital signs and mental status
- Signs and symptoms (e.g., pain, discoloration, bleeding, delirium, weakness, loss of vision, etc.)
- Unusual occurrences

This information also should be documented in the resident's record and a copy should accompany the resident to the hospital, if transferred.

The increased acuity of residents being admitted to long-term care settings means that emergency conditions are likely to be experienced. Nurses must be prepared to respond competently to these situations to ensure that residents receive proper care and reduce the likelihood of complications.

18

End-of-Life Care

Although many individuals enter long-term care facilities for rehabilitation and return to the community, most will spend the remainder of their lives in these settings. This reality, combined with the advanced age of residents, mean that death is hardly a rare occurrence. It is essential that long-term care nurses understand the importance of addressing the holistic needs of residents, their loved ones, and staff as residents experience the dying process.

This chapter should enable you to:

1. Describe stages of grief
2. List challenges faced by a resident's family members and staff when the resident is dying
3. Describe actions to provide support to dying residents
4. Identify the types of advance directives
5. Describe physical needs of the dying and related nursing care
6. Identify specific practices related to death and dying of persons of various religions and cultures

CHALLENGES ASSOCIATED WITH END-OF-LIFE CARE

Although death is a natural and expected part of life, few individuals are prepared to face this situation. People often are at a loss as to how to address the needs of the dying individual, as well as those affected by the person's death.

A variety of emotional reactions can be triggered by the reality that one is near the end of life. These were first described as five stages of grief by Elisabeth Kübler-Ross in the 1960s (Table 18.1). In addition to the possibility that residents may demonstrate signs reflective of

---

TABLE 18.1 Stages of Grief Experienced During the Dying Process

Denial and isolation	Resident avoids topic of death and may withdraw from others. This serves to afford resident time to mobilize defenses. It is important to allow resident sufficient time and not force discussions about death and dying.
Anger	Hostility and rage are felt as resident begins seriously thinking about reality of death. Often, family and staff closest to resident are recipients of this displaced anger. Resident needs to release tension by venting feelings. A useful approach is to accept the anger without judgment or feeling personally hurt.
Bargaining	Resident may try to extend life by seeking compromises or trade-offs (e.g., *"I will give a large donation to the church if I can live one more year"*; *"If I can live to see my grandchild born I will then be willing to die"*). Many times bargaining is done through prayer. Support is needed during this period, as well as protection to ensure that resident is not taken advantage of by quacks or others who offer unrealistic cures or life extensions.
Depression	A form of mourning occurs as resident considers the losses that will be faced. Support and the presence of others—even if this means sitting in silence for extended period of time—are needed. Human contact through hand holding and massages can be especially helpful.
Acceptance	As resident comes to terms with death he or she may be able to discuss it and begin to address issues openly. Support is needed as resident expresses feelings and discusses plans.

Adapted from Kübler-Ross, E. (1969).
Note: Not all dying persons experience every stage, nor will they progress through each stage in an orderly manner.

these stages, residents who are near the end of life may experience anxieties and fears related to issues such as:

- Pain and how will it be relieved
- Their ability to be alert and communicate
- How their loved ones will manage and react
- The amount of control they will have over their care
- Unresolved conflicts with friends or family members
- The degree to which their desires for their funeral and disposition of possessions are followed
- The mystery of what lies ahead after physical death occurs

Family members and others who have a close relationship with the dying resident often find themselves navigating new waters. They may be:

- Distressed at seeing the declining status of their loved one
- Uncertain about whether or how to discuss issues pertaining to the impending death
- Uncomfortable with the thoughts about their own mortality that may arise
- Feeling powerless at not being able to change the situation
- Experiencing effects of grieving
- Feeling overwhelmed by the decisions and tasks they face related to their loved one's care, funeral arrangements, and fulfilling the person's wishes

Consideration also must be given to the challenges faced by staff. They may:

- Be stressed by the dying process and death of residents with whom they have shared close relationships,
- Lack skills needed to provide support to dying residents and their loved ones,
- Feel distressed if the spiritual or religious beliefs of dying residents conflicts with their own
- Need support as they cope with their own grieving
- Become uncomfortable as they consider their own mortality and that of their family members

EMOTIONAL SUPPORT

Support will need to be provided to dying residents, their loved ones, and staff as part of end-of-life care. Residents at the end of life can benefit from:

- *Regular contact with family and friends.* This can be encouraged by ensuring that the resident is comfortable, clean, and well groomed during times when visitors will be present. Suggesting activities or areas of the facility that the resident and visitors can enjoy can prove helpful, as can having refreshments available for them. Contact with those meaningful in his or her life can afford the resident the opportunity for closure.

- *Normal interactions.* Visitors may be reluctant to touch, talk, or behave normally in the presence of the resident. They may need to be encouraged to behave the way they always have around the resident.
- *Close attention to pain control and physical needs.* The resident needs to be aware that as his or her condition changes, efforts will be made to promote comfort and to fulfill needs that the resident may no longer be able to meet independently.
- *Treatment with dignity.* The resident should be afforded respect in communication and care delivery.
- *Spiritual support.* Be it visits from clergy, the ability to pray in private, or respect for one's lack of belief in God, the resident's spiritual needs should be honored and he or she assisted in meeting them, as necessary.
- *Hope.* Hope can be inspired by keeping the resident engaged with others and offering new experiences that are possible based on the resident's condition (e.g., assisting the family with planning a party within the facility at which a family member's birthday can be celebrated). Hope also can be inspired by helping the resident to identify the impact he or she has had on others and the legacy he or she is leaving.

Sensitivity must be shown to the ways in which people from various cultures behave when their loved ones are dying and the unique practices in which they may engage. Table 18.2 describes some of

TABLE 18.2 Cultural Practices at the End of Life

Cultural Group	Beliefs and Practices Related to Death
African American	Emotional displays (e.g., collapsing, screaming) are common in reaction to death
Cubans, Filipinos, Mexicans	Large group of relatives and friends remain with dying person, place religious artifacts around person, light candles as a means of guiding the spirit to the afterlife; family members may have strong emotional and hyperkinetic reactions to learning of loved one's death
Haitians	All family members attempt to gather at bedside and pray; family members may cry uncontrollably
Indians, Hindus	Death rites are performed by a priest assisted by eldest son and other male relatives; women may display loud wailing

(continued)

TABLE 18.2 Cultural Practices at the End of Life (*continued*)

Cultural Group	Beliefs and Practices Related to Death
Japanese	Family members gather at time of death and stay at bedside; eldest son directs activities
Koreans	Family members gather at time of death, stay at bedside, and assist with care
Navajo Indians	Family and friends do not talk directly about person who is dying but discuss issue in the third person as talking about death to the person implies that one wishes him or her to die
Puerto Ricans	Head of family receives notice of death and communicates it to others; family members may want to stay with and touch body before it is removed
Vietnamese	Flowers are not placed in the dying person's room as they are considered part of the rites of the dead

these practices. It must be remembered that these views and practices may not be displayed by all individuals of the same culture. Through assessment, the practices and needs of individuals as they navigate the issues of death and dying can be identified and incorporated into the plan of care.

ADVANCE DIRECTIVES

Some of the difficulties families and staff face can be reduced when residents have advance directives. Advance directives are legally binding documents that help families and the health care team understand the desires of an individual related to care and treatment if that individual is unable to express those desires. The two major types of advance directives are a *living will,* which offers specific instructions concerning treatment preferences and end-of-life care, and *durable power of attorney,* in which a person (referred to as a health care proxy, surrogate, agent, or attorney-in-fact) is appointed to make health care decisions for the individual should the individual be unable to express his or her own treatment wishes. Not only do advance directives assist others in making important decision, but also they empower residents to determine their future end-of-life care.

Nurses should ensure that residents have advance directives and, if they do not, refer them to a social worker who can guide them to legal counsel or other sources of help in developing legally sound advance directive documents for their state.

ESSENTIAL FACTS

The Patient Self-Determination Act of 1991 requires that health care organizations:

- Inform residents of their right to make health care decisions and to refuse treatment
- Ask residents if they have completed an advance directive
- Provide written information about the state's provisions for implementing advance directives
- Include a copy of the resident's advance directive in his or her medical record

PHYSICAL SYMPTOMS AND CARE

As an individual is near death basic physical functions can be altered, which can have an impact on comfort and well-being. Table 18.3 lists some of the major physical symptoms and nursing measures that can be of benefit in managing them. Regular assessment is necessary because symptoms may change as the resident's function continues to decline and, consequently, nursing actions will need to be adjusted accordingly.

Signs of imminent death need to be identified, including:

- Decrease in blood pressure
- Rapid, weak pulse
- Dyspnea, periods of apnea
- Slower or no pupillary response to light
- Loss of vision and hearing (hearing is one of last senses to be lost)
- Cold extremities
- Profuse perspiration
- Pallor, mottling of skin
- Bladder and bowel incontinence
- Agitated delirium

TABLE 18.3 Nursing Actions Related to Physical Symptoms at the End of Life

Symptom	Nursing Actions
Dry oral cavity	Provide frequent oral hygiene Offer ice chips, hard candies Review medications for those that may contribute to symptoms (e.g., alpha-receptor antagonists, anticholinergics, antidepressants, antipsychotics) and discuss possible nonpharmacological substitutes with physician and pharmacist

(continued)

TABLE 18.3 Nursing Actions Related to Physical Symptoms at the End of Life (*continued*)

Symptom	Nursing Actions
Poor intake	Identify and address underlying cause (e.g., anorexia, nausea, low energy) Consult with dietician regarding dietary change and provision of frequent, smaller portioned meals Provide oral hygiene before meals Assist with feeding as needed Encourage family members to bring special foods that resident is known to enjoy Provide a pleasant, odor-free environment for mealtime Discuss the benefits and burdens of providing artificial nutrition and hydration with both resident and health care team *As ceasing to eat often occurs several days prior to death, consult with health care team as to discontinuing food intake. In addition, some residents may make the decision to stop eating as a means of hastening death. Family members and caregivers may need reassurance that resident will not suffer more from this decision as lack of intake leads to ketosis, which depresses hunger sensations and causes euphoria in some people.*
Dysphagia	Consult with dietician about a pureed diet Offer small, frequent amounts of food and fluids
Nausea	Consult with physician about use of an antiemetic or the herb ginger, which has antiemetic properties
Dyspnea	Elevate head of bed and position resident in a chair to provide maximum comfort and ease of breathing Schedule activities to allow rest between activities Administer oxygen as ordered Administer medications as ordered (e.g., atropine or furosemide can reduce bronchial secretions; narcotics can blunt medullary response and control symptoms)
Constipation	Prevent, as possible Incorporate juices and food items known to stimulate bowel movements in resident
Diarrhea	Assess for possible fecal impaction Consult with physician regarding antidiarrheal medication
Skin breakdown	Keep skin clean and dry Reposition resident frequently enough to prevent signs of pressure
Fatigue	Schedule activities to provide rest between activities Provide assistance with care

(*continued*)

TABLE 18.3 Nursing Actions Related to Physical Symptoms at the End of Life (*continued*)

Symptom	Nursing Actions
Pain	Assess location(s), type, intensity (on a scale of 0 to 10), pattern (intermittent, continuous), duration, and resident's description of pain; factors that make pain better and worse; analgesics currently used and that have been used in the past; resident's goal for pain relief
	Consider cultural and language barriers to resident's expression of pain
	Prevent pain from occurring by administering analgesics on a regular schedule and assessing when pain returns; develop a schedule to administer analgesics prior to the anticipated time of onset of pain
	Monitor severity of pain to assist in determining the need for a change in dosage or type of analgesic administered
	Use nonpharmacological measures to relieve pain, such as guided imagery, massage, acupressure, healing touch, diversion

All caregivers should be familiar with imminent signs of death and report them promptly. Recognizing that death is near can enable family and friends who want to be with the resident when death occurs to be notified. In addition, the resident or family may have expressed the desire to have clergy called when death is near.

ESSENTIAL FACTS

Family and friends of the resident who is near death should be encouraged to continue talking to and touching the resident, even if the resident is unresponsive.

SPIRITUAL SUPPORT

ESSENTIAL FACTS

A person who denies believing in or practicing any religion can still be highly spiritual. Religion is a set of beliefs that is expressed through doctrine, rites, and rituals while spirituality is the sense that there is a nonphysical dimension that connects one to something greater than oneself. For some individuals spirituality can consist of belief in a specific deity and certain practices, while for others it can be expressed through belief in a vague higher power or connection with Mother Earth.

As death approaches, spiritual needs may become of greater importance to the resident. Residents may feel they need to make peace with God, ask forgiveness, or take steps to ensure they can have a religious funeral even if their religious practices had lapsed. Asking residents if they wish to have a visit from clergy or members of a specific faith community can be beneficial. Families also can benefit from spiritual support as they face the death of their loved ones.

It is important to be aware of the end-of-life practices of various religions so that they can be supported (Table 18.4). As with cultural practices, there is variation in how individuals of the same religion practice their faith, so obtaining insights into the resident's and family's practices through assessment is essential.

TABLE 18.4 Religious Practices at the End of Life

Religious Affiliation	Beliefs and Practices Related to Death
Baptist	Prayer; communion
Buddhist	Last rites by a Buddhist priest; forgiveness is encouraged to aid in dying with peace; after death body is left alone as long as possible to avoid disturbing consciousness during transition from death to new life
Catholic	Prayer; last rites by a priest
Christian Scientist	Visit from a Christian Science reader
Eastern Orthodox (Greek, Russian)	Prayer; communion; last rites (Holy Unction) by a priest; cremation is not allowed
Episcopalian	Prayer; communion; confession; last rites
Friends (Quakers)	Individual communicates with God directly; no belief in an afterlife
Hindu	Visit by a priest to perform ritual of tying a thread around the neck or wrist; water is put in the mouth; family cleanses body after death; cremation is accepted
Jewish	After death, body is washed by an Orthodox Jew; someone stays with body until it is buried; cremation is not allowed
Lutheran	Prayer; last rites
Mormon	Baptism and preaching to deceased
Muslim	Confession; after death family prepares body; body must face Mecca
Pentecostal	Prayer; communion
Presbyterian	Prayer; last rites

AFTER THE DEATH

Long-term care facilities have policies and procedures related to care of the deceased, and these should be followed. In addition, consideration should be given to the needs of those who have suffered the loss of the resident—including family, friends, other residents, and staff. Some measures that can be beneficial include:

- Having a memorial service in which family, friends, other residents, and staff can reflect on the deceased resident's life and share their feelings
- Including a small table in the lobby upon which is placed a photograph of the deceased resident, a copy of the obituary, and a book in which people can write memories and messages to survivors
- Creating a poster that can be hung on the unit that announces the resident's death and highlights of his or her life

These measures assist with the grief of those close to the deceased person. They also demonstrate to other residents that one is not forgotten immediately when death occurs.

Residents With Dementia

═19═

Overview of Dementia

As most residents of long-term care facilities are of advanced age and the prevalence of dementia increases with age, it is not surprising that residents with dementia constitute a significant portion of the long-term care population. This reality demands that long-term care nurses be skilled at caring for residents with dementia.

This chapter should enable you to:

1. List major types of dementia
2. Describe measures used to diagnose dementia
3. List characteristics associated with mild, moderate, and advanced dementia
4. Describe the nurse's role in assessing individuals with cognitive dysfunction

TYPES OF DEMENTIA

Dementia is a general term that describes brain pathologies in which there is a progressive irreversible decline in cognitive function. Memory, orientation, judgment, reasoning, attention, language, and problem solving are affected. As the disease progresses personality changes are noted, along with inappropriate behaviors and impairments in self-care abilities. Eventually all aspects of functioning are affected.

There are several major types of dementia (Table 19.1), with Alzheimer's disease being the most common. Research and improved brain imaging have aided in differentiating dementias; however, it still is challenging to diagnose the type of dementia at an early stage.

TABLE 19.1 Types of Dementia

Type	Description
Alzheimer's disease	Most common type of dementia Characterized by presence of neuritic plaques and neurofibrillary tangles in cortex It can be years before brain changes cause symptoms, which develop gradually and progress at different rates among affected persons In addition to affecting cognitive function, personality, behavior and general function are affected
Vascular dementia	Can be rapidly progressive when caused by small cerebral infarctions that result in localized or diffuse damage to brain, or gradual in onset due to the cumulative effects of minor infarcts Associated with risk factors such as smoking, hypertension, hyperlipidemia, inactivity, and a history of stroke or cardiovascular disease
Frontotemporal dementia	Characterized by neuronal atrophy affecting frontal lobes of brain In early stage behavioral and personality changes are noted more than cognitive ones Abstract thinking and speech and language skills are impaired more so than memory initially Pick's disease is most common form
Lewy body dementia	Involves subcortical pathology and presence of Lewy body substance in cerebral cortex Onset is slow, with a progressive decline in cognition Fluctuations in mental status are common Incidence is higher among people who have a family member with dementia

---

(continued)

TABLE 19.1 Types of Dementia (*continued*)

Type	Description
Creutzfeldt–Jacob disease	An extremely rare dementia that is believed to originate from a slow virus Symptoms appear and progress rapidly, and tend to be more diverse than in Alzheimer's disease Psychotic behavior, heightened emotional lability, memory impairment, loss of muscular function, muscle spasms, seizures, and visual disturbances are classic symptoms Death typically occurs within 1 year of diagnosis
Others	Dementia can result from trauma, toxins, alcoholism, AIDS, and Parkinson's disease

ESSENTIAL FACTS

According to the Centers for Disease Control and Prevention (2014a), more than five million Americans have Alzheimer's disease. Between 25% and 50% of people over age 85 will exhibit signs of Alzheimer's disease. By 2050, the number of people with Alzheimer's disease is expected to more than double due to the growing population of older adults.

DIAGNOSING DEMENTIA

Despite advancements made in imaging and other diagnostic tests it is difficult to diagnose the type of dementia until the symptoms have progressed. The diagnosis of dementia is usually established by the history and presence of cognitive impairment, such as impairments in:

- Ability to acquire and retain new information
- Reasoning and judgment
- Language
- Visuospatial abilities (e.g., ability to identify common items)
- Mood, personality, behavior (e.g., mood swings, socially inappropriate behavior)

The presence of two or more of these impairments is the usual criterion for establishing the presence of dementia (McKhann et al., 2011). Physical examination and blood tests are done to rule out other conditions that could affect cognition and behavior.

As Alzheimer's disease affects a majority of individuals who have dementia, considerable attention has been paid to obtaining a greater understanding of this type of dementia. Revised diagnostic guidelines for Alzheimer's disease have designated three stages of the disease (National Institute on Aging, 2011):

- *Preclinical:* This is a stage that exists before clinical symptoms are apparent but brain changes can be detected through positron emission tomography (PET) scans and cerebrospinal fluid (CSF) analysis. As the relationship between the brain changes and the risk for developing Alzheimer's disease is uncertain, the guidelines for this stage only apply to research.
- *Mild cognitive impairment (MCI):* In this stage memory problems are present, although the person is able to function independently, and biomarkers associated with the disease are present, including elevated levels of tau or decreased levels of beta-amyloid in the CSF, reduced glucose uptake in the brain as determined by PET, and atrophy of certain areas of the brain as seen with structural magnetic resonance imaging (MRI). Like the preclinical stage, the guidelines for this stage are primarily for research and use in specialized clinical settings.
- *Alzheimer's dementia:* This final stage of the disease is most relevant for clinical settings as it outlines the methods physicians should use to evaluate the causes and progression of the disease. Rather than viewing memory loss as the most central characteristic of the disease, the guidelines states that the first symptom that the person may present could be a decline in other aspects of cognition, such as word-finding, visual/spatial issues, and impaired reasoning or judgment.

The guidelines are flexible to anticipate changes that could come from new technologies and advances in understanding of biomarkers and the disease process itself.

STAGES

Different types of dementia can progress at different rates; however, characteristics associated with the various stages of progression (mild, moderate, severe) can help in understanding where the resident is in the trajectory of the disease. These stages and characteristics are as follows:

Mild:

- Routine activities become more difficult to perform
- Judgment, decision-making, and problem-solving abilities are impaired
- There is less engagement in work and social activities
- Processing of spatial and visual information is more challenging

- Personality and mood changes may be present
- The person may be aware of changes and become depressed or withdrawn

  Moderate:

- Worsening of cognitive function; increased confusion occurs
- Disorientation to time and place is present
- Mood changes may be more apparent; delusions and hallucinations may be present

  Advanced:

- All areas of cognition are impaired
- The person has difficulty recognizing familiar people and places
- Sleep–wake cycle is altered
- Physical function and mobility are impaired; there is increased need for assistance with all activities of daily living
- Significant personality changes occur
- Behavioral problems are displayed

NURSING AND DEMENTIA

Although not responsible for diagnosing and staging dementia, nurses play a role in providing information that can assist these processes. Attentiveness during routine interactions and care can assist in assessing mental status and recognizing abnormalities and changes. Observations include:

- Attention to grooming, appropriateness of dress, body language, general behavior
- Appropriateness of speech and language
- Affect
- Responses to questions

In addition, formal tests of cognitive function are part of the assessment. A variety of tools can be used which typically assess:

- *Orientation:* The person's knowledge of his or her own name, current location, date, time of day, and season.
- *Language:* Appropriateness of speech and responses; ability to name objects that are pointed to or repeat phrases.
- *Memory:* Ability to recall three unrelated words (e.g., dog, cup, bed) immediately and then at an interval thereafter.
- *Attention and concentration:* Ability to spell the word *world* backward or to count backward from 100 by 7s.
- *Executive function:* Ability to describe what two words have in common (e.g., apple and banana, shoe and sock, coffee and tea) or to list

in a minute as many words as possible that start with a particular letter.

- *Ability to follow three-stage command:* Ability to follow instructions to do three basic acts, such as "pick up the piece of paper, fold it in half, and hand it to me".
- *Judgment:* After being given a situation that requires simple problem solving, the person's ability to describe what actions he or she would take (e.g., if fire was seen coming out of the bathroom). As an alternative, the person can be asked to explain the meaning of a saying such as *an ounce of prevention is worth a pound of cure.*
- *Visuospatial functioning:* Ability to draw the face of a clock or copy a simple diagram when requested.

It also is important for nurses to note changes in physical status as these may be responsible for cognitive changes. Infections, hyperglycemia, hormonal imbalances, tumors, pain, adverse drug reactions, and fluid and electrolyte imbalances are among the conditions that can alter mental status. Identifying and reporting changes in vital signs, output, energy, coloring, and appetite can assist in diagnosing and treating a reversible underlying problem. (See Chapter 16 for a discussion of delirium.)

Chapters 20 and 21 review nursing actions related to communication and clinical challenges of residents with dementia.

20

Communication Challenges

Difficulties with communication often are an early and notice-able symptom associated with dementia. There may be prob-lems recalling words or names, understanding new terms, and following conversation. Although these types of problems can happen to those with normal cognition periodically, in people with dementia they occur frequently and are often very notice-able to others. As the disease progresses all facets of verbal and nonverbal communication are affected. It is important to estab-lish effective strategies to communicate with residents who have dementia in order to identify changes in status, monitor the appropriateness of care, promote continued relationships with significant others and socialization, and facilitate the highest possible quality of life for residents.

This chapter should enable you to:

1. List communication problems that could be evident in residents with mild and advanced dementia
2. Describe effective techniques to facilitate communication in residents with dementia
3. Identify ways in which residents with dementia communicate health care changes nonverbally
4. List signs that could communicate the presence of pain in residents with dementia

COMMUNICATION CHALLENGES WITH MILD DEMENTIA

In the early stage of dementia communication problems may be missed or attributed to "growing older" or "feeling stressed." For example, the person may:

- Not recall the name of a friend or the town in which he or she grew up
- Be unable to recall the exact name for an item and substitute a word that is associated with it (e.g., calling a sofa a chair, a watch a clock, a microwave a machine); phrases such as "that thing" or "the whatchamacallit" may be used to substitute for the intended word
- Use improper grammar or pronunciation
- Lose his or her train of thought in the middle of a sentence
- Have difficulty following a discussion or the plot of a movie
- Be easily distracted by noise and activity in the immediate environment

ESSENTIAL FACTS

In the early stage of dementia, those affected often are aware of their communication problems and can become frustrated and embarrassed by them. This can lead to withdrawal from social activities and depression over the changes they notice in themselves.

These communication problems can occur before any memory deficits are apparent or the disease is recognized. As a result, people close to the individual may become impatient and frustrated, and attribute the communication problems to a lack of interest or attentiveness rather than a disease process.

At this stage, it is useful for those close to the resident to use techniques to facilitate communication, such as:

- Assessing communication ability and appropriate level for communication
- Giving clear, simple instructions
- Providing ample time for the person to process and respond
- Offering the correct word when the person cannot recall it
- Writing down instructions and important information
- Avoiding complex words and sentences
- Facing the individual when speaking
- Controlling environmental noise and distractions

Simplifying communication can be helpful to someone with a dementia but it is important not to oversimplify or treat the resident in a childlike manner. Assessing speech and language is essential to developing a communication style that is appropriate for the individual based on his or her level of function. Regular reassessment of cognition, speech, and language assists in adjusting the approach as needed. Effective communication strategies for the resident should be shared with family members and caregivers.

COMMUNICATION CHALLENGES AS DEMENTIA PROGRESSES

As dementia progresses, so do the communication deficits in residents with this disease, as evidenced by:

- Frequent use of the same words or phrases
- Inability to understand what is said
- Difficulty understanding written communication
- Talking about things from the past rather than current events
- Inability to remember the names of people close to them
- Putting thoughts together in a disorganized manner
- If bilingual, reverting to their native language
- Using made-up words or sounds
- Pointing and nodding rather than using words to express needs
- Losing the train of thought in the midst of verbalizing

Although these are common communication challenges, individuals may vary in the specific problems they display and the manner in which the problems progress. This reinforces the need to assess the resident's response to communication and verbal and nonverbal communication abilities on an ongoing basis and adjust approaches accordingly. Additional actions that could prove useful are outlined in Box 20.1.

Box 20.1   Tips to Effective Communication With Residents Who Have Dementia

- *Identify yourself.* Even if the resident sees you routinely, when you approach say "Hi Mrs. Jones, I'm your nurse Sally Smith.

(continued)

Box 20.1 *(continued)*

- *"Face the person and make eye contact before speaking.* If the person is seated or in bed, bend down to be on eye level.
- *Show patience and a willingness to understand.* Pay attention to what the resident is saying and do not interrupt. Allow time for the resident to process and respond.
- *Use simple sentences and language.* Avoid combining multiple ideas or using lengthy sentences.
- *Give one instruction or comment at a time.* Rather than presenting several steps or ideas, offer them singularly. For example, instead of saying "Take off your clothes, put on your pajamas, go to the bathroom, and then get into bed," first state "Take off your clothes," and when that is done, instruct the resident to "Put on your pajamas," etc.
- *Paraphrase.* Identify specific words or phrases that are difficult for the resident to understand and substitute others that are more readily understood. For example, if the resident does not understand what is meant by "Would you like to go to the activity?" substitute "Would you like to listen to music?"
- *Reframe negative statements into positive ones.* Instead of telling the resident not to do something, offer a statement that indicates what he or she should do. For example, instead of stating "Don't dig in your roommate's dresser," say "Come here and walk down the hall with me."
- *Try to guess the word the resident is attempting to find.* If the resident keeps saying things like "I want that thing to carry stuff" or "Give me one of those paper things," ask "Do you want a bag?"
- *Give direct instructions.* When something is framed as a question it implies a choice. Rather than asking, "Would you like your shower now?", which could trigger a negative response, state, "It's time for your shower now."
- *Avoid asking questions that the resident is unable to answer.* This can frustrate and cause stress for the resident. If it appears that the resident is having difficulty answering a question, offer a clue.
- *Use visual cues to support verbal communication.* Use calendars and clocks; write information (e.g., name of caregiver) on a dry erase board; write down information on paper.

(continued)

Box 20.1 (continued)

- *Try to understand and address the resident's feelings.* The resident who says something like, "My little girl needs me" may be missing his or her family or role as a father or mother. Ask the resident, "What things did you do with your little girl?"
- *Stimulate communication by noticing items in the resident's room or new clothing.* If the resident has a new photo of a grandchild on his or her dresser, offer a comment such as "You must be excited to have a new grandchild."
- *Pay attention to nonverbal clues.* Notice if the resident appears anxious or eager to withdraw, which could mean he or she feels overwhelmed by the situation, or if he or she is rubbing a part of the body, which could indicate the presence of pain. Be aware of your own body language and facial expressions, as well.

NONVERBAL COMMUNICATION

Residents with dementia often are unable to verbalize symptoms that could enable others to recognize a change in status or presence of pain. Behaviors and body language become important clues to the presence of problems. Changes in health status can be demonstrated by:

- Heavy or noisy breathing
- Pacing
- Blinking, watery eyes
- Changes in the ability to walk or transfer
- Change in appetite or food intake
- Change in sleep pattern
- Disinterest in activities usually enjoyed
- Touching a body part
- Weakness (general or on one side of the body)
- Discoloration (general or in one area)
- New or increased falling

Box 20.2 lists possible signs of pain in people with dementia.

In addition to being a means by which residents express status and reactions, nonverbal communication can communicate messages *to* residents. Touch is a powerful communicator of caring. Holding a hand, stroking a cheek, hugging, and massaging are among the ways in which touch conveys caring and provides comfort. While therapeutic for many residents, touch can be discomforting to others or

Box 20.2 Signs that Could Indicate Pain in Residents With Dementia

- Moaning, groaning, sighing, crying
- Wrinkled brows, eyes clenched shut
- Restlessness, wandering, pacing, rocking back and forth
- Tense posture
- Guarded movements
- Worsening of confusion
- Resisting care
- Becoming verbally or physically abusive
- Poor appetite, refusal of food
- Refusal to participate in activities and care, increased dependency
- Changes in vital signs

trigger undesirable reactions. For example, residents with a history of being abused may become anxious when touched by others; some may misinterpret a caring hug as a sexual advance and respond with inappropriate touching. Reactions to touch should be assessed and this information used to determine effective use of this therapeutic tool.

Dementia significantly affects the ability to communicate. Despite its challenges, communication remains important in the care and quality of life of residents. Skill in interpreting verbal and nonverbal communication can assist in identifying signs and symptoms that could easily be missed. Effective measures to communicate with residents who have dementia can enhance their sense of well-being and promote maximum comfort.

21

Special Clinical Challenges

Any long-term care resident can present clinical challenges, but residents with dementia pose special challenges due to their reduced ability to protect themselves from harm, altered methods of communicating needs, and unsafe behaviors related to impaired cognition. In addition to problems that can arise affecting residents' ability to meet daily needs, safety, and quality of life, there are challenges resulting from the way others may treat residents with dementia. Beyond ensuring that these residents are safe and have basic needs fulfilled, nurses also must promote care and interactions that are person centered.

This chapter should enable you to:

1. Identify factors that contribute to and interventions that address the following concerns in residents with dementia:
   - Wandering
   - Aggressive behavior
   - Poor nutrition and hydration
   - Sleep disturbances
2. List actions that can promote dignity in residents with dementia

WANDERING

ESSENTIAL FACTS

Wandering involves leaving a safe environment in which one is supposed to be to travel to an inappropriate place. It can indicate restlessness, discomfort in the current environment, or an intent to fulfill a purpose, such as the belief that one has to pick up a child from school.

Wandering is one of the most common behavioral problems in residents who have dementia and is exhibited by most persons with the disease at some point. It can occur due to the brain's inability to recognize or interpret the environment. Other factors that can cause residents to wander include:

- Pain
- Uncomfortable environmental temperature
- Adverse medication reactions (e.g., antipsychotics, antidepressants)
- Hunger or thirst
- Overstimulation or insufficient stimulation (noise, colors, lighting)
- Need for physical activity
- Constipation
- Thinking that there is purpose to fulfill (e.g., go to a job, visit a friend, find a lost child)

ESSENTIAL FACTS

It is essential that residents wear identification bracelets and that there be a current photograph of them in the record to assist with their identification should they wander away from the facility.

When wandering or pacing appears as a new behavior, it should not be assumed to be a "normal" feature of the disease. The resident should be assessed for conditions that could have triggered the behavior, such as a reaction to a medication or an infection.

For many residents with dementia, wandering is a chronic issue. Although interventions should be individualized, there are some general approaches that be used to prevent and reduce wandering, as well as foster safety, including:

- Placing the resident in a supervised area where he or she can be regularly observed
- Regularly checking on the resident

- Consistently assigning the same caregivers to care for the resident
- Controlling environmental noise
- Maintaining a stable environmental temperature
- Distracting the resident if he or she indicates the need to leave for some illogical purpose (e.g., thinking she needs to go to school).
- Placing stop signs on doors, protective gates, or Velcro-secured ribbons across doorways to discourage exit
- Installing bells or signals on doors to alert when a resident attempts to exit
- Ensuring the environment is free from clutter that could trip the resident while pacing

ESSENTIAL FACTS

Consistent assignment of staff, by which staff care for the same residents most or all of the time, reduces the anxiety residents with dementia may experience in adjusting to a new person and promotes continuity and consistency of care.

AGGRESSIVE BEHAVIOR

ESSENTIAL FACTS

Data from the U.S. Bureau of Labor Statistics shows that nursing assistants experience more physical violence than any other institutionally based caregiver, with more than half of certified nursing assistants (CNAs) being victims of assault and battery at least once every week (Centers for Disease Control and Prevention, 2014).

Aggressive behavior is an act that threatens or actually causes harm to other people or objects. It can consist of hitting, scratching, biting, grabbing, kicking, or throwing an item. In people with dementia, these behaviors are not typically intentionally planned to cause harm but, rather, result from feeling threatened or overwhelmed in a situation. For example, the caregiver may take the resident to the shower room and prepare to put him or her in the shower. The shower room may appear as a strange and frightening place to the resident, who may become agitated and kick, punch, or bite in an effort to resist this unknown threat.

As aggressive behaviors can cause harm to staff and residents, a proactive approach to prevent them is advisable and could include measures such as:

- Learning about the resident's history (e.g., past routines, activity and care preferences, words and actions that triggered negative responses)
- Determining if certain individuals or situations trigger aggressive behavior
- Identifying triggers for aggressive behavior and plans to avoid them
- Approaching the resident in a calm manner
- Avoiding situations that overwhelm or overstimulate the resident
- Offering the resident basic choices
- Explaining actions before proceeding to take them
- Being alert to signs that aggression is building, such as angry facial expression, increasing loudness of voice, use of threatening or obscene language, making fists, raising and swinging arms, pounding the fist on a table or wall, or throwing items
- Gently but firmly telling the resident to stop if aggressive behaviors are displayed
- Backing away and protecting yourself and others if the resident tries to attack

ESSENTIAL FACTS

Studies have shown that using dementia-appropriate communication styles reduces behavioral symptoms in these residents (Kim, Woods, Mentes, et al., 2014).

POOR NUTRITION AND HYDRATION

A variety of nutrition-related challenges can appear in residents with dementia. Depressed appetite and thirst sensations can reduce food intake; the ability to handle utensils and feed oneself can be decreased; chewing and swallowing may be more difficult; and the person may forget when and how to eat.

The dietician should be consulted for a determination of the appropriate diet and frequency of intake. It can be useful for caregivers to:

- Set up the tray in a similar manner for each meal
- Cut food into pieces that are easy for the resident to chew and swallow
- Guide the resident through eating with one-stage commands (e.g., put the meat on your fork, put it in your mouth, chew it up)

- Remind the resident to chew and swallow
- Remind the resident to take drinks of fluid throughout the day
- Monitor weight and food and fluid intake

ESSENTIAL FACTS

It is useful for an occupational therapist to perform a functional cognitive assessment to determine the resident's current and potential level of function, as well as approaches that can maximize function.

SLEEP DISTURBANCES

Approximately half the residents with dementia will experience sleep disturbances as a result of changes in the brain or other conditions (e.g., pain, adverse drug reactions, dyspnea). These disturbances can be evidenced by:

- Reversal of sleep patterns
- Frequent awakening during the night
- Daytime sleepiness or nodding off

Because of the potential for adverse reactions, sedative-hypnotics should be used with extreme caution and, preferably, only on a short-term basis. Nonpharmacological measures to promote sleep should be used, such as:

- Engaging the resident in physical activity during the day
- Adhering to a consistent schedule for bedtime
- Relieving pain
- Offering exposure to sunlight or full-spectrum lighting during waking hours
- Ensuring that the bedroom is conducive to sleep (dim lighting, soft music, comfortable temperature)
- Providing aromatherapy with essential oil of lavender (*Note:* Synthetic lavender may offer a fragrance but will not induce the physical reaction produced by the essential oil)
- Avoiding stimulating drinks and activities late in the day
- Providing a massage at bedtime

PRESERVING DIGNITY

As dementia progresses, the affected individuals become like strangers living within the shell of the bodies that once housed them. Their personalities and behaviors may hardly resemble those of the people they once were. Their disorganized thought processes, inappropriate communication, inattention to grooming, incontinence, and unusual behaviors can cause others to view them as less than normal—and treat them as such. Nurses are challenged to prevent these residents from being treated in dehumanizing, disrespectful ways. Care plans and actions that contribute to promoting dignity and respect of residents with dementia include:

- Learning about and sharing their history and unique characteristics
- Building on the remaining capacities
- Allowing them to do as much for themselves as possible
- Learning about and respecting personal preferences
- Offering choices, even if they are minor
- Addressing them by their preferred names
- Not laughing or making fun of their behaviors, and discouraging others from making fun of them
- Assisting them in staying involved with friends and family (e.g., assisting with grooming prior to a visitor's arrival, suggesting activities that visitors can do with the resident, offering communication tips)

Nurses can promote the highest possible quality of life in residents with dementia by preventing complications, maximizing existing function, and honoring the value of the person within them.

Management and Leadership

22

Foundations of Leadership and Management

Long-term care nurses carry a wide range of responsibilities such as overseeing the care provided to residents, determining staffing needs, developing assignments for staff, assuring compliance with regulations and standards, monitoring quality, ordering supplies, identifying and reporting risks, and facilitating problem solving. Many of these responsibilities demand knowledge and skills that go beyond those of basic nursing practice—they demand management and leadership competencies.

This chapter should enable you to:

1. Describe the differences between management and leadership
2. List major leadership styles
3. Describe strategies to enhance communication
4. List steps in effective delegation
5. List methods that can be used in performance appraisal
6. Describe measures for managing complaints
7. List methods to improve time management

DIFFERENTIATING LEADERSHIP AND MANAGEMENT

Despite their many overlapping features, leadership and management are different concepts. The complexities of the nursing department demand both leaders and managers. Typically, nurses in administrative roles, such as the director of nursing, function as the department's leaders whereas those who ensure the daily tasks to provide care and keep the units flowing, such as charge nurses or unit nurse managers, function as managers. Leaders also can possess management responsibilities and skills; likewise, managers, as well as people who do not carry management titles, can demonstrate leadership. Table 22.1 outlines differences in the function of leaders and managers.

TABLE 22.1 Comparing Leadership and Management

	Leaders	Managers
General focus	• Equip and inspire others to achieve and improve departmental and personal goals	• Supervise others in accomplishing daily work consistent with accepted standards
Authority	• Derives from position title and role, as well as ability to inspire others to follow one's lead	• Derives authority from position title and role
Functions	• Cast vision for department • Set direction for operations • Determine and advocate for needed resources • Plan based on identified needs and trends • Analyze operations and outcomes • Motivate employees • Introduce changes that improve overall or long-range care and working conditions • Seek ways to improve department operations • Network with external sources to stay abreast of changes	• Maintain operations • Plan and delegate tasks to a group of employees • Supervise those to whom tasks are delegated for adherence to desired standards • Develop resident care plans • Monitor outcomes against plans • Revise plans as needed • Correct undesired staff performance • Assure systems are properly functioning to accomplish daily tasks
Risk-taking	• Take reasonable risks to achieve a higher level of performance for department	• Avoid risks and seek to assure work is achieved within current expectations

Critical thinking is an important skill for both leaders and managers. Assumptions and current practices need to be reviewed on an ongoing basis to consider their continued effectiveness and determine whether better approaches can result in improvements. Leaders and managers need to display the behaviors they desire and expect in staff, such as a positive attitude, team spirit, openness to learn, and adherence to high standards.

ESSENTIAL FACTS

The fact that someone holds a leadership position does not necessarily mean that person is functioning as a leader. It requires more than a title to be a leader. Likewise, employees without a formal leadership title or role can demonstrate leadership skills.

STYLES OF LEADERSHIP

Various styles can be used to lead a department or team to accomplish goals. Some of the common leadership styles include:

- *Autocratic/authoritarian:* This leader makes decisions and orders staff to perform tasks with little or no input from them. Staff are controlled through rewards and punishments.
- *Laissez faire:* At the opposite extreme from the autocratic leader is the one who exercises little control and direction and allows staff to make their own decisions, giving direction only when requested.
- *Democratic/participative:* In between the extremes of excessive control and no control is the democratic/participative leader who consults with staff to obtain their input and allows them to make decisions within defined parameters. While offering staff the right to have control over specific areas, this leader ultimately accepts and holds responsibility.
- *Inconsistent:* Perhaps the most difficult type of leader for staff to work with is this one, whose style is unpredictable and can vary day to day.

It is useful for nurses to consider the style that reflects their leadership and evaluate the pros and cons. For example, a laissez-faire style could work well with a group of mature, highly credentialed nurses who have demonstrated the ability to make sound decisions and fulfill their responsibilities competently. However, a group of young, newly prepared nursing assistants with no work experience or those who have demonstrated poor performance may require a leader who is more autocratic.

Good leadership is not about being an authority figure, giving orders, correcting others, and getting the tasks done at any cost, but rather, creating a climate that encourages and recognizes the best in staff so that they will function at their best.

COMMUNICATION SKILLS

During the average day employees are given their assignments, care plans are utilized, supplies are ordered, dietary substitutions are requested, residents' changes in status are reported, physicians are informed of the results of laboratory tests, residents express their needs, visitors' questions are answered, new policies are announced, and the incoming shift is informed of issues that will need their attention. Multiple communications transpire during the average day.

If communication were as simple as Person A sending a message and Person B receiving it, considerably fewer communication problems would occur. Unfortunately, many variables can interfere with the effectiveness of communication, including:

- *Fluency in the language used for communication:* Reading a memo written in English when English is one's second language can hinder communication.
- *Choice of words:* Complex language can be used which the recipient does not understand; additionally, charged words or phrases can block communication.
- *Relationship of parties involved:* Individuals who have had disagreements may not be open to hearing each other.
- *Prejudices:* A person who has prejudices toward a person of a different race, ethnicity, gender, or sexual orientation may block or minimize what that person says.
- *Assumptions based on past experiences:* A supervisor who through deeds or actions contradicts his or her words may not be trusted by staff and, as a consequence, may no longer receive important information that would otherwise have been shared.
- *Stress:* People may speak without thinking, be insensitive, or block out communication when stressed.

The following strategies can enhance the effectiveness of communication:

- *Know what you want to express.* Before speaking or writing think through the purpose and content of the communication.
- *Select the best means of communicating the message.* Verbal communication may be quick and personal in some situations; in others

the time invested in writing a formal memo could prove useful for future reference. Along this line, consider the risks associated with selecting one form of communication over another. For example, e-mailing information about a resident's laboratory results to a physician may be quick and preferred by the physician, but it risks exposing confidential resident information if the communication is sent to an unintended receiver by mistake and lacks the accepted legal record of the transaction.

- *Be as simple and direct as possible.* State the message in as few words as possible. The purpose of most work-related communication is not to demonstrate the writing skill or eloquence of the writer but rather to deliver a message. Complicated words or phrases can be difficult for some people to understand.
- *Ensure that actions are consistent with words.* If you send a memo stating that a new policy will be implemented on a specific date, make sure that the groundwork has been done to allow this to happen.
- *Minimize the number of layers through which the communication must travel.* Every additional layer of receiver and sender in the communication process increases the risk for miscommunication.
- *Encourage two-way communication:* If the administration sends a memo to employees concerning a change in the benefit package, provide a means for employees to ask questions and offer feedback. Determine the method (e.g., memo, staff meeting, one-to-one meeting, intercom) that is most effective and appropriate for the communication.
- *Maintain a healthy balance of communication.* Insufficient communication can cause uncertainty about policies, philosophy, and operations, leading employees to make incorrect assumptions about what is desired of them. It also can cause them to feel as though they are not important to the facility. At the other extreme, information overload can cause employees to block out new communication. Employees need sufficient communication to know what is expected of them and to remain current about major activities in the organization.

ESSENTIAL FACTS

Remember that listening is a crucial communication skill. Avoid being so absorbed in forming a response in your mind that you miss what currently is being said. Also, pay attention to what is not being said, as when a person responds "okay" but his or her body language reflects otherwise.

DELEGATION

Delegation refers to the transfer of responsibility to another person. Each state's nurse practice act specifies the type of functions that can be delegated. Caution is necessary when considering delegation to ensure that the person delegating the function has the authority to do so and that the function is delegated to an appropriate staff member. For example, a nursing assistant cannot delegate to a nurse, nor can a registered nurse (RN) delegate a function that must be done by an RN, such as assessment, to a licensed practical or vocational nurse (LPN/LVN). Nurses should be familiar with their state's nurse practice act to ensure that they do not violate it when they delegate. Keep in mind that while an RN can delegate a task to an LPN, such as developing an assignment sheet for a team of nursing assistants, the RN has the ultimate responsibility for its completion.

ESSENTIAL FACTS

Performing a nursing assessment and developing nursing diagnoses are activities within the RN's scope of practice and cannot be delegated to an LPN/LVN. LPNs/LVNs can make observations and collect data, but they cannot conduct the assessment.

Box 22.1 describes steps to consider in delegation.

Box 22.1   Steps in Delegation

- Review your state's nurse practice act and your facility's policies related to tasks that can be delegated to various levels of staff.
- Be clear on the task that needs to be accomplished, and the time and resources it requires.
- Assess whether the person to whom the task is being delegated possesses the necessary skills, knowledge, time, and resources to complete the task.
- Give specific directions, including the degree to which you want to be kept abreast of progress, such as if the person should perform the task:
  - Without any need for follow up with you
  - Informing you when it is completed
  - Reporting to you when each step of the task is completed to obtain approval for the next step
- Offer feedback when the task is completed.

PERFORMANCE APPRAISAL

Nurses who supervise other employees are responsible for monitoring and evaluating those employees' performance. Methods to use in this effort include:

- Direct observation of employees' activities
- Periodic checks; spot checks
- Feedback from other employees, residents, and visitors
- Attendance records
- Incident and accident reports
- Reports of quality improvement assessments
- Employees' self-evaluations

Evaluations should be made based on a compilation of all performance over a designated period of time and not the most recent events. This composite is aided by maintaining records that document specific observations and occurrences which can then be used to construct a general assessment of performance over time. Maintaining such records also offers support if an employee challenges an issue. For example, if the performance appraisal includes a statement that the employee has a problem completing assignments before the end of the shift and the employee challenges this, the specific dates on which this occurred can be offered.

Although positive performance and areas in need of improvement are reviewed in an annual performance appraisal, offering employee feedback throughout the year is beneficial in correcting performance problems and reinforcing positive performance.

ESSENTIAL FACTS

Coaching skills can prove useful in assisting employees to improve performance. The traditional approach to correcting performance problems often involves the manager informing the person of what was done incorrectly and how to correct the situation. In the coaching approach, there is a partnership between the manager and employee in which the manager states the problem and helps the employee use his or her own abilities to think through strategies to correct it. The coaching approach encourages employees to be active participants in problem solving, enables them to develop goals that they can realistically achieve, respects their capabilities to solve problems, and promotes their growth.

MANAGING COMPLAINTS

Complaints are not uncommon in long-term care settings. Residents are living with health conditions that often produce discomfort, disability, and dependency, causing them to be sensitive to treatment that they view as less than perfect. Family members may be guilty, anxious, and depressed at the status of their loved ones, causing them to be extra sensitive to situations that even hint at being adverse to their relatives. Owing to the widespread negative image of long-term care facilities among many in the public, some family members may assume staff need close scrutiny to ensure that adequate care is given to their loved one, while others may hold unrealistic expectations about care. Staffing shortages and heavy work demands can have an impact on staff, resulting in less-than-positive responses by employees. All of these factors can lead to unfounded, as well as valid, complaints.

Nurses must be prepared to manage complaints. This begins by preventing situations in which complaints can arise. Measures that can assist in complaint prevention include:

- *Addressing resident and visitor requests promptly.* If requests cannot be met as desired, offer a reasonable explanation for the reason.
- *Giving realistic commitments.* If a resident states that he would like a shower and the nursing assistant has to shower another resident first, the nursing assistant should state "I'll be able to shower you in a half hour after I have finished showering someone else," rather than "Okay, I'll be right with you."
- *Minimizing surprises.* If a plumbing problem is causing baths and showers to be delayed, inform the residents of this before their regular bathing times. Likewise, if a resident has experienced an incident, advise the family of this before they visit so that they are not caught by surprise.
- *Anticipating needs.* If a resident's daughter visits at noon daily and likes to take her mother to the activity room at that time, be sure the mother is bathed, dressed, and out of bed by then.

Despite the best intentions and actions, some complaints will arise. When they do it is beneficial to:

- Listen to the complaint completely, without interrupting or offering explanations.
- Clarify the issue (e.g., "You say that when you asked the nursing assistant to help she ignored you and left the room?" or "You say your father's coat was here yesterday but is now missing?").
- Focus on the issue without reacting to accusations or emotionally charged statements.
- Acknowledge the person's feelings without placing blame (e.g., "I can understand your anger at not getting help when you asked

for it" or "It is upsetting to not be able to find your father's coat when it is needed").

- Offer assistance in solving the problem (e.g., "I'm sorry this happened and will talk with the nursing assistant to find out why you were not helped" or "I'll go through all the closets on the unit to see if we can find your father's coat.")
- If the situation escalates, contact your supervisor or administrator.
- Follow up to ensure that a satisfactory resolution has been achieved.

ESSENTIAL FACTS

It is beneficial to maintain written records of complaints and their resolution, and to periodically review them to identify trends or problems with specific units or employees.

TIME MANAGEMENT

Because there are regular demands on nurses' time and a finite number of hours in a day, it is essential to learn to manage time effectively. It is important to understand that working long hours and being busy all the time do not necessarily equate to effectiveness and high productivity. A helpful first step to effective time management is to perform a self-assessment in which time-wasting behaviors can be identified (Box 22.2).

Box 22.2   Checklist of Time-Wasting Behaviors

___ Beginning the day with no agenda or plan
___ Not prioritizing activities
___ Addressing issues as they occur rather than by priority
___ Feeling the need to be part of and control most activities
___ Reading or handling the same piece of mail several times
___ Not having or using a private work area for office activities (e.g., documenting, planning)
___ Having a cluttered desk
___ Being diverted from current activity to address other issues as they arise
___ Multitasking
___ Allowing the behaviors of others to delay or divert plans or activities

(continued)

Box 22.2 *(continued)*

___ Being reluctant to delegate
___ Lacking good delegation skills
___ Being unrealistic in evaluating work that can be accomplished in given time or by given staff, or both
___ Desiring excessive control
___ Answering all incoming calls without screening
___ Holding and attending unnecessary or poorly run meetings
___ Allowing discussion of nonagenda items during meetings
___ Being nonassertive
___ Engaging in gossip or the discussion of personal problems during work hours
___ Lacking the knowledge or skill to complete assignments
___ Procrastinating
___ Failing to engage in good self-care practices

It is useful to improve personal time management practices, as well as to aid other members of the team in improving theirs. Effective time management can have a positive impact on job productivity, satisfaction, and morale, and enable individuals to have more time and energy available for personal life. Useful strategies to consider in improving time management include:

- *Planning.* Consider activities that need to be done throughout the year (e.g., reviewing procedure manual, completing annual evaluations, compiling reports) and plot them on a calendar. Use a daily calendar and begin each day with a plan based on scheduled activities and priorities. Be realistic about what can be accomplished (e.g., it is unrealistic to expect to finish all work within an 8-hour shift if you have to care for four residents, each of whom will require over an hour of your time, and also administer medications for the entire unit).
- *Prioritizing.* Determine if the activity is urgent or nonurgent, important, or unimportant. There can be many important tasks but they do not all have to be done as soon as possible.
- *Delegating.* Resist feeling that delegation is an imposition or will cause others to view you negatively. Appropriately assigning tasks to others can aid in getting tasks accomplished and relieving you of tasks that do not necessarily require your personal involvement. It also can help others to grow in their jobs.
- *Controlling interruptions.* Establish a work area where you can address paperwork and planning activities without being disturbed. Have calls screened.

- *Conducting meetings effectively.* Avoid traps such as routinely holding a meeting every Tuesday at 2 p.m. simply because the facility has always held the meeting then; conducting a meeting of a large group when only a few of those attending could have completed a necessary preliminary task; or allowing people to go off on tangents during the meeting. Ensure that an agenda is prepared beforehand for the meeting and that it is followed.
- *Engaging in good self-care practices.* Eat a well-balanced diet and obtain adequate rest and sleep. Build time in your schedule for exercise and leisure activities. Learn how to set limits.

23

Determining Staffing Needs

Nursing staff provide a majority of services to residents in long-term care facilities and constitute most of the employee population. Because the nursing department is the backbone of long-term care, an incorrect number and mix of nursing staff members can threaten quality of care and interfere with the efforts of other disciplines.

As the major department, nursing also is responsible for a significant portion of the facility's budgetary expenditures. The operations, competencies, and stability of the nursing department can have an impact on the facility's total fiscal health. Long-term care nurses, particularly those in administrative roles, need to be able to determine staffing needs in order to meet residents' care demands, properly utilize various levels of staff, and demonstrate fiscal responsibility.

This chapter should enable you to:

1. List factors influencing staffing needs
2. Determine productive and nonproductive time
3. Describe methods for estimating hours per resident day (HPRD)
4. Calculate the number of full-time equivalent (FTE) employees needed based on three approaches: census, HPRD, and employees' productive time

FACTORS INFLUENCING STAFFING NEEDS

ESSENTIAL FACTS

Regulations covering long-term care facilities offer minimum staffing requirements. The staffing level that may be needed to care for the specific resident population of a given facility could be considerably higher than those minimums based on a variety of factors that influence staffing needs. Staffing at minimum levels when more hours and a different level of nursing personnel are needed could ultimately be costly in terms of higher survey deficiencies, incident rates, complications, turnover, and hospital readmissions.

Facilities, even those with similar bed size and physical layout, can vary in their staffing needs. Factors that influence staffing needs include:

- *Resident acuity.* The number and type of health conditions in need of management; complexity of treatments required; and dependency level, mental status, and behavior of residents are considered when determining staffing needs.
- *Average census.* A facility operating at a census of 80% of its bed capacity will have different staffing needs than if all beds are consistently filled.
- *Physical plant.* Unit layouts can affect staffing. If there are 30 beds on a wing with supply, utility, and medication rooms at the far end of the hall, staff may need to invest more time obtaining supplies and equipment than if the unit is smaller sized. Individual showers and tubs in each room save more time than the use of a single shower and tub room on the unit.
- *Availability of support services.* A housekeeper assigned to the unit can address housekeeping needs as they arise, thereby saving nursing staff from either doing the cleaning or taking the time to call the housekeeping department. Laundry staff who deliver linens to the rooms and remove dirty linens from the unit likewise save nursing staff from doing these tasks, as do dietary staff who deliver meals directly to residents rather than just delivering food carts to the unit.
- *Staff profile.* Experienced employees may require less supervision and be more productive than inexperienced ones. Registered nurses (RNs) may provide for greater efficiency because

they are able to do tasks that other levels of nursing personnel cannot do.

- *Scheduling realities.* There can be restrictions on how many hours or consecutive days employees can work.
- *Nonproductive time.* Employees are not present for all of the 2,080 potential hours that they could work (i.e., 40 hours times 52 weeks) due to nonproductive time (i.e., time off for vacation, holidays, personal leave, sick time, etc.). Because benefit packages vary, facilities can differ in the nonproductive time of employees. In addition, average sick time utilization can vary and affect how many hours employees actually are available to work.
- *Model of care.* Facilities that have implemented culture change programs may offer residents more flexibility in deciding their bathing, eating, and activity schedules, which can influence staffing. Likewise, facilities that employ nursing assistants who function in broader capacities by preparing meals, doing laundry, and performing light housekeeping duties may require a higher number of nursing assistants.

Nurses need to be sensitive to the fact that nonnursing professionals who develop the facility's budget may lack an understanding of the factors that affect staffing and work from the assumption that all facilities of similar bed size can be staffed similarly. In addition, budget developers may not understand the number of nonnursing tasks that the nursing department performs, which affects staffing needs. Nurses need to educate these individuals about the factors affecting staffing needs in their individual facilities to ensure that adequate staffing is budgeted.

DETERMINING HPRD

The first step in determining a facility's unique staffing needs is to calculate the average hours of care residents need for a 24-hour period, known as the *hours per resident day (HPRD)*. At times, staff are able to estimate HPRD fairly well based on experience. For example, they may know that residents who require complete assistance need X hours of care, those who need partial assistance need Y hours of care, and those who are fairly independent need Z hours of care. Although this knowledge provides useful guidance, a tool to estimate HPRD, such as the one shown in Box 23.1, may still be useful. The unique features of the individual facility can contribute to differences in categories considered and the weight given to each level of dependency.

Box 23.1 Sample Method for Calculating Daily Hours of Nursing Care Based on Residents' Needs

Step One: Determine the dependency of each resident in each of the care areas.

Care Area	Resident Totally Independent; Requires No Assistance	Resident Partially Dependent/ Impaired; Requires Minor or Occasional Assistance	Resident Totally Dependent/ Impaired; Requires Total Assistance
Bathing	1	2	3
Dressing/ grooming	1	2	3
Eating	1	2	3
Drinking	1	2	3
Transferring	1	2	3
Ambulation	1	2	4
Repositioning	1	2	4
Communication	1	2	3
Cognitive function	1	3	6
Behavior	1	3	3
Vision	1	2	3
Hearing	1	2	3
Pressure ulcer risk	1	2	3
Bladder elimination	1	2	5
Bowel elimination	1	2	3
Drug administration	1	2	3
Treatment (list and score each)	1	2	3
Subtotals			

Total All Columns =

(continued)

Box 23.1   *(continued)*

Step Two: Calculate the hours per resident day (HPRD) required by the resident.

Multiply the total of all columns by 5:

Total of all columns = _____ × 5 = _____

Take the product obtained and divide by 60 to get the HPRD:

$$60)\overline{\text{HPRD}}$$

Step Three: Determine the average HPRDs needed for the unit or department.

Add all the residents' HPRDs together and divide by the number of residents:

$$\text{Number of residents})\overline{\text{Total HPRDs}}^{\text{Average HPRD}}$$

ESSENTIAL FACTS

It is useful to monitor and reassess HPRD regularly as significant changes in this variable will affect staffing. For example, if the HPRD averaged 4.5 in January and in March increased to 6.0 because residents with more acute health problems were admitted, staffing may need to be increased or admission of high-acuity residents restricted.

USING HPRD TO DETERMINE NUMBER OF STAFF REQUIRED

Once the average HPRD are known, the number of staff required to provide those hours must be determined. As mentioned, productive and nonproductive times can vary among facilities; therefore, it is essential that the employee productive time for a facility be determined. Box 23.2 outlines the steps to determining productive time.

After determining the average productive hours per employee, the next step is to calculate how many *full-time equivalent (FTE) employees* will be needed to provide the determined HPRD. This is done by dividing the productive hours per employee into the total number of hours required for the department or unit. Box 23.3 demonstrates this.

Box 23.2 Determining Productive Time

Step One: Identify the total annual nonproductive hours. (The human resources department should be able to assist in providing this information.)

Category	Hours
Holidays	
Average vacation days	
Average sick time utilization	
Educational days	
Other (list)	
TOTAL	

Step Two: Determine the average annual productive hours per employee.

$$2080 \text{ maximum annual working hours} = \frac{\text{Total nonproductive hours}}{\text{Annual productive hours}}$$

Box 23.3 Determining Full-Time Equivalent (FTE) Employees Needed

Step One: Multiply the average hours per resident day (HPRD) by the total number of residents to obtain the total hours of care required daily. (This can be calculated for the entire nursing department or a specific unit.)

_____ Total residents × _____ HPRD = _____ Total daily hours of nursing care

Step Two: Obtain the annual hours of nursing care required by multiplying the total daily nursing care hours by 365 days.

_____ Total daily nursing care × 365 = _____ Total annual hours of nursing care

Step Three: Determine how many full-time equivalents (FTEs) are required to provide the hours of care by dividing nonproductive time into the total annual hours of nursing care.

$$\text{Productive hours} \overline{) \dfrac{\text{FTEs required}}{\text{Total annual HPRD}}}$$

The following example shows how this works in one facility:

- The facility has 125 residents who have been determined to need an average of 5.5 HPRD. Based on this calculation, the annual average of nursing hours required is 250,937.5:

$$125 \text{ residents} \times 5.5 \text{ HPRD} = 687.5 \text{ HPRD daily}$$
$$\times 365 \text{ days} = 250,937.5 \text{ hours/year}$$

- The FTE employees' average annual nonproductive time is 152 hours:

$$
\begin{array}{l}
10 \text{ Vacation days} \\
5 \text{ Average sick days} \\
3 \text{ Personal leave days} \\
\underline{1 \text{ Education day}} \\
19 \text{ Total nonproductive days} \times 8 \text{ hours} = \\
152 \text{ annual nonproductive hours}
\end{array}
$$

- Based on the nonproductive hours, the average productive hours per employee is 1928.

$$
\begin{array}{l}
2,080 \text{ Total possible working hours} \\
\underline{- 152 \text{ Nonproductive hours of the facility's employees}} \\
1,928 \text{ Productive hours per employee annually}
\end{array}
$$

- The number of FTE employees required to provide the hours needed per year is 130.15, rounded to 130 FTEs.

$$\frac{250,937.5}{1,928} = 130.15 \text{ FTEs required}$$

When developing the actual schedule it may be discovered that several more FTEs are needed to meet the daily quota owing to factors such as the number of consecutive days an employee can work without having a day off, part-time staffing , and so on.

ESSENTIAL FACTS

Consideration must be given not only to the number of FTEs required, but also to how the FTEs are allocated among RNs, licensed practical nurses (LPNs), and nursing assistants. Regulatory requirements and resident acuity levels are important considerations in determining the type of staff who fill the FTE requirements.

MONITORING STAFFING

Unexpected absences do occasionally occur, causing staffing levels to be lower than ideal. For this reason it is useful to consider the absolute minimum staffing level at which the department or unit can work. For example, a unit may be staffed as follows on the day shift:

> 1 RN, 2 LPNs, 7 nursing assistants

It may be determined that occasionally, a minimum staffing level could be:

> 1 RN, 2 LPNs, 6 nursing assistants
> or
> 1 RN, 1 LPN, 7 nursing assistants

Staff would not be replaced if these minimums could be met; however, if staffing fell below those levels, replacement would be necessary.

All nurses who are responsible for staffing should understand these conditions so they can ensure that minimum staffing levels are met and also avoid replacement of staff when the unit could function with reduced staffing for one shift.

It is valuable to monitor staff satisfaction, resident satisfaction, survey results, incidents and accidents, pressure ulcer development, absenteeism, and turnover as problems noted in these areas could be associated with insufficient staff.

24

Surveys

The Centers for Medicare and Medicaid Services (CMS) has been designated by the Secretary of the Department of Health and Human Services (HHS) to ensure that facilities comply with regulations and that they do so by conducting surveys. Federal regulations describe the minimum standards that a facility must meet. A state can add regulations that also must be complied with. CMS typically has regional offices that conduct surveys with state regulatory divisions.

There is nothing mysterious about what will be evaluated during a survey. The regulations clearly state the standards that must be met, and the survey will determine if the facility is in compliance. To assure compliance with regulations, nurses should be familiar with regulations and adhere to practices that support them.

This chapter should enable you to:

1. Describe four types of surveys that examine resident care
2. List severity levels and scope of deficiencies
3. Describe standards that nursing homes are required to meet as stated in regulations

TYPES OF SURVEYS

There are four types of surveys that facilities have that examine resident care (Centers for Medicare and Medicaid, 2014d):

- *Standard survey:* These unannounced surveys are conducted every 9 to 15 months from the last survey date.
- *Abbreviated standard survey:* In addition to a standard survey, a shorter standard survey can be done based on a complaint or change in ownership or administrative staff.
- *Extended survey:* If substandard quality of care (SQC) is discovered during a standard survey, additional policies and procedures are reviewed either prior to the exit conference of within 2 weeks of the survey. An SQC consists of a deficiency with a scope and severity of F, H, I, J, K, or L in regulations pertaining to quality of care, quality of life, or resident behavior/facility practices. If a facility is found to have an SQC, its ability to train nursing assistants is suspended for a period of time.
- *Partial extended survey:* If during an abbreviated standard survey an SQC is identified, nursing services, physician services, and administrative policies and procedures related to the problem area will be reviewed.

If deficiencies were found during a survey, the facility develops a plan of correction that specifies the actions that will be taken to correct the deficiencies. A follow-up survey will then be done to determine if the plan of correction was effective.

In addition to the resident-centered surveys, the Occupational Safety and Health Administration (OSHA) performs surveys to assess the facility's compliance with workplace safety regulations. Among the areas they will examine are workplace accidents and injuries, bloodborne pathogens, and compliance with the Americans with Disabilities Act.

SEVERITY LEVELS AND SCOPE OF DEFICIENCIES

ESSENTIAL FACTS

If the survey has discovered that a facility is not in compliance with the regulation, an F-tag (federal tag) number will be cited. This number corresponds to the regulation number as it was published in the Federal Register and differs from the regulation number. For example, the regulation number for Residents' Rights is 483.10; however, F-151 refers to noncompliance of the Exercise of Rights. Similarly, the regulation number for Resident Assessment is 483.20, but F-272 cites a deficiency related to Comprehensive Assessment.

When deficiencies are identified during the survey they are assigned a level of severity, which is defined as follows:

- Level 1: No actual harm with potential for minimal harm
- Level 2: No actual harm with potential for more than minimal harm that is not immediate jeopardy
- Level 3: Actual harm that is not immediate jeopardy
- Level 4: Immediate jeopardy to resident health or safety

ESSENTIAL FACTS

"Immediate jeopardy" is a situation in which the facility's non-compliance with one or more requirements of participation:

- Has caused, or is likely to cause, serious injury, harm, impairment, or death to a resident; and
- Requires immediate correction, as the facility either created the situation or allowed the situation to continue by failing to implement preventive or corrective measures.

A determination is made as to the scope of the deficiency:

- Isolated: Only one or a few residents are affected and/or a limited number of staff are involved and/or the situation occurred in a limited number of locations
- Pattern: More than a limited number of residents are affected and/or more than a limited number of staff are involved and/or the situation occurred in several locations and/or the same residents have been affected by repeated occurrences of the practice
- Widespread: The situation is pervasive throughout the facility or represents a systemic failure that affected or has the potential to affect a large number of residents

ESSENTIAL FACTS

After the survey findings have been shared, the facility develops a plan of correction that states the actions that will be taken to address each cited deficiency. These plans should be realistic and incorporated into routine plans to comply with the regulations at all times.

AREAS SURVEYED

Surveys are based on the standards stated in the regulations. By being familiar with the regulations, nurses can be proactive in assuring compliance. Highlights of long-term care facility regulations are presented in Table 24.1, which concludes this chapter.

Surveys are a means of assuring that the care residents receive meets acceptable standards and the facility is a safe environment for residents and employees. It must be remembered, however, that regulations state *minimum* standards and that surveys will only focus on those basic requirements. Nurses need to strive for higher standards that incorporate best practices and support optimal care and operations.

TABLE 24.1 Selected Sections of Federal Long-Term Care Facility Regulations

483.10 Resident Rights

A resident has the right to:

- Be informed about what rights and responsibilities he or she has
- Determine if he or she wishes to have the facility manage his personal funds
- Choose a physician and treatment, and participate in decisions and care planning
- Privacy and confidentiality
- Voice grievances and have the facility respond to those grievances
- Examine survey results
- Work or not work
- Privacy in sending and receiving mail
- Visit and be visited by others from outside the facility
- Use a telephone in privacy
- Retain and use personal possessions to the maximum extent that space and safety permit
- Share a room with a spouse, if that is mutually agreeable
- Self-administer medication, if the interdisciplinary care planning team determines it is safe
- Refuse a transfer from a distinct part, within the institution

483.12 Admission, Transfer, and Discharge Rights

The facility may not transfer or discharge the resident unless:

- The transfer or discharge is necessary to meet the resident's welfare and the resident's welfare cannot be met in the facility
- The transfer or discharge is appropriate because the resident's health has improved sufficiently so the resident no longer needs the services provided by the facility
- The safety of individuals in the facility is endangered
- The health of individuals in the facility would otherwise be endangered
- The resident has failed, after reasonable and appropriate notice, to pay for a stay at the facility, or
- The facility ceases to operate

(continued)

TABLE 24.1 Selected Sections of Federal Long-Term Care Facility Regulations (*continued*)

483.15 Quality of Life

The facility must promote care for residents in a manner and in an environment that maintains or enhances each resident's dignity and respect in full recognition of his or her individuality.

The resident has the right to:

- Choose activities, schedules, and health care consistent with his or her interests, assessments, and plans of care; interact with members of the community both inside and outside the facility; and make choices about aspects of his or her life in the facility that are significant to the resident
- Organize and participate in resident groups in the facility
- Participate in social, religious, and community activities that do not interfere with the rights of other residents in the facility
- Reside and receive services in the facility with reasonable accommodation of individual needs and preferences, except when the health or safety of the individual or other residents would be endangered
- Receive notice before the resident's room or roommate in the facility is changed.

The facility must provide for an ongoing program of activities designed to meet, in accordance with the comprehensive assessment, the interests and the physical, mental, and psychosocial well-being of each resident.

483.20 Resident Assessment

A facility must make a comprehensive assessment of a resident's needs, using the Resident Assessment Instrument (RAI) specified by the state.

When required, a facility must conduct a comprehensive assessment of a resident as follows:

- Within 14 calendar days after admission, excluding readmissions in which there is no significant change in the resident's physical or mental condition
- Within 14 days after the facility determines, or should have determined, that there has been a significant change in the resident's physical or mental condition
- Not less than once every 12 months

A facility must assess a resident using the quarterly review instrument specified.
A facility must maintain all resident assessments completed within the previous 15 months in the resident's active record.
The assessment must accurately reflect the resident's status.
A registered nurse must conduct or coordinate each assessment with the appropriate participation of health professionals.
A registered nurse must sign and certify that the assessment is completed.

(*continued*)

TABLE 24.1 Selected Sections of Federal Long-Term Care Facility Regulations (*continued*)

Each individual who completes a portion of the assessment must sign and certify the accuracy of that portion of the assessment.

The facility must develop a comprehensive care plan for each resident that includes measurable objectives and timetables to meet a resident's medical, nursing, and mental and psychosocial needs that are identified in the comprehensive assessment.

A comprehensive care plan must be:

- Developed within 7 days after the completion of the comprehensive assessment
- Prepared by an interdisciplinary team, that includes the attending physician, a registered nurse with responsibility for the resident, and other appropriate staff in disciplines as determined by the resident's needs, and, to the extent practicable, the participation of the resident, the resident's family or the resident's legal representative, and
- Periodically reviewed and revised by a team of qualified persons after each assessment

When the facility anticipates discharge a resident must have a discharge summary that includes:

- A recapitulation of the resident's stay
- A postdischarge plan of care that is developed with the participation of the resident and his or her family, which will assist the resident to adjust to his or her new living environment

483.25 Quality of Care

Each resident must receive and the facility must provide the necessary care and services to attain or maintain the highest practicable physical, mental, and psychosocial well-being, in accordance with the comprehensive assessment and plan of care.

A resident's abilities in activities of daily living should not diminish unless circumstances of the individual's clinical condition demonstrate that diminution was unavoidable.

To ensure that residents receive proper treatment and assistive devices to maintain vision and hearing abilities, the facility must, if necessary, assist the resident in making appointments, and by arranging for transportation to and from the office of a practitioner specializing in the treatment of vision or hearing impairment or the office of a professional specializing in the provision of vision or hearing assistive devices.

The facility must ensure that a resident who:

- Enters the facility without pressure sores does not develop pressure sores unless the individual's clinical condition demonstrates that they were unavoidable; and a resident having pressure sores receives necessary treatment and services to promote healing, prevent infection and prevent new sores from developing

(*continued*)

TABLE 24.1 Selected Sections of Federal Long-Term Care Facility Regulations (*continued*)

- Enters the facility without an indwelling catheter is not catheterized unless the resident's clinical condition demonstrates that catheterization was necessary; and a resident who is incontinent of bladder receives appropriate treatment and services to prevent urinary tract infections and to restore as much normal bladder function as possible
- Enters the facility without a limited range of motion does not experience reduction in range of motion unless the resident's clinical condition demonstrates that a reduction in range of motion is unavoidable; and a resident with a limited range of motion receives appropriate treatment and services to increase range of motion and/or to prevent further decrease in range of motion
- Displays mental or psychosocial adjustment difficulty, receives appropriate treatment and services to correct the assessed problem; and a resident whose assessment did not reveal a mental or psychosocial adjustment difficulty does not display a pattern of decreased social interaction and/or increased withdrawn, angry, or depressive behaviors, unless the resident's clinical condition demonstrates that such a pattern is unavoidable
- Has been able to eat enough alone or with assistance is not fed by nasogastric tube unless the resident's clinical condition demonstrates that use of a nasogastric tube was unavoidable; and a resident who is fed by a nasogastric or gastrostomy tube receives the appropriate treatment and services to prevent aspiration pneumonia, diarrhea, vomiting, dehydration, metabolic abnormalities, and nasal-pharyngeal ulcers and to restore, if possible, normal eating skills

The facility must ensure that the resident environment remains as free from accident hazards as is possible; and each resident receives adequate supervision and assistance devices to prevent accidents.

Based on a resident's comprehensive assessment, the facility must ensure that a resident maintains acceptable parameters of nutritional status, such as body weight and protein levels, unless the resident's clinical condition demonstrates that this is not possible; and receives therapeutic diet when there is a nutritional problem.

The facility must provide each resident with sufficient fluid intake to maintain proper hydration and health.

Each resident's drug regimen must be free from unnecessary drugs.

The facility must ensure that:

- Residents who have not used antipsychotic drugs are not given these drugs unless antipsychotic drug therapy is necessary to treat a specific condition as diagnosed and documented in the clinical record, and
- Residents who use antipsychotic drugs receive gradual dose reductions, and behavioral interventions, unless clinically contraindicated, in an effort to discontinue these drugs
- The facility is free of medication error rates of 5% or greater; and residents are free of any significant medication errors

(*continued*)

TABLE 24.1 Selected Sections of Federal Long-Term Care Facility Regulations (*continued*)

483.30 Nursing Services

The facility must have sufficient nursing staff to provide nursing and related services to attain or maintain the highest practicable physical, mental, and psychosocial well-being of each resident, as determined by resident assessments and individual plans of care.

The facility must provide services by sufficient numbers of each of the following types of personnel on a 24-hour basis to provide nursing care to all residents in accordance with resident care plans.

Except when waived, the facility must:

- Designate a licensed nurse to serve as a charge nurse on each tour of duty
- Use the services of a registered nurse for at least 8 consecutive hours a day, 7 days a week
- Designate a registered nurse to serve as the director of nursing on a full time basis (The director of nursing may serve as a charge nurse only when the facility has an average daily occupancy of 60 or fewer residents.)

483.65 Infection Control

The facility must establish and maintain an Infection Control Program designed to provide a safe, sanitary and comfortable environment and to help prevent the development and transmission of disease and infection.

483.75 Required Training of Nursing Aides

A facility must not use any individual who has worked in the facility as a nurse aide:

- For more than 4 months, on a full-time basis, unless that individual is competent to provide nursing and nursing related services; and that individual has completed a training and competency evaluation program, or a competency evaluation program approved by the State as meeting the requirements of; or that individual has been deemed or determined competent
- For less than 4 months as a nurse aide in that facility unless the individual is a full-time employee in a state-approved training and competency evaluation program; has demonstrated competence through satisfactory participation in a state-approved nurse aide training and competency evaluation program or competency evaluation program; or has been deemed or determined competent

Before allowing an individual to serve as a nurse aide, a facility must receive registry verification that the individual has met competency evaluation requirements unless the individual is a full-time employee in a training and competency evaluation program approved by the state; or the individual can prove that he or she has recently successfully completed a training and competency evaluation program

(*continued*)

TABLE 24.1 Selected Sections of Federal Long-Term Care Facility Regulations (*continued*)

or competency evaluation program approved by the state and has not yet been included in the registry. Facilities must follow up to ensure that such an individual actually becomes registered.

The facility must complete a performance review of every nurse aide at least once every 12 months, and must provide regular in-service education based on the outcome of these reviews. The in-service training must be sufficient to ensure the continuing competence of nurse aides, but must be no less than 12 hours per year; address areas of weakness as determined in nurse aides' performance reviews and may address the special needs of residents as determined by the facility staff; and for nurse aides providing services to individuals with cognitive impairments, also address the care of the cognitively impaired.

The facility must ensure that nurse aides are able to demonstrate competency in skills and techniques necessary to care for residents' needs, as identified through resident assessments, and described in the plan of care.

483.75 Staff Qualifications

The facility must employ on a full-time, part-time, or consultant basis those professionals necessary to carry out the provisions of these requirements.

Professional staff must be licensed, certified, or registered in accordance with applicable state laws.

483.75 Quality Assessment and Assurance

A facility must maintain a quality assessment and assurance committee consisting of the director of nursing services; a physician designated by the facility; and at least 3 other members of the facility's staff.

The quality assessment and assurance committee meets at least quarterly to identify issues with respect to which quality assessment and assurance activities are necessary; and develops and implements appropriate plans of action to correct identified quality deficiencies.

The state or the Secretary may not require disclosure of the records of such committee except insofar as such disclosure is related to the compliance of such committee with the requirements of this section.

Source: Centers for Medicare and Medicaid Services. (2014d).

25

Legal Aspects

Nursing practice in any setting carries its share of risks. In long-term care settings the risks are increased due to the vulnerability and multiple pathologies of the population served, range of treatments that are utilized, high number of unlicensed nursing employees involved in care that must be supervised, and, in many settings, low staffing levels. To further compound risks there are situations in which nurses may be asked by residents and families for advice for issues pertaining to making end-of-life decisions, developing or changing wills, obtaining power of attorney, and managing resources. To protect the people they care for, their employers, and themselves nurses must be knowledgeable about laws pertaining to their practice and ensure that they are practicing in a manner consistent with them.

This chapter should enable you to:

1. List sources of laws
2. Describe actions that could potentially cause legal problems or liability related to:
   - Abuse
   - Advance directives
   - Assault and battery
   - Competency
   - Confidentiality
   - Consent
   - Defamation

- Do-not-resuscitate orders
- False imprisonment
- Incidents and accidents
- Malpractice
- Restraint use
- Supervisory responsibilities
- Telephone orders
3. Describe actions to promote a legally sound practice

SOURCE OF LAWS

All citizens, regardless of their state or setting, must adhere to a variety of laws. Additional laws apply to licensed health care workers and specific settings of practice. Laws arise from:

- *Constitutions:* Government bodies can grant rights to citizens (e.g., freedom of speech, right to vote), as well as grant powers and place limits on government agencies.
- *Statutes:* Local, state, and federal governments can enact laws, such as nurse practice acts.
- *Regulations:* Administrative agencies at the state and federal levels can enact laws that specify the conditions that must be met for certain activities (e.g., regulations that describe the standards that a facility must meet to be licensed and receive reimbursement from government health insurance programs).
- *Court decisions:* Decisions from cases in state or federal courts can establish precedents that must be followed.

ESSENTIAL FACTS

Practice acts exist for registered nurses, licensed practical/ vocational nurses, nursing assistants, advanced practice nurses, and medication aides. They describe the educational requirements, licensure requirements, scope of practice, appropriate title that can be used, and consequences of not abiding by the act. Nurses need to ensure that their practice is consistent with their license and that they do not delegate tasks to or allow tasks to be performed by employees whom they supervise that are outside the legal scope of practice of those employees. The National Council of State Boards of Nursing's website (www.ncsbn.org) lists contact information for every state's board of nursing that can aid in obtaining information on practice acts within a specific state.

There are public and private laws. *Public laws* are those involving the government and individuals, institutions, or businesses, such as the laws involving murder, discrimination, and safety standards for health care facilities. *Private laws* are those involving private parties, such as employment contracts and malpractice. The government can fine, jail, or revoke a license when a person or business is found guilty of violating a public law. Individuals can sue for damages when there in a court-determined violation of a private law.

SPECIFIC LEGAL RISKS

Abuse

ESSENTIAL FACTS

Abuse can consist of doing or threatening to do physical, psychological, financial, or sexual harm.

The vulnerability of the population served in long-term care settings is a factor that heightens their risk of being abused. Several major categories of abuse are recognized (Centers for Medicare and Medicaid Services, 2014a):

- *Physical abuse:* Hitting, slapping, pinching and kicking; also includes controlling behavior through corporal punishment.
- *Verbal abuse:* The use of oral, written or gestured language that willfully includes disparaging and derogatory terms to residents or their families, or within their hearing distance, regardless of their age, ability to comprehend, or disability.
- *Mental abuse:* Humiliation, harassment, threats of punishment or deprivation.
- *Sexual abuse:* Sexual harassment, sexual coercion, or sexual assault.
- *Involuntary seclusion:* Separation of a resident from other residents or from her or his room or confinement to her or his room (with or without roommates) against the resident's will, or the will of the resident's legal representative.
- *Neglect:* Failure to provide goods and services necessary to avoid physical harm, mental anguish, or mental illness.
- *Misappropriation of property:* The deliberate misplacement, exploitation, or wrongful, temporary or permanent use of a resident's belongings or money without the resident's consent.

Residents can experience any of these forms of abuse by staff, family members, friends, other residents, and visitors. For example, a nursing assistant may tell a resident that if he continues to press the call light he will be evicted from the facility, or a visitor may obtain a resident's signature under the pretense that it is required by the government when that signature actually will be used to steal funds from a resident's account.

Abuse may be reported by residents; however, there are situations in which the resident is unable or reluctant to report the abuse. Nurses need to be aware of signs that could be consistent with abuse, such as:

- Unexplained bruises or injuries
- New anxiety, depression, or suspicious demeanor
- Reluctance to answer questions about injuries or unusual occurrences
- Withdrawal
- Fearful or anxious reaction when a specific person is present
- Excoriation, bruising, bleeding, or pain in the genital area
- Reports of being visited by someone who requested money, had them sign papers, or obtained personal information from them
- Reports of being threatened or harmed

All suspected or known abuse must be reported. Nurses need to be familiar with the reporting process in their specific states.

Advance Directives

Competent individuals can develop a legally binding document known as an advance directive that describes their desires about care at a future time. Two common forms of advance directives are:

- *Durable power of attorney:* A legal term that allows an individual to designate a person (known as a proxy, decision maker, agent surrogate, or attorney-in-fact) who can communicate the individual's preferences if the individual is unable to independently do so
- *Living will:* A document stating the type of medical treatment that the individual would and would not want should the individual not be able to express preferences

Nurses need to ask residents if they have advance directives and ensure that these documents are included in the record for reference.

The Patient Self-Determination Act, enacted by Congress in 1990 and implemented in 1991, requires health care organizations to:

- Ask residents if they have completed an advance directive
- Inform residents of their right to make health care decisions and refuse treatments
- Provide written information about their state's provisions for implementing advance directives
- Include documentation of residents' advance directives in their medical records
- Educate the staff and community about advance directives

Assault and Battery

Intentionally threatening to cause physical harm to another individual is considered assault. This can occur when a caregiver says to a resident, "I'm going to break your fingers if you keep unbuttoning your shirt." Even if the caregiver has no intention of doing so and is merely using the threat to get the resident to comply, if the resident believes the threat could be carried out, this is a case of assault.

Battery is the act of touching someone without his or her consent. Performing a procedure without the resident's consent or removing an intoxicated visitor from the building by pulling him by the arm are examples of battery.

Competency

Unless a court of law has judged a person to be incompetent, the person is considered competent and has the right to make his or her own decisions. In long-term care settings situations may exist in which a resident is unable to make decisions in a competent manner but has not been legally judged incompetent. Although there may be family members who offer to make decisions on the resident's behalf or claim that they have always been looked to for decision, unless there is written proof that they have been named as a proxy or been appointed as a guardian, they should not be allowed to make decisions for the resident. In these situations, family members or other responsible parties should be advised to file a petition with the probate court to determine the resident's competency and have a guardian appointed.

There are different forms of guardianship:

- *Guardian of person:* The guardian has legal authority to consent to or refuse care and treatment for the resident.
- *Guardian of property (limited guardianship, conservatorship):* The guardian has the authority to represent the resident in legal transactions and manage financial matters but does not have the authority to make decision related to medical treatment.
- *Plenary guardianship (committeeship):* The person serves as guardian of person and guardian of property.

ESSENTIAL FACTS

Guardianship differs from power of attorney, which allows a competent individual to appoint someone to make decisions and represent them. Power of attorney can be limited, giving authority for the person to represent the individual only for specific matters. Usually, power of attorney is no longer valid if the individual granting it becomes incompetent. A durable power of attorney provides a mechanism for power of attorney to be continued or initiated should the individual become incompetent.

To ensure that residents are properly protected and that actions are consistent with the law, residents and their families should be referred to legal counsel for these matters. Nurses need to ensure that they are respecting residents' wishes and that decisions are made by persons with the authority to do so by asking to see actual copies of documents that grant decision-making authority rather than just relying on verbal assurances. Copies of these documents should be placed in the resident's health record.

Confidentiality and Privacy

Residents have the right to have the information in their medical records and other information pertaining to their status and care kept confidential. This is granted by federal law through the Health Insurance Portability and Accountability Act of 1996 (HIPAA).

HIPAA protects the rights of all Americans to privacy of their medical records and other health information provided to health care providers and health plans. As part of this act, individuals have a right to access their medical records and determine how their personal health information is used and disclosed. Violation of these rights could result in civil and criminal penalties. HIPAA does not prevent the sharing of information in the case of state-required reporting of infectious diseases.

There are additional federal laws to protect residents' privacy that afford them the right to use a telephone in private, privately communicate with visitors, and send and receive mail unopened.

Nurses should ensure that no staff member or visitor violates a resident's privacy; examples of violations of a resident's privacy include:

- A resident's relative who is not a legal guardian looking at the resident's medical record or discussing the resident's care with staff
- A nurse writing an article that identifies residents by name without their consent
- A visitor photographing several residents without their consent and posting the photos on Facebook

Consent

Health care providers and facilities need written consent to perform specific procedures. Typically, residents sign consent forms upon admission that grants permission for the facility to perform routine and customary services (e.g., administering medications, conducting examinations, bathing). Anything that exceeds basic care (e.g., moderate to high-risk diagnostic procedures, surgery, use of anesthesia, participation in research) requires that specific consent be obtained.

Consent must be informed and to ensure that it is, the resident must be offered, on a level and in a language he or she can understand, a full written and verbal description of the procedure, its purpose, steps that will occur, alternatives, expected consequences, possible side effects, and risks. Legal guardians grant consent for residents who have been judged to be legally incompetent.

Residents should not be coerced into granting consent. If they refuse, this should be documented. The policy of the facility in these circumstances should be followed.

Defamation

Defamation consists of writing or saying something to a third party that injures a person's reputation.

ESSENTIAL FACTS

Libel is the written form of defamation; slander is the verbal form.

Sharing the work history of a former employee with her new employer without the employee's consent, posting on Facebook that a coworker has a sexually transmitted disease, and documenting in a resident's record that her son probably is stealing her money are examples of situations that could result in liability for defamation.

Do-Not-Resuscitate (DNR) Orders

There are situations in long-term care in which a decision is made to not provide cardiopulmonary resuscitation should a resident's cardio-pulmonary function cease. Such a decision not to take action requires a physician's order. A decision during a care planning conference by the team not to resuscitate should the need arise or to do a "slow code" does not suffice for the physician's order.

The decision to resuscitate or not resuscitate should be discussed with the competent resident as part of the admission process; the health care proxy can offer guidance for the incompetent resident. The preference should be expressed in the advance directive, which becomes part of the medical record.

False Imprisonment

False imprisonment involves detaining or restraining a competent person without good cause. A competent resident who wishes to leave the facility against medical advice has the right to do so. Likewise, an employee who is suspected of a wrongdoing cannot be detained in the facility until the police arrive if he wants to leave.

There are special provisions for health care facilities to detain residents who have certain contagious diseases or have psychiatric conditions that cause them to be at risk of harming themselves or others.

Incidents and Accidents

Anything that occurs out of the ordinary is considered an incident. This can include a fall, one resident hitting another, or administration of an incorrect medication. An unintentional injury that results from an incident is an accident. A fracture that resulted from a fall, a broken nose that occurred when one resident hit another, and an adverse reaction to an incorrectly administered medication are examples of accidents.

When documenting incidents and accidents only facts and what is observed should be documented. For example, if the nurse hears a scream and upon entering a resident's room finds the resident on the floor, the notation should not be "Resident fell on floor" as it was not observed. Instead, the notation should be "Resident found on floor next to bed. Resident states she knelt on floor to find a necklace she dropped and couldn't raise herself."

The facility policy and procedure for documenting incidents and accidents should be closely adhered to.

Malpractice

An individual can sue for malpractice if there is a deviation from a standard of care that results in harm to the individual. Malpractice can involve *commission,* which results when a procedure is incorrectly performed, or *omission,* which results when a procedure that should have been performed was not done. Commission or omission of an act alone does not support a claim of malpractice. For malpractice to occur the following conditions must be present:

- *Negligence:* The action fails to meet acceptable standards. Sources of standards include regulations, professional associations, and evidence-based guidelines.
- *Duty:* A relationship exists between the resident and the person charged with negligence whereby the person has formally agreed to provide services.
- *Injury:* Physical or mental harm occurs as a result of the negligence.

ESSENTIAL FACTS

> With the growing complexity and diversity of the long-term care resident population, nurses need to ensure that they are familiar with all standards affecting their practice and perform competently.

Restraint Use

The Omnibus Budget Reconciliation Act (OBRA) includes a regulation stating that nursing home residents have the right to be free from physical or chemical restraints imposed for the purposes of discipline or convenience and not required to treat the resident's medical condition. Anything that physically or chemically limits a resident's movement is considered a restraint. This includes Geri Chairs, side rails, antipsychotic medications, safety belts, and protective vests.

When a resident displays behavior that could result in injury for himself or others there are actions to take before considering the use of restraints, beginning with assessing possible causes for the behavior. Pain, an adverse drug reaction, and fever are among the underlying factors that could contribute to unusual behaviors; correcting the cause could eliminate the behavior. If no treatable cause is identified lowering the bed and placing a mat on the floor alongside it to buffer a fall, providing more supervision by caregivers, and using behavior modification are among the alternatives to restraints that can be used.

ESSENTIAL FACTS

> In addition to violating residents' rights, the inappropriate use of restraints can result in liability for resident neglect and false imprisonment.

Supervisory Responsibilities

Nurses can be liable for the wrongful actions of employees whom they supervise. This liability is derived from the legal doctrine of *respondeat superior*, from the Latin term meaning "let the superior reply." The nurse is not responsible for wrongful acts committed by an employee that are beyond the employee's job description, that the employee has not been assigned to do, or that are against the law. However, the nurse could be liable if he or she has assigned a task to the employee that the employee is not competent or licensed to perform or if the nurse failed to properly supervise the employee.

Telephone Orders

As medical staff typically are not on the premises of long-term care facilities at all times, nurses must rely on telephone communication to obtain orders. There are several risks associated with telephone orders, such as:

- Insufficiently assessing the resident, which compromises the ability to communicate adequate information about the resident's status
- Providing insufficient information about the resident's status, current medications, and care activities when talking with the physician
- Not understanding or fully hearing what is being said
- Communicating through someone other than the physician (e.g., office staff)
- Accepting and implementing an order than seems inappropriate
- Documenting the order inappropriately

If understanding the order is a problem or the order seems inappropriate, it can help to have a third party on the line to listen and witness the communication. Having the physician fax the order or, if acceptable to the facility, e-mail the order, can promote accuracy of the communication. If the telephone communication will be recorded, the physician must be informed that the recording is being made unless special recording equipment is used that makes all parties on the call aware that a recording is being made.

A nurse should question orders that seem inappropriate. If the physician is firm about the order and the nurse believes it to be inappropriate, the nurse should call the medical director for validation. Telephone orders should be signed within 24 hours.

Facilities should have policies that state who can call a physician and accept a telephone order and what actions should be taken if there are problems or concerns.

PROMOTING A LEGALLY SOUND PRACTICE

Because of the risks present in long-term care nursing, nurses must be knowledgeable about laws affecting their practice, current on evidence-based best practice, and proactive in assuring they practice in a legally sound manner. Tips to promote a legally sound practice are offered in Box 25.1.

Box 25.1 Tips for a Legally Sound Practice

- Be familiar with the practice acts governing you and other nursing employees. Ensure that you are functioning within your scope of practice and that you delegate tasks to others that are within their scope of practice.
- Follow the facility's policies and procedures. If you detect that a policy or procedure does not reflect current best practice, take action to ensure it is updated.
- Maintain the confidentiality of residents' records and personal information.
- Ensure proper consent to release or share information about residents.
- Maintain the confidentiality of employees' records. Do not provide a reference for a current or former employee without the written consent of that employee.
- Be familiar with residents' normal status and promptly report and act on changes in status.
- Ensure that care plans are based on residents' assessed needs, are realistic, and are followed.
- Supervise the activities of employees to whom tasks have been delegated; correct their performance problems promptly.
- Promptly report all suspected or actual abuse to the appropriate agency.
- Report malfunctioning or broken equipment or systems.
- Validate unclear or inappropriate orders with the physician or nurse practitioner. Consult with the medical director if, after seeking validation, the order remains and you still question its accuracy.
- Identify residents before administering medications or treatments.
- If you identify that the type or number of nursing staff is inadequate to meet residents' care needs, collect facts to support your assessment and discuss with administration.
- When documenting:
  - Write legibly.
  - Be objective. Feelings and opinions have no place in residents' records, employees' evaluations, and other official forms of documentation.
  - Document signs and symptoms but do not make medical diagnoses. It is not within the scope of nursing to make medical diagnoses. State observations and clinical findings.

(continued)

Box 25.1 *(continued)*

- When documenting incidents, avoid making suppositions and conclusions. Document only what you witness and observe. If you did not actually see an injury to a resident occur, state what you found when you came upon the scene. If the resident or someone else offers an explanation, record it in quotes, indicating who made the statement.
- Use only accepted abbreviations.
- When making corrections, do not obliterate the original entry. Draw a single line through the error and date, time, and initial the error, along with a notation that it was an error.
- State the date and time of the notation, and sign it.

26

Self-Care

Nurses who work in any setting face stress in their daily work; in long-term care facilities there are unique factors that heighten stress even more. Because of the potentially harmful effects of stress, nurses need to be proactive in engaging in self-care practices so that they do not suffer ill consequences from stress and to enable them to be effective in their roles. Also, by engaging in positive self-care practices, nurses serve as role models to other staff, which can promote improvements in their health status and an optimally functioning team.

This chapter should enable you to:

1. Describe unique factors contributing to stress in long-term care settings
2. List the effects of stress
3. Describe four measures to promote self-care

FACTORS CONTRIBUTING TO STRESS IN LONG-TERM CARE

When most people consider highly stressful care settings, emergency departments, intensive care units, and surgical suites most likely would lead the list. Often, people unfamiliar with the realities of long-term care settings assume nursing in these sites is uncomplicated, routine, and low stress. However, as nurses who work in these settings know, there are many factors that contribute to long-term care facilities being highly stressful places to work, such as:

- *The need to be competent in multiple areas:* Unlike hospital specialty units that require staff to be competent in one clinical specialty (e.g., cardiac care, emergency medicine, gynecology), long-term care settings have residents with a wide range of conditions. Nurses must have the knowledge and skills related to multiple specialties to competently care for residents. In addition, many long-term care nurses also fill managerial roles which demand a unique set of competencies.
- *The need to provide person-centered care:* In most acute care settings, care is determined by the treatment that is considered best for the condition. The treatment and related care are provided with little regard for addressing psychosocial, spiritual, and other personal issues. In contrast, long-term care involves a holistic approach in which the physical, emotional, mental, social, and spiritual needs and preferences of residents are considered. This requires adjustments to ideal care strategies so that services are individualized and address long-term needs.
- *The long-term relationships with residents:* When faced with difficult patients in a hospital or outpatient setting, nurses may be able to avoid becoming highly stressed about the situation because they know the encounter is of limited duration. This is not the case for nurses in long-term care settings, who know that challenging residents usually are likely to be with them for an extended period. Even if residents are not difficult, the long-term nature of the relationship can produce stress when residents with whom nurses have developed relationships experience worsening health or die.

RESPONSE TO STRESS

ESSENTIAL FACTS

The work of Hans Selye in the 1950s laid the foundation for the growth of knowledge about stress. Selye identified two different types of stress: **eustress**, which is positive, motivating, and has pleasant effects (e.g., a surprise birthday party), and **distress**, which is negative—the bad stress (e.g., having someone you love diagnosed with a terminal illness). When stress is discussed what is being referred to is usually the distress type, which produces the negative effects.

When confronted with a stressor the body reacts by activating the sympathetic nervous system, which stimulates the release of epinephrine and norepinephrine and triggers the fight-or-flight response. The heart rate increases, as does the rate and depth of respirations. Production of glucose is boosted, causing an increase in the amount of glucose and oxygen available for organs and tissues. The stress response also stimulates the heightened release of aldosterone and cortisol. The results affect multiple dimensions of the person and include:

- Increased pulse and blood pressure
- Tightness of the chest
- Anorexia, gastric upset, nausea, diarrhea
- Headache
- Urinary frequency
- Disinterest in sex
- Accident-proneness
- Irritability, angry outbursts, emotional instability
- Restlessness
- Poor concentration, forgetfulness, poor judgment, inattention to detail
- Decreased social involvement
- Reduced productivity, increased lateness and absenteeism, accident-proneness, low morale

If unrelieved or poorly managed, stress can lead to serious health conditions. For this reason, nurses need to engage in positive health practices that can strengthen their ability to manage stress.

SELF-CARE TIPS

Self-Assessment of Health Practices

Nurses have been educated in the principles of good health practices; however, that does not mean that they follow these practices themselves. Getting insufficient sleep, eating junk food, feeling too exhausted to exercise, and putting everyone else's needs ahead of their own are not uncommon practices of nurses. It usually is not the lack of knowledge, but the lack of commitment to self-care that is the challenge. To be effective nurses need to eat a proper diet, exercise, obtain adequate rest, and follow other positive health practices, in addition to being attentive to their emotional and spiritual well-being.

Nurses can find it beneficial to perform a periodic self-assessment of how well they are meeting their basic needs. Box 26.1 provides a tool that can be used to guide this self-evaluation. It could prove

Box 26.1   Self-Assessment of Basic Needs

Need	No Related Signs or Symptoms	Related Signs, Symptoms, or Unhealthy Habit	Factors Contributing to Signs, Symptoms, or Unhealthy Habit	Corrective Action
Respiration/ Circulation				
Nutrition/ Hydration				
Elimination				
Movement				
Rest				
Immunity				
Comfort				
Socialization/ Relationships				
Recreation				
Solitude				
Safety				

useful for nurses to allocate a few hours, find a quiet place, and critically review their health status.

After identifying problems, realistic actions can be planned to improve health. Writing the actions on an index card and placing that card in an area that is regularly seen (e.g., dresser, desk, or dashboard) can provide regular reminders of intended corrective actions.

Connecting With Others

Human beings are relational and intended to live in community with others. The richness of nursing staff's connections in their personal lives provides fertile soil to grow meaningful connections with residents. Yet, as basic and common as relationships can be, they can be quite challenging. Among the major challenges nursing staff may face are:

• Finding and protecting the time and energy to connect with others in meaningful ways

- Having little in reserve to invest in nurturing relationships with friends and family due to the physical, emotional, and mental energies exerted in a typical workday
- Displacing work-related stress to significant others, thereby interfering with positive personal relationships
- Working excessive overtime due to concern for residents' welfare or employer pressure, leaving precious little time and energy to do anything more in off hours than attend to basics

Strained personal connections are the weeds of untended relationship gardens.

The allocation of time and energy requires the same planning as the allocation of any finite resource. Ignoring this reality puts one at risk for suffering the consequences of poor relationships. Recognizing that there always will be activities that vie for time and energy, nurses need to take control and develop practices that reflect the value of personal relationships. This can involve limiting the amount of overtime worked to no more than X hours each week, dedicating every Thursday evening to dining out with the family, or blocking out Sunday afternoons to visit or telephone friends. Expressing intentions through understood "personal policies" (e.g., informing a supervisor that you will work no more than one double shift per month) and committing time on your calendar (e.g., blocking off every Sunday afternoon for "friends' time") increase the likelihood that significant relationships will receive the attention they require.

Spirituality

Time and energy also must be protected to afford ample time for connecting with one's God, higher power, or other source of spirituality. The spiritual grounding resulting from this connection enables nursing staff to better understand and serve the spiritual needs of residents. Spiritual connection can be enhanced through prayer, fasting, attending church or temple, engaging in Bible or other holy book studies, taking periodic retreats, and practicing days of solitude and silence.

Connecting With Self

Connection with self is essential to nurses' self-care, and examples of strategies to facilitate this process include:

- *Sharing life stories:* Every adult has a unique and rich storehouse of experiences that have been cemented into the life in which he or she dwells. Oral sharing of life stories with others helps people gain self-insight and put experiences into a perspective that affords meaning. As people share stories, they begin to see that theirs are not the only lives that have been less than ideal, sprinkled with pain, or have unfolded in unintended ways. Writing one's life story is a powerful means of reflection that affords a permanent record that can be revisited and reconsidered as one gains deeper wisdom about one's self and others. The process of sharing life stories can be particularly meaningful for long-term care nurses in their work with older residents who often have interesting life histories that they are eager to share—and that frequently can offer rich life lessons.

- *Journaling:* Writing personal notes in a journal or diary can facilitate reflection on one's life. These writings differ from written life stories in that they record current activities and thoughts rather than past history. An honest written account of feelings, thoughts, conflicts, and behaviors can help people learn about themselves and work through issues.

- *Meditating:* The ancient practice of meditation has helped people sort out thoughts and gain clarity of direction for ages. Many nurses find meditation challenging because the nature of their work consists of *doing*—and multitask doing, at that! However, periods of *being still* enable nurses to offer an optimum healing presence to their patients. The physiological responses associated with the deep relaxation achieved during meditation have many health benefits (e.g., improved immunity, reduced blood pressure, and increased peripheral blood flow).

ESSENTIAL FACTS

There are several techniques that can be used for meditating; individuals vary in their preference for the different forms of meditation. Some people may focus on a word or prayer, whereas others may choose to have no intentional thought and to be open to whatever thoughts drift into their minds. Essential elements to any form of meditation are a quiet environment, comfortable position, and calm and passive attitude.

To many nurses and other caregivers, particularly women, taking a few days off "to do nothing" seems like a luxury that cannot be afforded. Yet, unless nursing staff want their interactions with residents to be solely mechanical (i.e., task oriented), they must treat themselves as more than machines. Their bodies, minds, and spirits must be restored and refreshed periodically if they are to offer holistic care, and retreats offer an ideal means to achieve that. During the retreat, one can spend time on activities that can aid in achieving peace and clarity, such as meditating, journaling, expressing oneself creatively through art, and praying. If life circumstances prevent a multiday or even a full-day retreat, a partial-day retreat can be planned within one's home by establishing peace and privacy (e.g., sending children off; asking roommates to stay away for the morning; unplugging telephones; turning off the computer; or placing an out-of-order sign on the doorbell) and allocating time in retreat-type activities. The charge that a retreat provides to one's physical, emotional, and spiritual batteries will more than compensate for the tasks that were postponed.

ESSENTIAL FACTS

A retreat is a withdrawal from normal activities. It can be structured or unstructured, guided by a leader or self-directed, and taken with a group or alone. Although retreats are offered in exotic locations that offer lavish provisions, they need not be luxurious or expensive. Whatever the location or structure, key elements of the retreat experience include a respite from routine responsibilities; freedom from distractions (telephones, e-mails, children, and doorbells); no one to care for and worry about other than self; and a quiet place.

COMMITTING TO A DYNAMIC PROCESS

Self-care is an ongoing process that demands active attention. However, knowing the actions that support self-care is only the beginning. Committing to engaging in one's self-care completes the picture. This may mean that limits are set on the amount of overtime worked to adhere to an exercise schedule or that one is willing to face the uncomfortable feelings experienced during the process of reflecting on less than pleasant life experiences. Sacrifices, unpopular decisions, and discomfort can result when one chooses to "work on oneself." Yet, it is this inner work that contributes to nurses being effective healers and models of healthy aging practices.

References

American Association for Long Term Care Nursing. (2014). *Position descriptions and core competencies* (3rd ed.). Cincinnati, OH: Author.

American Geriatrics Society 2012 Beers Criteria Update Expert Panel. (2012). The American Geriatrics Society updated Beers criteria for potentially inappropriate medication use in older adults. *Journal of the American Geriatrics Society, 60*(4), 616–631.

Bergstrom, M., Allman, R. M., & Carlson, E. D. (1994). *Treatment of pressure ulcers.* Clinical Practice Guideline No. 15, AHCPR Pub No 95-0652. Rockville, MD: U.S. Department of Health and Human Services, Public Health Service, Agency for Health Care Policy and Research.

Carboni, J. D. (1990). Homelessness among the institutionalized elderly. *Journal of Gerontological Nursing, 7,* 32–37.

Centers for Disease Control and Prevention. (2014a). Dementia/Alzheimer's Disease. Retrieved May 25, 2014, from http://www.cdc.gov/mentalhealth/basics/mental-illness/dementia.htm

Centers for Disease Control and Prevention. (2014b). Occupational violence. Retrieved May 2, 2014, from http://www.cdc.gov/niosh/topics/violence/

Centers for Medicare and Medicaid Services. (2014a). Interpretive guidelines. *State operations manual,* appendix PP—Guidance to surveyors for long term care facilities: Abuse. 42 C.F.R. §483.13, F223, F224, F225, F226 [Online]. Retrieved June 2014, from http://www.cms.gov/Regulations-and-Guidance/Guidance/Manuals/Downloads/som107ap_p_ltcf.pdf

Centers for Medicare and Medicaid Services. (2014b). *State operations manual,* appendix PP—Guidance to surveyors for long term care facilities: Quality of care. 42 C.F.R. §483.25. Retrieved March 15, 2014, from http://www.cms.gov/Regulations-and-Guidance/Guidance/Manuals/downloads/som107ap_pp_guidelines_ltcf.pdf

Centers for Medicare and Medicaid Services. (2014c). *State operations manual, appendix PP—Guidance to surveyors for long term care facilities: Resident rights.* 42 C.F.R. §483.10. Retrieved March 15, 2014, from http://www.cms.gov/Regulations-and-Guidance/Guidance/Manuals/downloads/som107ap_pp_guidelines_ltcf.pdf

Centers for Medicare and Medicaid Services. (2014d). *State operations manual, Appendix PP—Guidance to surveyors for long term care facilities.* Retrieved May 5, 2014, from http://www.cms.gov/Regulations-and-Guidance/Guidance/Manuals/downloads/som107ap_pp_guidelines_ltcf.pdf

Commonwealth Foundation. (2014). Modeling and measuring nursing home reform: The culture change staging tool. Retrieved February 1, 2014, from http://www.commonwealthfund.org/Innovations/Tools/2005/Nov/Modeling-and-Measuring-Nursing-Home-Reform--The-Culture-Change-Staging-Tool.aspx

Eden Alternative. (2014). Eden Alternative: Our ten principles. Retrieved January 15, 2014, from http://www.edenalt.org/our-10-principles

Hohmann, N., Hohmann, L., & Kruse, M. (2014). The impact of combined use of fall-risk medications and antithrombotics on injury severity and intracranial hemorrhage among older trauma patients. *Geriatric Nursing, 35*(1), 20–25.

Kim, H., Woods, D. L., Mentes, J. C., Martin, J. L., Moon, A., & Phillips, L. R. (2014). The nursing assistants' communication style and the behavioral symptoms of dementia in Korean-American nursing home residents. *Geriatric Nursing, 35*(2), S11–S16.

Kübler-Ross, E. (1969). *On death and dying.* New York, NY: Macmillan.

McKhann, G. M., Knopman, D. S., Chertkow, H., Hyman, B. T., Jack, C. R., Kawas, C. H., . . . Phelps, C. H. (2011). The diagnosis of dementia due to Alzheimer's disease: Recommendations from the National Institute on Aging–Alzheimer's Association workgroups on diagnostic guidelines for Alzheimer's disease. *Alzheimer's & Dementia, 7*(3), 263–269.

Misiorski, S., & Rader, J. (2004). *Getting started: A pioneering approach to culture change in long-term care organizations.* Rochester, NY: Pioneer Network.

National Institute on Aging. (2011). Alzheimer's diagnostic guidelines updated for first time in decades. Retrieved May 1, 2014, from http://www.nia.nih.gov/newsroom/2011/04/alzheimers-diagnostic-guidelines-updated-first-time-decades

National Pressure Ulcer Advisory Panel. (2007). NPUAP pressure ulcer stages/categories. Retrieved December 24, 2014, from http://www.npuap.org/resources/educational-and-clinical-resources/npuap-pressure-ulcer-stagescategories/

Norton, D., McLaren, R., & Exton-Smith, A. N. (1962). *An investigation of geriatric nursing problems in the hospital.* London, UK: National Corporation for the Care of Old People.

Pioneer Network, (2011, April). Positive outcomes of culture change: The case for adoption. *Tools for Change, 1*(2). Retrieved March 1, 2014, from http://www.pioneernetwork.net/Data/Documents/Tools%20for%20Change-Adoption%20v3.pdf

Pioneer Network. (2014). What is culture change? Retrieved March 1, 2014, from https://www.pioneernetwork.net/CultureChange/Whatis/

Sommer, R. (1961). Symptoms of institutional care, *Social Problems, 8,* 254.

Recommended Reading

Adelman, R. (2013). Assisted living lawsuits: An ounce of prevention is worth a pound of cure. *Geriatric Nursing, 34*(2), 166–169.

Allen, J. (2010). The POLST: Advocating for assisted living residents' end-of-life wishes. *Geriatric Nursing, 31*(3), 234–235.

Allen, J. (2011a). Assisted living nurse competencies. *Geriatric Nursing, 32*(5), 387–391.

Allen, J. (2011b). Resident care decisions in assisted living: Who is in charge? *Geriatric Nursing, 24*(1), 146–147.

Allen, J. (2013). Expanding the INTERACT to assisted living: Reducing unnecessary hospitalizations and readmissions. *Geriatric Nursing, 34*(1), 84–85.

American Geriatrics Society 2012 Beers Criteria Update Expert Panel. (2012). The American Geriatrics Society updated Beers criteria for potentially inappropriate medication use in older adults. *Journal of the American Geriatrics Society, 60*(4), 616–631, Table 2.

Ashcraft, A. S., & Owen, D. C. (2014). From nursing home to acute care. Signs, symptoms, and strategies used to prevent transfer. *Geriatric Nursing, 35*(4), 316–320.

Ayello, E. A., & Sibbald, R. G. (2012). Preventing pressure ulcers and skin tears. In M. Boltz, E. Capezuti, T. Fulmer, & D. Zwicker (Eds.), *Evidence-based geriatric nursing protocols for best practice* (4th ed., pp. 298–323). New York, NY: Springer Publishing.

Bakerjian, D. (2014). Pets impact on quality of life, a case study. *Geriatric Nursing, 35*(2), 160–163.

Balas, M. C., Casey, C. M., & Happ, M. B. (2012). Comprehensive assessment and management of the critically ill. In M. Boltz, E. Capezuti, T. Fulmer, & D. Zwicker (Eds.), *Evidence-based geriatric nursing protocols for best practice* (4th ed., pp. 600–627). New York, NY: Springer Publishing.

Barnum, B. S. (2006). *Spirituality in nursing: From traditional to new age.* New York, NY: Springer Publishing.

Beck, C., Buckwater, K. C., Dudzik, P. M., & Evans, L. K. (2011). Filling the void in geriatric mental health: The Geropsychiatric Nursing Collaborative as a model for change. *Nursing Outlook, 59*(4), 236–241.

Belker, L. B., McCormick, J., & Topchik, G. S. (2012). *The first time manager* (6th ed.). New York, NY: American Management Association.

Boltz, M. (2012). The family caregiver: An untapped resource. *Geriatric Nursing, 33*(2), 137–139.

Brous, E. (2012). Legal clinic: Common misconceptions about professional licensure. *American Journal of Nursing, 112*(10), 55–60.

Burfield, A. H., & Cooper, J. W. (2014). Assessing pain and falls risk in residents with cognitive impairment: Associated problems with overlooked assessments. *Annals of Long-Term Care, 22*(5), 36–40.

Burt, T. (2013). Palliative care of pressure ulcers in long term care. *Annals of Long-Term Care, 21*(3), 20–28.

Chappell, N. L., Kadlec, H., & Reid, C. (2014) Change and predictors of change in social skills of nursing home residents with dementia. *American Journal of Alzheimer's Disease and Other Dementias, 29*(1), 23–31.

Charalambous, A., Chappell, N. L., Katajisto, J., & Suhonen, R. (2012). The conceptualization and measurement of individualized care. *Geriatric Nursing, 33*(1), 17–27.

Cho, E., Lee, N. J., Kim, Y., & Stumpf, N. (2011). The impact of informal caregivers on depressive symptoms among older adults receiving formal home health care. *Geriatric Nursing, 32*(1), 18–28.

Choi, M., Lee, J., Kim, S., Kim, D., & Kim H. (2012). Nurses' knowledge about end-of-life care: Where are we? *Journal of Gerontological Nursing, 42*(6), 61–65.

Coggins, M. D. (2014). Medication-related ototoxicity. *Today's Geriatric Medicine, 7*(3), 6–7.

Cohen, C. J., Auslander, G., & Chen, Y. (2010). Family caregiving to hospitalized end-of-life and acutely ill geriatric patients. *Journal of Gerontological Nursing, 36*(8), 42–50.

Daft, R. (2013). *Management.* Mason, OH: South-Western Cengage Learning.

D'Amico, A. K. (2014). Resilience strategies for geriatric care teams. *Today's Geriatric Medicine, 7*(3), 26–27.

Dellefield, M. E., & Magnabosco, J. L. (2014). Pressure ulcer prevention in nursing homes: Nurse descriptions of individual and organization level factors. *Geriatric Nursing, 35*(2), 97–104.

deVries, K. (2013). Communicating with older people with dementia. *Nursing Older People, 25*(4), 30–37.

DiBartolo, M. C. (2012). Dementia revisited. *Journal of Gerontological Nursing, 38*(5), 46–51.

Dossey, B. M., & Keegan, L. (2012). *Holistic nursing: A handbook for practice* (6th ed.). Sudbury, MA: Jones & Bartlett.

Drick, C. A. (2014). At last: Moving into person-centered care. *AHNA Beginnings, 34*(1), 6–9.

Eliopoulos, C. (2012). *Nursing administration manual for long term care facilities.* Glen Arm, MD: Health Education Network.

Eliopoulos, C. (Ed.) (2013). *Invitation to holistic health* (3rd ed.). Sudbury, MA: Jones & Bartlett.

Eliopoulos, C. (2014a). *Culture change nurse coordinator manual.* Glen Arm, MD: Health Education Network.

Eliopoulos, C. (2014b). *Nursing administration of long-term care facilities* (9th ed.). Glen Arm, MD: Health Education Network.

Enderlin, C. A., McLeskey, N., Rooker, J. L., Steinhauser, C., D'Avolio, D., et al. (2013). Review of current conceptual models and frameworks to guide transitions of care in older adults. *Geriatric Nursing, 34*(1), 47–52.

Epps, F. (2014). The relationship between family obligation and religiosity on caregiving. *Geriatric Nursing, 35*(2), 126–131.

Fanus, K., Huddelston, R., Wisotzkey, S., et al. (2014). Embracing a culture of safety by decreasing medication errors. *Nursing Management, 45*(3), 16–19.

Farrell, D., Brady, C., & Frank, B. (2011) *Meeting the leadership challenge in long term care. What you do matters.* Baltimore, MD: Health Professions Press.

Fick, D. M., & Resnick, B. (2012). 2012 Beers Criteria update: How should practicing nurses use the criteria? *Journal of Gerontological Nursing, 38*(6), 3–5.

Fick, D. M., Kolanowski, A. M., Hill, N. L., Yevchak, A., & DiMeglio, B. (2013). Using standardized case vignettes to evaluate nursing home staff recognition of delirium and delirium superimposed on dementia. *Annals of Long-Term Care, 21*(9), 34–38.

Francis, D. C., & Lahaie, J. M. (2012). Iatrogensis: The nurse's role in preventing patient harm. In M. Boltz, E. Capezuti, T. Fulmer, & D. Zwicker (Eds.), *Evidence-based geriatric nursing protocols for best practice* (4th ed., pp. 200–228). New York, NY: Springer Publishing.

Gaugler, J. E. (2014). The process of adult day service use. *Geriatric Nursing, 35*(1), 47–54.

Gaugler, J. E., Potter, T., & Pruinelli, L. (2014). Partnering with caregivers. *Clinical Geriatric Medicine, 30*(3), 493–515.

Gordon, M. (2013). Care demands by families and family healthcare proxies: A dilemma for palliative care and hospice care staff. *Annals of Long-Term Care, 21*(5), 42–46.

Gordon, M. (2014). When should antipsychotics for the management of behavioral and psychological symptoms of dementia be discontinued? *Annals of Long-Term Care, 22*(4), 24–29.

Gould, R. L., Coulson, M. C. & Howard, R. J. (2012). Efficacy of cognitive behavioral therapy for anxiety disorders in older people: A meta-analysis and meta-regression of randomized controlled trials. *Journal of the American Geriatrics Society, 60*(2), 218–229.

Grant, P. D., & Ballard, D. (2011). *Law for nurse leaders: A comprehensive approach.* New York, NY: Springer Publishing.

Gray-Miceli, D., & Quigley, P. A. (2012). Fall prevention: Assessment, diagnoses, and intervention strategies. In M. Boltz, E. Capezuti, T. Fulmer, & D. Zwicker (Eds.), *Evidence-based geriatric nursing protocols for best practice* (4th ed., pp. 268–297). New York, NY: Springer Publishing.

Hahn, J. E. (2012). Minimizing health risks among older adults with intellectual and/or developmental disabilities: Clinical considerations to promote quality of life. *Journal of Gerontological Nursing, 38*(6), 11–17.

Hall, S., Dodd, R. H., & Higginson, I. J. (2014). Maintaining dignity for residents of care homes: A qualitative study of the views of care home staff, community nurses, residents and their families. *Geriatric Nursing, 35*(1), 55–60.

Halperin, J. L., & Malhotra, J. K. (2014). Implications of new oral anticoagulants for stroke prophylaxis in elderly patients with atrial fibrillation. *Annals of Long Term Care, 22*(5), 28–33.

Harahan, M. F., Sanders, A., Stone, R. I., Bowers, B. J., Nolet, K. A., et al. (2011). Implementation and evaluation of LVN LEAD: A leadership and supervisory training program for nursing home charge nurses. *Journal of Gerontological Nursing, 37*(6), 26–33.

Hieb, M. (2006). *Inner journaling through art journaling. Learning to see and record your life as a work of art.* Philadelphia, PA: Jessica Kingsley.

Hotsel, B. K., Carmody, J., Vangel, M., Yerramsetti, S. M., et al. (2011). Mindfulness practice leads to increases in regional brain gray matter density. *Psychiatry Research: Neuroimaging, 181*(1), 36–43.

Houde, S. C., Melillo, K. D., & Holmes, R. (2012). The patient-centered medical home. *Journal of Gerontological Nursing, 38*(3), 12–16.

Howe, E. E. (2014). Empowering certified nurse's aides to improve quality of work life through a team communication program. *Geriatric Nursing, 35*(2), 132–136.

Howland, R. H. (2011). Update on newer antipsychotic drugs. *Journal of Psychosocial Nursing and Mental Health Services, 49*(4), 13–15.

Johnson, R. A., & Bibbo, J. (2014). Relocation decisions and constructing the meaning of home: A phenomenological study of the transition into a nursing home. *Journal of Aging Studies, 30*(8), 56–63.

Jones A. L., Harris-Kojetin L., & Valverde, R. (2012). *Characteristics and use of home health care by men and women aged 65 and over.* National Health Statistics Reports; No. 52. Hyattsville, MD: National Center for Health Statistics.

Joosse, L. L. (2011). Sound levels in nursing homes. *Journal of Gerontological Nursing, 37*(8), 30–35.

Kagan, S. H. (2011). Patient and family-centered care. Is there individualized care here? *Geriatric Nursing, 32*(5), 365–367.

Kapp, M. B. (2010). *Legal aspects of elder care.* Sudbury, MA: Jones & Bartlett.

Kenneley, I. (2014). *Clostridium difficile* infection is on the rise. *American Journal of Nursing, 114*(3), 62–67.

Kim, S. S., Hayward, R. D., & Kang, Y. (2013). Psychological, physical, social, and spiritual well-being similarities between Korean older adults and family caregivers. *Geriatric Nursing, 34*(1), 35–40.

Kleba, P. A., & Flak, N. L. (2014). The Elder Justice Act: What nurses need to know. *American Journal of Nursing, 114*(9), 65–68.

Kofoed, N. A. (2011). Reflective practice for personal and professional transformation. *Journal of Christian Nursing, 28*(3), 132–138.

Lane, A. M., & Hirst, S. P. (2012). Are gerontological nurses apathetic about apathy in older adults. *Journal of Gerontological Nursing, 38*(1), 22–28.

Langemo, D. (2012). General principles and approaches to wound prevention and care at end of life: An overview. *Ostomy and Wound Management, 58*(5), 24–34.

Legg, T. J., & Adelman, D. S. (2011). Diagnosis: Dementia. Psychiatric referral versus federal regulations: A balancing act for long-term care nurses. *Journal of Gerontological Nursing, 37*(11), 24–27.

Lu, D. F., & Herr, K. (2012). Pain in dementia: Recognition and treatment. *Journal of Gerontological Nursing, 28*(2), 8–13.

Maltoni, M., Scarpi, E., & Rosati, M. (2012). Palliative sedation in end-of-life care and survival: A systematic review. *Journal of Clinical Oncology, 30*(12), 1378–1383.

Markowitz, D. (2013). *Self care for the self aware: A guide for highly sensitive people, empaths, intuitives, and healers.* Bloomington, IN: Balboa Press.

Martin, D., Kripalani, S., & DuRapau, V. J. (2012). Improving medication management among at-risk older adults. *Journal of Gerontological Nursing, 38*(6), 36–37.

McCusker, M., Ceronsky, L., Crone, C., Epstein, H., Greene, B., Halvorson, J., et al. (2013). *Palliative care for adults.* Bloomington, MN: Institute for Clinical Systems Improvement (ICSI).

McKenzie, G., Teri, L., Pike, K., LaFazia, D., & van Leynseele, J. (2012). Reactions of assisted living staff to behavioral and psychological symptoms of dementia. *Geriatric Nursing, 33*(2), 96–104.

Menzel, P. T., & Chandler-Cramer, M. C. (2014). Advance directives, dementia, and withholding food and water by mouth. *Hastings Center Report, 44*(3), 23–37.

Miller, C.A. (2012). *Essentials for dementia care.* New York, NY: Springer Publishing.

Mion, L. C., & Sandhu, S. K. (2014). Screening for dementia in hospitalized older adults: Try the Mini-Cog. *Geriatric Nursing, 35*(4), 313–315.

Mitsch, A. L. (2013). Antidepressant adverse drug reactions in older adults: Implications for RNs and APNs. *Geriatric Nursing, 34*(1), 53–60.

Mitty, E. (2012). Advance directives. In M. Boltz, E. Capezuti, T. Fulmer, & D. Zwicker (Eds.), *Evidence-based geriatric nursing protocols for best practice* (4th ed., pp. 579–599). New York, NY: Springer Publishing.

Mitty, E. L., & Post, L. F. (2012). Health care decision making. In M. Boltz, E. Capezuti, T. Fulmer, & D. Zwicker (Eds.), *Evidence-based geriatric nursing protocols for best practice* (4th ed., pp. 562–578). New York, NY: Springer Publishing.

Mueller, C., Burger, S., Rader, J., & Carter, D. (2013). Nurse competencies for person-directed care in nursing homes, *Geriatric Nursing, 34*(2), 101–104.

Palmer, J. L. (2012). Caregivers' desired patterns of communication with nursing home staff—just TALKK. *Journal of Gerontological Nursing, 38*(4), 47–54.

Palmer, J. L. (2013). Preserving personhood of individuals with advanced dementia: Lessons from family caregivers. *Geriatric Nursing, 34*(3), 224–229.

Patterson, S. M., Hughes, C., Kerse, N., Cardwell, C. R., & Bradley, M. C. (2012). Interventions to improve the appropriate use of polypharmacy for older people. *Cochrane Database System Review, 16*(5), CD008165.

Patz, S. (2014). Holistic assessment in person-centered care. *AHNA Beginnings, 34*(1), 10–11, 22.

Pickering, C. E. Z., & Rempusheski, V. F. (2014). Examining barriers to self-reporting of elder abuse in community dwelling older adults. *Geriatric Nursing, 35*(2), 120–125.

Ray, K., & Meyer, S. (2014). Moving toward a more objective peer review process. *Nursing Management, 45*(1), 52–54.

Reich, J. (2012). Becoming whole: The role of story for healing. *Journal of Holistic Nursing, 30*(1), 16–23.

Resnick, B., & Mitty, E. (Eds.) (2009). *Assisted living nursing: A manual for management and practice.* New York, NY: Springer Publishing.

Richardson, C. (2012). *The art of extreme self-care: Transform your life one month at a time.* Carlsbad, CA: Hay House.

Rose, K. M., & Williams, I. C. (2011). Family matters. Family quality of life in dementia. *Journal of Gerontological Nursing, 37*(6), 3–4.

Rosenbloom, D. A., & Fick, D. M. (2014). Nurse/family caregiver intervention for delirium increases delirium knowledge and improves attitudes toward partnership. *Geriatric Nursing, 35*(3), 175–181.

Rosted, E., Poulson, I., Hendriksen, C., Petersen, J., & Wagner, L. (2013). Testing a two step nursing intervention focused on decreasing rehospitalizations and nursing home admission post discharge from acute care. *Geriatric Nursing, 34*(6), 477–485.

Ruppar, T. M., Dobbels, F., & DeGeest, S. (2012). Medication beliefs and antihypertensive adherence among older adults: A pilot study. *Geriatric Nursing, 33*(2), 89–95.

Scala, E. (2012). *Back to the basics: A nurse's pocket guide to self-care.* Amazon. com: Createspace.

Schaeffer, J. (2014). Assessing aspirin efficacy for heart patients. *Today's Geriatric Medicine, 7*(3), 10–11.

Simonson, W. (2014). New sedative/hypnotic dosing guidelines. *Geriatric Nursing, 35*(4), 306–307.

Slaughter, S. E., Morgan, D., & Drummond, N. (2011). Functional transitions of nursing home residents with middle-stage dementia: Perspectives of family members and nurses. *Journal of Gerontological Nursing, 37*(5), 50–59.

Solberg, L. M., Plummer, C. E., May, K. N., & Mion, L. C. (2013). A quality improvement program to increase nurses' detection of delirium on an acute medical unit. *Geriatric Nursing, 34*(1), 75–79.

Specht, J. T. (2011). Promoting continence in individuals with dementia. *Journal of Gerontological Nursing, 37*(2), 17–21.

Stefanacci, R. G. (2013). Care coordination today: What, why, who, where, and how? *Annals of Long Term Care, 21*(3), 38–42.

Stefanacci, R. G., & Spivack, B. S. (2014). Determining the future of long-term care. *Annals of Long Term Care, 22*(5), 24–27.

Steis, M. R., & Fick, D. M. (2012). Delirium superimposed on dementia: Accuracy of nurse documentation. *Journal of Gerontological Nursing, 38*(1), 32–42.

Stuart, R. L., Wilson, J., Bellaard-Smith, E., Brown, R., Wright, L., Vandergraaf, S., & Gillespie, E. E. (2012). Antibiotic use and misuse in residential aged care facilities. *Internal Medicine Journal, 4*, 1445–1459.

Sullivan, E. J. (2012) *Effective leadership and management in nursing* (8th ed.). Upper Saddle River, NJ: Prentice Hall.

Tuck, I., Johnson, S. C., Kuznetsova, M. I., McCrockli, C., Baxter, M., & Bennington, L. K. (2012). Sacred healing stories told at the end of life. *Journal of Holistic Nursing, 30*(2), 69–80.

Turner, S. A. (2014). Recent developments in long term care/hospice relationships. *Geriatric Nursing, 35*(1), 63–64.

Van der Ploeg, E. S., Walker, H., & O'Connor, D. W. (2014). The feasibility of volunteers facilitating personalized activities for nursing home residents with dementia and agitation. *Geriatric Nursing, 35*(2), 142–146.

Vann, A. S. (2013). Three important actions for Alzheimer's caregivers. *Annals of Long-Term Care, 21*(10), 37–38.

Vann, A. S. (2014). Advising Alzheimer's caregivers about assisted living. *Annals of Long-Term Care, 22*(1), 17–20.

Vogelsmeier, A. (2011). Medication administration in nursing homes: RN delegation to unlicensed assistive personnel. *Journal of Nursing Regulation, 2*(3), 49–55.

Wan, T. T. H., Breen, G. M., Zhang, N. J., & Unruh, L. (2010). *Improving the quality of care in nursing homes. An evidence-based approach.* Baltimore, MD: Johns Hopkins.

Wang, J. J. (2012). A structural model of the bio-psycho-socio-spiritual factors influencing the development towards gerotranscendence in a sample of institutionalized elders. *Journal of Advanced Nursing, 67*(12), 2628–2636.

Wehling, M. (2012). *Drug therapy for the elderly.* New York, NY: Springer Publishing.

White, D. L., Cartwright, J., & Lottes, J. (2012). Long-term care nurse role models in clinical nursing education: The ECLEPs experience. *Journal of Gerontological Nursing, 38*(1), 43–51.

Wierman, H. R., Wadland, W. R., Walters, M., Kuhn, C., & Farrington, S. (2011). Nonpharmacological management of agitation in hospitalized patients. *Journal of Gerontological Nursing, 37*(2), 44–48.

Wiglesworth, A., Mosqueda, L., Mulnard, R., Liao, S., Gibbs, L., & Fitzgerald, W. (2010). Screening for abuse and neglect of people with dementia. *Journal of the American Geriatrics Society, 58*(3), 493–500.

Wiley, B., & Osterberg, C. M. (2014). Strategies for reducing falls in long-term care. *Annals of Long-Term Care, 22*(1), 23–32.

Zarowitz, B. J. (2013). Comprehensive medication review: Coming soon to a nursing home near you! *Geriatric Nursing, 34*(1), 62–65.

Resources

Adult Day Care

National Adult Day Services Association
www.nadsa.org

Assessment Tools

Hartford Institute for Geriatric Nursing—Try This *series*
www.hartfordign.org/practice/try_this/

Assisted Living

American Assisted Living Nurses Association
www.aalna.org

Common Risks

Agency for Healthcare Research and Quality
Pressure Ulcers in Hospitals: A Toolkit for Improving Quality of Care
www.ahrq.giv/researchltc/pressureulcertoolkit

Braden Scale for Predicting Pressure Ulcer Risk
www.bradenscale.com/braden

Centers for Disease Control and Prevention
Clostridium difficile *prevention strategies*

www.cdc.gov/hai/organisms/cdiff/Cdiff_settings.html

Hartford Institute for Geriatric Nursing
Try This: Best Practices in Nursing Care to Older Adults Issue 8, Fall Risk
    Assessment: Hendrich II Fall Risk Model

www.hartfordign.org/resources/education/ tryThis.html

National Pressure Ulcer Advisory Panel
www.npuap.org

Culture Change

Artifacts of Culture Change Tool
www.pioneernetwork.net/Providers/Artifacts/

The Commonwealth Fund in New York City

Offers a video showing examples of culture change
www.cmwf.org/topics/topics_show.htm?docid=372482.

Eden Alternative
www.edenalt.org

Green House Project
www.ncbcapitalimpact.org

Pioneer Network
www.PioneerNetwork.net

Dementia

Alzheimer's Association
www.alz.org

Lewy Body Dementia Association
www.lbda.org

National Institute on Aging, Alzheimer's Disease Education and Referral Center
www.nia.nih.gov/alzheimers

Documentation

Health IT Adoption Toolkit
www.hrsa.gov/healthit/toolbox/HealthITAdoptiontoolbox/PrivacyandSecurity/
securityrisks.html

Medicare and Medicaid Regulations
www.cms.gov

National Council State Board of Nursing
www.ncsbn.org/index.htm

State Boards of Nursing—for nurse practice acts
(see individual state websites)

End-of-Life Care

Advance Directives by State
www.caringinfo.org/i4a/pages/index.cfm?pageid=3289

Hartford Institute for Geriatric Nursing
Try This: Assessing Pain in Older Adults *www.hartfordign.org/resources/*
education/tryThis.html.

Families

National Consumer Voice for Long Term Care
www.theconsumervoice.org

National Family Caregivers Association
www.nfcacares.org

General

Children of Aging Parents
www.caps4caregivers.org

National Association of Area Agencies on Aging
www.n4a.org

National Association of Professional Geriatric Care Managers
www.caremanager.org

National Eldercare Locator
www.eldercare.gov

National Hospice and Palliative Care Organization
www.nho.org

Home Health Care

National Association of Home Care
www.nahc.org

National Citizens Coalition for Nursing Home Reform
www.nccnhr.org

Visiting Nurse Associations of America
www.vnaa.org

Legal Resources

American Association of Retired Persons (AARP) Elder Law Forum
www.aarp.org/research/legal-advocacy/

American Bar Association Senior Lawyers Division
www.abanet.org/srlawyers/home.html

Hartford Institute for Geriatric Nursing

Elder Mistreatment. Geriatric Nursing Protocol. Detection of Elder Mistreatment

*www.consultgerirn.org/topics/elder_mistreatment_and_abuse/want_to_
know_more*

National Academy of Elder Law Attorneys
www.naela.com

National Center on Elder Abuse
www.elderabusecenter.org

National Senior Citizens Law Center
www.nsclc.org

Nursing Home Abuse/Elder Abuse Attorneys Referral Network
www.nursing-home-abuse-elderly-abuse-attorneys.com

Long-Term Care Nursing Responsibilities

American Assisted Living Nurses Association
www.alnursing.org

American Association for Long Term Care Nursing
www.LTCNursing.org

American Association for Nurse Assessment Coordination
www.aanac.org

American Nurses Association Scope of Practice
www.nursingworld.org/sop

Medication Safety

American Geriatrics Society Beers List Guidelines and Clinical Tools
www.americangeriatrics.org/health_care_professionals/clinical_practice/
*   clinical_guidelines_recommendations/2012*

Food and Drug Administration
Medications and You: A Guide for Older Adults

www.fda.gov/Drugs/ResourcesForYou/ucm163959.htm

Minimum Data Set

Centers for Medicare and Medicaid Services—MDS forms and instructions
www.cms.gov

Nursing Homes

American Association for Long Term Care Nursing
www.ltcnursing.org

American Nurses Association Council on Nursing Home Nurses
www.nursingworld.org

American Public Health Association, Section on Gerontological Health
www.ph.ucla.edu/ghsnet/

Leading Age
www.LeadingAge.org

National Association of Directors of Nursing Administration in Long-Term Care
www.nadona.org

Person-Centered Care

BeliefNet
www.beliefnet.com

Duke Center for Spirituality, Theology, and Health
www.dukespiritualityandhealth.org

Eden Alternative
www.edenalt.org

Green House Model
www.thegreenhouseproject.org

Pioneer Network
www.pioneernetwork.org

Regulation of Nursing Homes

Assisted Living Regulations
www.ahcancal.org/ncal/resources/Pages/AssistedLivingRegulations.aspx

Centers for Medicare and Medicaid Services
www.cms.gov

Survey and Certification—Guidance to Laws and Regulations
www.cms.gov/Medicare/Provider-Enrollment-and-Certification/Guidancefor
*   LawsAndRegulations*

National Council of State Boards of Nursing
www.ncsbn.org/government.htm

Nursing Home Compare
www.medicare.gov/nursinghomecompare

Reimbursement for Long-Term Care

Medicaid
www.Medicaid.gov

Medicare
www.Medicare.gov

Program for All-Inclusive Care of the Elderly (PACE)
www.medicare.gov/Nursing/Alternatives/Pace.asp

Index